The Dialogic Species

EUROPEAN PERSPECTIVES
A Series of the Columbia University Press

THE DIALOGIC SPECIES

*A Linguistic Contribution
to the Social Sciences*

CLAUDE HAGÈGE

Translated by Sharon L. Shelly

COLUMBIA UNIVERSITY PRESS
NEW YORK

Columbia University Press wishes to express its appreciation of assistance given by the government of France through le Ministère de la Culture in the preparation of this translation.

L'Homme du Paroles: Contribution linguistique aux sciences humaines, copyright © 1985, Librairie Arthème Fayard; translation copyright © Columbia University Press 1990

Columbia University Press
New York   Oxford
Copyright © 1990 Columbia University Press
All rights reserved

Library of Congress Cataloging-in-Publication Data
Hagège, Claude, 1936–
[Homme de paroles. English]
The dialogic species : a linguistic contribution to the social sciences / Claude Hagège ; translated by Sharon L. Shelly.
p.   cm. — (European perspectives)
Translation of: L'homme de paroles.
Includes bibliographical references.
ISBN 0-231-06760-7 (alk. paper) : $35.00
1. Linguistics. I. Title. II. Series.
P121.H2413   1990
410—dc20   89-13923
CIP

Casebound editions of Columbia University Press books are Smyth-sewn and printed on permanent and durable acid-free paper

Printed in the United States of America
c 10 9 8 7 6 5 4 3 2 1

Contents

v

Contents

Preface

The period immediately following World War II saw a rapid worldwide expansion of the theoretical study of speech and languages as a source of knowledge about man. For some time, in fact, linguistics held a kind of dominion over the other social sciences. Because its focus seemed to reach the very heart of the human species, and because it had invented for itself a rigorous and ordered form of discourse, linguistics was considered a model. Its refined formulations did indeed appear to rise above subjectivity and naive metaphor.

In the past fifteen years, however, this dominance has been questioned. For some, in fact, the situation has been reversed. Recent impressive advances in sociology, anthropology, and psychology, for example, seem to relegate language specialists to a sort of menial rear guard which produces overly technical research without always keeping its promises of momentous revelations about the human condition.

We cannot help but be surprised at this state of affairs: for whatever destiny awaits humanity in the third millennium—suddenly so imminent—we may say with certainty that these last days of the twentieth century are truly the age of language, just as they are the age of great discoveries about the cosmos, robots, the atom, or genetics. From sound recording and radio to television, books, and the press, from the most imposing summit meeting to the humblest private telephone conversation, it is clear that the dazzling progress of communication, the computer revolution, and the unlimited extension of social contact (all processes which permit a qualified triumph over time through reduction of space) infinitely increase the possible uses of language, whether spoken, written, or broadcast. For the past quarter of a century, the human species has been immersed in a gigantic ocean of words and sentences.

It is therefore important to redefine the role of language in the definition of the human species. It is a singular faculty, one whose manifestations (words and sentences) assail us even as they constitute natural instruments for our socialization and, perhaps, obstacles to our solitude. The goal of this book is to reveal the contribution that linguistics may still make to the elucidation of humanity, that strange object of study for the "social" sciences, whose status is so difficult to define. With mischievous and obscure consistency, the human race presents itself as a clearly definable phenomenon, only to thwart our efforts with eternally *in*consistent behavior. This may in fact be a hopeful sign. For despite all the machines for self-destruction that we create, despite all the clouds that our ambiguous genius releases to trouble the atmosphere above us and our descendants, we remain a species capable of the most radical reversals. We are, further, endlessly bent upon *surprising ourselves*, if only through the aptitude discussed in this book: the stubborn determination to converse with our peers, a resolute will to exchange. The primary exchange, which constitutes the basis of all others, is that of words. If humanity is defined as *homo sapiens*, or "knowing man," it is originally and primarily as *homo loquens*, "speaking man."

This book, which combines reflection with empirical data, is built upon a progressive theme developed in three stages. First, we show the present state of some of the principal directions of research on speech (part 1); next, the elements which establish the importance of the contribution of linguistics to knowledge about the human species (part 2); and finally, the linguistic theory of humanity and society which may be constructed upon these foundations (part 3). An interactive conception, which we will call *discursive* (Fr. *dialogal*), underlies this enterprise and determines its primary orientation.

In the first section, "On Certain Advances in Linguistics; or, The Human Profile," I first show that the faculty of speech, *initially recorded in the genetic code,* soon took on a significant social aspect, making it more and more difficult to characterize this faculty in terms of pure innateness, or as independent of the languages in which it is realized; hence the hypothesis of an original diversity of *languages,* as opposed to the uniqueness of *speech* as an aptitude (chapter 1, "Unity of Species, Plurality of Languages"). The importance of these social factors, and the reciprocal relation linking them to biological schemata, are next demonstrated through the study of a type of natural experimentation quite rare in the social sciences: the genesis of creoles (chapter 2, "The Creole Laboratory"). After this external examination, I apply the same dialectical method to the study of the internal properties which, in the domains of phonetics, grammar, and lexicon, seem to be candidates for universality—or, on the contrary, serve as criteria for the distinction of human languages into various types (chapter 3, "Language Universals and Typological Differences"). Finally, I show that the invention of writing, while fixing invariants in silent form and encouraging the anonymous or deferred encoding of traces—a procedure which is vulnerable to esthetic excess—has not, however, challenged the preeminence of orality linked to the diversity of the social contexts of speech (chapter 4, "Writing and Speaking").

Part 2, "Applications, or Universe, Discourse, and Society," provides an anthropological orientation for the results of part 1. The study of the signs (words) which constitute languages reveals that the pressures of group life engender more or less coherent linguistic structures, oriented toward the transmission and interpretation of messages useful for all— although this stability is periodically challenged by individual desires and expressive needs (chapter 5, "The Territory of the Sign"). In similar fashion, we see that linguistics contributes to anthropology by showing how the autonomy of language with respect to thought on one side, the universe on the other, and finally to logical systems, is linked to discourse features (chapter 6, "Language, Reality, and Logic"); this same link is evident in the order by which discourse articulates the world (chapter 7, "Word Order and World Order"). Finally, the examination of discourse behavior provides knowledge about humanity which may facilitate cultural or political exploitation: in short, the power of language is a means to political power (chapter 8, "Wordmasters").

Part 3, "Theoretical Goals or Our Dialogical Nature," appears as the natural conclusion of this itinerary. Applied first to the utterance as a phenomenon of production and interpretation, this theoretical construction outlines three complementary approaches (chapter 9, "The Three Viewpoints Theory"). The debate is then broadened into a general perspective on the discourse relation and the human properties it defines (chapter 10, "Socio-Operative Linguistics; or, Toward a Theory of Communication"). The importance of social factors leads to the development of a central theme, which is the phenomenon of linguistic variation (chapter 11, "Speech Fluctuation"). We end with a consideration of the drive which linguists, through their theoretical models, seek to justify (chapter 12, "Love of Languages").

It was in early 1982 that I conceived the central idea of this book: linguistics cannot continue along its present path of isolated complacency, when language and speech are in fact so essential to the human species. Under the present circumstances, it is indeed a challenge to produce a broadly accessible study of the results of a science which, in trying to construct reasoned discourse about humanity, has taken on a rather austere profile. In attempting to meet this challenge, I have been greatly encouraged by the dedication and goodwill of Odile Jacob, who has also been an attentive reader and has offered me many useful suggestions.

I am grateful as well to all those who have devoted their time and efforts to assisting and advising me, especially A. Dufour, J. Duvaut, M. and F. Gasser, S. Platiel, and N. Revel-Macdonald.

By the Same Author

Esquisse linguistique du tikar (Cameroun). Paris: Société d'études linguistiques et anthropologiques de France, 1969.

La langue mbum de Nganha (Cameroun): Phonologie, Grammaire. Paris: Société d'études linguistiques et anthropologiques de France, 1970, 2 vols.

Profil d'un parler du Tchad. Paris: Geuthner, 1973.

Le problème linguistique des prépositions et la solution chinoise, avec un essai de typologie à travers plusieurs groups de langues. Collection linguistique publiée par la société linguistique de Paris. Louvain: Peeters, 1975.

La grammaire générative, Réflexions critiques. Collection Le Linguiste. Paris: PUF, 1976. *Critical Reflections on Generative Grammar.* A revised and expanded English translation. Chicago: Jupiter Press, 1981.

La phonologie panchronique (in collaboration with A. G. Haudricourt). Colletion Le Linguiste. Paris: PUF, 1978.

Le comox laamen de Colombie Britannique, présentation d'une lan-

gue amérindienne. Paris: Association d'ethnolinguistique amérindienne, 1981.

La structure des langues, Collection Que sais-je? Paris: PUF, 1982.

La réforme des langues: histoire et avenir (Language Reform: History and Future). In collaboration with I. Fodor, 3 vol. Hamburg: Buske, 1983–84.

Les catégories de la langue palau (Micronésie), une curiosité typologique. Munich: Fink, 1986.

Prefatory Note to the Second Edition

Certain readers of the first edition of this book, including several professional linguists, have been kind enough to offer me their constructive criticism. My desire to assimilate their suggestions has resulted in changes and corrections on about a dozen pages of this edition. While these modifications represent a very small portion of the book, the second edition is thus not entirely identical to the first. My thanks especially to S. Boucheron, J. Boulin, J. Deschamps, C. Jacques, K. Tommissen, C. Trocmé, and A. Sauvageot.

PART ONE

On Certain Advances in Linguistics

OR

The Human Profile

1

Unity of Species, Plurality of Languages

And the Flesh Was Made Word

Contrary to popular opinion, it is very likely that the immense diversity of currently existing languages cannot be traced to a single original language for all humanity. If there is uniformity, it is that of the language faculty particular to the human race, and not of the language itself. In the beginning, then, there must have been a single species (monogenesis of lineage), but not a single idiom (polygenesis of languages): such is the hypothesis set forward here.

It is no simple task to establish absolute historical beginnings. The more carefully we scrutinize the depths of the chasm in which we seem to see the emergence of the human species, the less simple becomes the task—both logically and with respect to the practical possibilities of transmission to the present. This is why any precise dating of "the moment at which humans appeared on earth" can have only the most speculative basis. On the other hand, the current state of anthropological research offers reasonable conjectures in favor of a prehistoric scenario whose principal stages may be retraced, although of course only along irremediably approximate lines. Four to five million years ago, the members of the genus *Homo* began to distinguish themselves more and more clearly from *Australopithecus,* who moreover did not become extinct and continued to live side by side with his descendant for some time. The appearance of the species *Homo habilis* may be placed at around 2.2 million years ago, between the Plio-Pleistocene (itself situated between the Tertiary and Quaternary periods) and the early Pleistocene. With *Homo habilis* began a very slow and irreversible movement of expansion, the fantastic adventure of which we are the present-day avatar. (Meanwhile, of course, we await further metamorphoses which are sometimes hinted at in science fiction—but about which science can tell us nothing!)

The region of the world in which, pending further revelations, the emergence of our ancient ancestor has been situated is eastern and southern Africa. Recent excavations have been particularly fruitful in three zones, constituting an almost continuous band: in Ethiopia, the sites of Melka Kunturé, Hadar (in the province of Wollo, in Afar country), and the Omo Valley; in Kenya, the eastern Turkana province; and in Tanzania, the Olduvai site. Of course, many peoples imagined these mythic Ethiopian confines to be the cradle of humanity long before evidence was supplied by the prehistoric discoveries of the modern epoch; and it was imagination—strengthened, of course, by contact with the sites and their inhabitants—that led the Greek historian Diodorus of Sicily (in the first century before Christ), who traveled extensively there, to reach the same conclusion. Nevertheless, we are today in possession of evidence that is more reliable than the ancient myths and tales.

At these three excavation sites, as well as at many prehistoric sites surrounding these deposits, teams of anthropologists[1] have revealed a considerable quantity of tools, which is to say fragments of stone crudely modified for scraping, piercing, chopping, gouging, etc. Of course, the existence of such tools does not mean that the primates who fashioned them were already representatives of the human species in the modern sense. Still, these primates are the very first living beings who may be associated with objects of their own making, and not only with biological properties. The invention and transmission of manufacturing techniques resulting from long experience, and the organization of a collective activity as important as hunting (upon which depended the survival of the species) imply capacities of symbolization as well as the emergence of consciousness and of a reflective awareness of emotion. As a corollary, we observe that cranial capacity increased greatly in comparison with that of *Australopithecus robustus* and *Australopithecus boisei*, the last of the Australopithecines. The temporal region and Broca's area, linked respectively to memory and language, were developing or emerging at the same time.

Only a unique ecological niche could be expected to combine the great number of conditions favorable to the perfecting of such a unique species. It is difficult to imagine how such a large and highly structured ensemble of factors could have been found identically realized in several distant regions. Moreover, it is only in eastern and southern Africa that vestiges attributed to *Homo habilis* have been discovered. Thus, given the present state of knowledge, we must presume this part of the world to be the cradle of humanity.

One problem remains, however. What process is at the origin of the essential properties which determine a new species—regardless of the chromosomic hypothesis we may use to sketch, for the final stage, their very rapid formation? Before the actual identification of the species, what events brought about the gradual emergence of hominids who must have possessed in their genetic code the aptitude for language, even if they did not immediately make use of it? Beginning in the upper Miocene, Africa appears to have undergone a climatic upheaval of decisive importance to the destiny of the developing human species. Extending over several hundreds of thousands of years, and despite some brief periods of remission, this climatic shift transformed the savannas of eastern Africa into regions of scanty steppes. This natural phenomenon precipitated the evolution which was to lead to *Homo habilis* and which we propose to interpret here in neo-Darwinian terms. In fact, forced to adapt themselves to the new environment which had irreversibly—although very slowly—imposed itself upon them, our ancestors developed more and more specific aptitudes in order to survive in a more and more hostile milieu, and this at the price of the irremediable loss of those individuals who did not succeed in adapting themselves. We may visualize this process by observing the drought which, today, and in precisely this same horn of East Africa, kills entire tribes and ravages their flocks, leaving behind only a desert landscape. We have considerable evidence of the characteristics that our ancestors then developed. Their endocranial capacity increased, resulting in a more and more "human" brow. Similar growth took place in the encephalic capacity and in the irrigation of the dura mater. Dentition became more even, showing clear traces of the omnivorous diet to which the species was constrained by the scarcity of vegetable

5

nourishment. The tools fashioned by these early humans attest to the growing complexity of their conceptualizations. Finally, there is every evidence that an environment hostile to their survival inspired a certain solidarity, creating a nucleus of social life and organization for the collective struggle against the threat of extinction. It is in this context —and at the same time as the related aptitude for life in society—that the faculty of *language* (but not yet, of course, its "immediate" use in the form of *languages* in the modern sense of the word) must have been associated with the genetic code of what, approximately 2.2 million years ago, was to become *Homo habilis.*

Can the "birth" of *Homo habilis* be more precisely defined? Can we establish the origin of the language faculty? The most cautious scholars prefer to assign it to a later stage of the history of the genus *Homo.* Perhaps it was during the middle Pleistocene, between 1.5 and 2 million years ago, the period in which a new species, *Homo erectus,* appeared, and during which endocranial capacity doubled, while tools became more and more regular and symmetrical. Perhaps it was even the period between the middle and upper Paleolithic (from two hundred thousand to thirty thousand years ago), which is—at last—the period of *Homo sapiens:* here we find relatively sophisticated techniques of stoneworking, traces of religious rites, the first evidence of burial and of funeral offertories, and cave drawings of increasing complexity which constitute very explicit monuments of abstract art and of ritual symbolism. In any case, humans may not have been able to use the faculty for language, which appears in the genetic code from the *Homo habilis* stage, until later. If the language faculty—whether or not it was first exploited in the form of gestural communication predating codes of diversified calls—can be assigned to the characteristics of *Homo habilis,* it is because all evidence indicates the very great complexity of their neurological organization. Consistent with this analysis is the idea that the physical, intellectual, and social characteristics of the species assume some means of communication.

Meanwhile, we have evidence of a fact of some importance for the debate on the origin of languages; a fact that we can interpret (again in neo-Darwinian terms) in light of natural selection constructing organisms of communication which show great diversity from their first appearance. A short time after speciation was complete, *Homo habilis* undertook vast migrations. Remains of mandibles and stone tools estimated at 1.6 or 1.8 million years old, dating therefore from the intermediate stage between *Homo habilis* and *Homo erectus* at the latest, have been found as far away from Africa as western Europe and eastern

Asia. These are vestiges of very ancient peregrinations of the human species. Judging from the observable traces of activity, the aptitude for language, while very probably already present at the time of these migrations, was nevertheless quite far from having produced linguistic communication in the modern sense.

Under these conditions, we may perhaps clarify some aspects of the origin of the language faculty. If we abandon the illusion of fixity that extends to prehistoric humans the characteristics of contemporary humanity, we may assume that the hundreds of thousands of years necessary for the emergence of the language faculty were followed by other vast periods during which it continued to develop. Similarly, we expect a reciprocal action which, as in all organisms studied by the life sciences, links innate faculties to milieu and history. This development is accompanied by a more and more complex structuring of the neocortex. Indeed, the latter, which with its some thirty billion neurons constitutes the seat of conceptual thought, invaded (but did not replace) older components: the archaic or reptilian brain, presumed center of the instincts, and the limbic system, seat of the emotions.[2]

Diversity and the Myth of Unity

We have seen that all evidence indicates virtual simultaneity of the birth of the species and the ancient migrations. Moreover, we can better sketch this vast adventure if we keep in mind the difference between the notions of speech faculty *(langage)* and language *(langue).*[3] Through a continuing series of improvements, the first more or less coded stammerings became regular formations; their repertories extended as the aptitude to symbolize became enriched with the more specific faculty of articulating thought in ordered signs expressed by combinations of sounds. But such an evolution itself assumes a considerable period of time and thus cannot have produced human *languages* in the contemporary sense of the term, until *after* the great migrations. Thus, in all likelihood, this process took place in several different geographical areas. The ecological milieu, nature and its sounds, vegetable and animal species as well as the sound phenomena they produced, were therefore quite diverse. Diverse also, in each living biocenosis (or community of interdependent beings), were the nuclei of social organization which were constituted, and, consequently, the first languages themselves. For, from the beginning, they were closely affiliated with these social organizations, although it is true that this relationship was gradually obscured by the progressive and arbitrary conventions that separate words and phrase structures from their original sources.

As to the universality of the "choice," by these dispersed prehistoric societies, of the vocal-auditory signifier to produce meaning when other routes were possible, this can certainly be explained. It was natural to extend the use of such organs as the nose, lips, and larynx, which already possessed nutritive, respiratory, and defensive functions, to that of communication. This is surely as true for our ancestors, who must have known such usage before the migratory period, as it is assumed to be for the higher animals, from mammals to birds, with whom their peregrinations placed them in contact in various environments. The concept of "natural" here has no metaphysical implication. We may perhaps reverse the old maxim that habit is "second nature": what we call nature may simply be first habit. But habit was strengthened by favorable factors, which better reflect the brilliant career of sound in the human adventure of language. Characteristic of the human species is the development of meanings which permit reception deferred in space (distance receptors, in Hall's terminology),[4] i.e., sight and hearing as opposed to touch, which determines more immediate close reception. We can understand why, of the distance receptors, hearing finally won out over sight, and the vocal-auditory character (transmitter-receptor) of human language dominated its visual character. Indeed, the latter characteristic is not always useful, since gestures are hardly, if at all, perceptible at night. The role of the gestural signifier, which was probably anterior to that of the sound signifier, has long been associated with the latter and remains, with variations among cultures, just as visible today. Due to the constraints of the physical world, however, gestures lost their primacy. Moreover, when distance is not too great, a total screen (caused by separation, relief, natural accident, etc.), while constituting an obstacle to sight, does not block auditory reception.

Finally, we note that the human species preferred sounds produced by exhalation, although the environment must have included species that produced sounds by inhalation of air, like the Equidae of today. The only place in the modern world where we find aspirated sounds, called "click consonants," and whose existence has never precluded expirated sounds, is South Africa: Hottentots, Bushmen, Zulus, and other populations speak click languages. There is no evidence that these African clicks are vestiges and that primitive humans began by using only sounds of this type. If we assume that the evolution of languages is cyclic and not linear, complex aspirated sounds could have been formed from simple sounds; and the evolution of articulations may progress from front to back after a phase of the cycle in which it progressed from back to front. In such a case, there would be no direct link between primitive clicks and clicks attested today. But it is not impossible that in certain regions of the globe to which our ancestors migrated, the very first phase of the cyclic history of langages included aspirated sounds.[5]

Thus, the adoption of the vocal-auditory route to communication is universal; it characterizes all organisms clearly manifesting the faculty of language. But it took place in areas of the world far enough apart that evolving human languages were, from the very beginning, distinct from one another. We can thus posit an original diversity of languages as perfectly compatible with the unity of the aptitude for language that enters into the definition of the species. It is clear that in positing this diversity, we call into question the myth of unity. Certainly, the uniqueness of mother-languages themselves is not assumed by all. Indo-Europeanists, for example, do not necessarily claim that a unique, original Indo-European language existed. But no matter how cautious the experts may be, the tenacious myth of unity has long inspired the speculation of amateurs.

Linguists attempt to reconstruct proto-languages family by family. And as divergences are reduced when we retrace them through time, we should in fact arrive at a smaller and smaller number of language prototypes. On the horizon before us, then, looms the myth of unity. Of course, we do not openly proclaim this dream of identity, for which all comparisons serve as pretexts. But the confusion between unity of origin of the human species and unity of the "first language" appears in the work of one of the great precursors of the comparativists: Leibniz. "There is nothing," says Theophilus to Philalethes,[6] "which conflicts with—indeed there is nothing which does not support—the belief in the common origin of all nations and in a primitive root-language." Yet, as we delve into the past, the distinction between similarity of languages with common ancestors, and borrowings between languages of different origins, continues to dwindle. Whatever artifice we use to subsume or precipitate it in a proposed whole, whatever nostalgia we may have for an original purity in complete harmony with the Creator, the diversity of languages resists the temptation of unity.

Speech and the Innate

The debate over innate and acquired behavior, in ignoring the dialectic of the relationship between the two, has already inspired many long and pointless academic disputes. The study of speech makes an important contribution to this discussion, for it emphasizes an intermediate link: the human ability to generate an infinite number of sentences, as implied by the concept of *competence* defined by Chomsky[7] (some of whose related intuitions, as we will later see, are more dubious). We shall assume that this natural aptitude of children is applied to the sentence models provided by those around them. However, if this link can in fact be recreated in ontogeny (child language learning), it is absent from the first moments of phylogeny (the birth of language in the species). In the latter case, social organization assumes some means of communication. Rudimentary at first, this process eventually (according to the most conservative estimates, not before the appearance of *Homo sapiens*) produced languages. But while we may assume that, originally, social life had biological roots in the human species, it is nonetheless clear that once group life began to develop, a permanent interaction of social and cerebral factors was established. This is why we will qualify in some measure the biologist's point of view: "It seems likely (but of course always hypothetical) that the development of the social bond, strongly increasing in the higher primates, is at first the *consequence* and not the cause of the growth of the neocortex."[8] While we accept this hypothesis, let us not forget that the author himself goes on to say: "We must not, however, exclude the possibility of a reverse contribution of the social milieu to the genetic evolution of the direct ancestors of man." Moreover, Changeux makes reference to the "significant variability of the organization of the cortex in relation to the cultural environment."[9]

Assuming, then, that biological encoding is not the only factor to consider, we must nonetheless acknowledge its importance. This point has inspired a great deal of research among specialists of the brain and of aphasia.[10] We need only remember that as early as 1861,[11] Broca had established a direct correlation between lesions of the left frontal lobe and the speech handicap which bears his name: in Broca's aphasia we find oral (and graphic) expression seriously impaired in a number of ways: slowness, substitutions and telescoping of words, and even more significant alterations of grammar. We know that hemispheric specialization of the cognitive systems is a characteristic which distinguishes the human brain from that of nonhuman primates. In addition, the biological roots of sensitivity to speech have been demonstrated by various research. Thus, it appears that the human cortex contains acoustic detectors specifically adapted to the distinctive features of language sounds: experiments carried out upon infants of 3 to 5 months show that they react positively to the oppositions *ba / pa* (voiced / unvoiced) or *ba / da* (labial / dental).[12]

Eventually, perhaps, we will achieve a better understanding of how the original diversity of languages assumed here correlates with the unity of the human species endowed with speech. One of the most promising avenues—and one of the least explored, no doubt because it requires a high level of competence in both linguistics and neurology— is the search for cerebral mechanisms involved in communication. Neurobiologists were carrying out rudimentary research in this area as early as 1962 (Hyden) and 1964 (Barbizet).[13] According to this work, the sensorial stimuli produced by an object or a notion reach the cortex via innumerable branching paths which constitute a sort of neuronic *metacircuit* unique to each object or notion. For every sign of a language, the metacircuit would then be the neurological trace of what, in linguistics, is called "meaning."

On the other hand, this meaning, as well as the structures of sentences, must be fixed by memory, which must integrate both the motor functions corresponding to the articulatory gestures of the speaker and the perceptive recognition linked to the reception of messages by the hearer. Hyden's hypothesis is the following: memory deposits or *engrams* are constituted in the brain, along the metacircuits, by modifications of the structures of the macromolecules of ribonucleic acid (RNA); these are distinct from the macromolecules of deoxyribonucleic acid (DNA), as shown, for example, by their effects in the case of retaining traces: genetic memory—that is, conservation through all descendance of properties linked to the genetic code—has its seat in the structure of DNA, and is virtually indestructible; while human memory, based in the structure of RNA, is notoriously faulty and uncertain. In any case, Hyden's hypothesis postulates the biochemical character of engrams,[14] and implies that memory, especially linguistic memory, is not simply the "mental function" of classical philosophers, but can be, through its material side, characterized as a general property of nerve tissue. This approach constitutes a serious challenge to the persistent idealism of certain social scientists, who, in pure scholastic tradition, remain indifferent to the biological roots of behavior.

Having recalled this general framework, we may suppose that en-

11

gram types vary with language types. Let us take only one example, which applies to the typological differences treated in chapter 3: that of languages with limited morphology, i.e., weak differentiation between words with related meanings and distinct functions. The engrams corresponding to this opposition between languages according to the complexity of their morphology must themselves be distinct. Moreover, word order (another distinctive factor) has an increased role in languages with limited morphology, where it must bear responsibility for the indication of variable functions (see chapter 7).

Neurological organization and processes, whose importance for linguistic communication we are only beginning to understand, are obviously common to the species and innate. This, however, does not exclude the relationship of reciprocal influence which links them to social behavior during the development of the species. Moreover, if we set aside for the moment the history of speech in the species and consider the facts according to the process of child language acquisition, we must then wonder about the nature of this faculty in humans today. The aptitude for self-expression, first through single words, then by arranging them in sentences, is not an entirely autonomous ability and cannot be dissociated from intelligence.

The sensory-motor stage of intelligence is not exclusively human and precedes speech in the development of children, as can be observed by their behavior: establishment of correspondences between objects, perception of order of succession, interlocking schemas, and other structures linked to general coordination of activity, and which will later be used linguistically.[15] Can we then deduce something about the abstract mechanisms constraining the form of grammars, mechanisms which the generativist theory considers to be universal and innate?[16] Even if we assume that these mechanisms have psychological reality, and are something other than purely general principles incorporated into the theoretical apparatus,[17] they would not be specific enough to make human speech appear distinct from other systems of communication. Children possess a knowledge of the structures of the world, and this knowledge reflects, independently of speech, the fact that they have a particular perceptive apparatus and live on the earth—both biological givens. In learning to speak, they learn, on the one hand, to use signs and combinations of signs to construct the linguistic expressions which make up their language; and, on the other hand, to apply these expressions concerning the world to the knowledge that they have of this world. It is the capacity for this dual learning process which, in the form of the faculty of language, has been inscribed in the code of the species from *Homo habilis* to *Homo sapiens* and which, in a similar but not identical manner (see chapter 2), is inscribed in the biology of the child.

Unlike what occurred at the dawn of the species, however, linguistic expression in the child does not arise entirely spontaneously. The hereditary transmission of a capacity to learn to speak, or even of a fixed schema regulating language, cannot suffice to explain language learning as we see it take place. Clearly, the language faculty cannot itself be learned. But how could this faculty in and of itself explain the acquisition of language between 22 months and 3 to 4 years, if the imitation of adults, interacting with the capacity to integrate what is imitated, did not play an essential role?

In the sixties, it was believed[18] that the linguistic environment of the child was characterized by poverty and numerous mistakes: thus it was easy to assume that the innate aptitude, faced with a rather mediocre exterior input, would have the decisive role almost to itself. Reality is otherwise: it is only in the first stages of life, between birth and the second year, that adults speaking to children use simple (but not impoverished) language: they tend to exaggerate intonational contours, raise vocal inflections, shorten sentences, limit syntactic relations, make liberal use of doubled syllables and other hypocoristic procedures, replace direct address ("you") with "he," "she," "baby," etc. Such tendencies are confirmed in the languages of the world where this type of communication has been studied, from Bengali (India) to Tzeltal (Guatemala) and including Lithuanian, Luo (Sudan), and French.[19] Children of all ages, however, are exposed as much to the discourse of adults among themselves, which they hear continually, as to that which adults address to them; besides, the characteristics which we have mentioned concern only the first stages of life. Three-year-olds, imitating adults, themselves speak "baby talk" with younger chidren. This extensive adaptation of communicative behavior may very well be a general property of the species, and even of related species, according to the specialists who teach sign language to apes: older chimpanzees, for example, slow their gestures when addressing younger ones.[20]

For subsequent stages, much research[21] has established that adults' sentences to children, from the moment the latter are no longer "infants" in the etymological sense (Lat. *in-fans*, "speechless"), are diverse and clearly structured, even in very different languages. As we might expect, utterances gain in complexity as the child grows.

One of the reasons for the continuing confusion in the innateness debate is that we do not always distinguish clearly between speech *(langage)* and languages *(langues)*. The difference between the two notions, necessary to the clarity of the discussion, was pointed out in the first part of this chapter. As we have seen, the facts suggest that only the speech faculty is innate. But certain modern theories of innateness go further. Thus generative grammar, which already assigns to this faculty the abstract mechanisms constraining the form of linguistic systems, attributes to it the specific domain of syntax as well. The latter is, in fact, characterized by a hierarchical organization of the elements of the sentence, whatever the language, whether in the case of the simplest two-word utterance (since the two must certainly have different functions in order to constitute a message and not a pure accumulation), or complex sentences with many conjunctive terms, in which the clauses are subordinated to each other, with frequent cases of embedding. The innateness theory claims that such hierarchical organization is inscribed in the genetic code, by virtue of principles like the transformational cycle: this principle states, for example, that in forming a complex sentence, a single series of transformations applies successively to what will be the lowest subordinate clause (in languages like English or French), then to the next highest, and so on up to the matrix.[22]

Yet such a conclusion is not inevitable. Suppose we further extend our application of neo-Darwinian ideas (in a partially metaphoric sense) to linguistics. We can then claim that these complex entities (produced by an evolution comparable to the biological one outlined in *The Origin of Species*) are hierarchically organized, according to their selective advantages, by a statistical—or even a logical—"necessity."[23] In most cases, in fact, the products of evolution—here, the sentences which languages allow us to formulate—are made up of constituents which are, or which derive from, elements that were originally free units, functioning independently as messages. The evolution toward complexity is thus quite natural, at least until the cyclic history of languages begins a reverse movement: the association of free units to form sentences with embedded structures is a response to the pressures of a system of communication which, through the evolution of social relations, creates the need for more and more complex formulations.

Thus, the syntactic hierarchies and other properties that the innateness models assign to the totality of languages, and assume to be written into the genetic code, may be expained in evolutionary terms without recourse to the innateness theory. The natural experimentation observed in creoles (chapter 2) confirms the role of social factors, the importance of which we will also see later when we study the general properties of languages (chapter 3), and discourse factors in relation to writing (chapter 4). Through this line of study we will be able to establish with more and more precision the true linguistic definition of the human species.

2

The Creole Laboratory

The Shadow of the Past

Like most of the social sciences, linguistics is unable to carry out trials on the actual genesis of its object of study. We can—and do—conduct all kinds of experiments on the acquisition of speech, on the production and audition of sounds, on the application of syntactic rules, and on the reception of messages. But it is not possible to reconstruct the birth of a language as a manifestation of the faculty of speech. Much could be learned from such an experiment if only it could be performed. If we could observe a language as it evolves from an absence of communication, we would be able to grasp the essential nature of our most human characteristic; we would also acquire crucial insights on the innateness debate.

And yet, might not this perfect experiment of which linguists often dream actually exist somewhere—hidden, yet within their reach? Within our field of inquiry lies a special group of languages: some linguists express no interest in them, while others, even when specializing in them, do not always have a clear idea of the insights such languages can bring to general considerations on speech. Pidgins and creoles seem to await integration into a coherent linguistic theory. And yet they appear (and we will separate the real from the apparent, below) to provide the opportunity, rare in the social sciences, for informal experimentation in a natural laboratory that spontaneously reproduces the conditions of birth. Linguistic theories that remain locked in the present are blind to the genesis of languages. Were it not for this barrier, the study of creoles could be promoted to the leading edge of the language sciences. But the conspicuous concern observed today in countries where creoles are spoken reflects economic and political, rather than scientific, motives. In most cases these are third world countries, former colonies to which the West, under the combined pressure of its bad conscience and its own interests, extends purely verbal signs of compassion.

But aside from the creolists, western linguists are mainly concerned with the "major languages" (French, English, Spanish, Portuguese) which, in the mouths of slave traders and colonists, provided the foundations of most of the early pidgins. They reject the notion of new (but hardly prestigious) beginnings based upon the genetic model applicable to any language, which creole types, however modest, can nevertheless illustrate. Behind the sublimated racism of these scholars, expressed by protestations of concern designed to stifle all dissent, lurks a powerful intellectual bigotry: could the Africans, the Asians, and the West Indians possibly have reproduced, in shortened form, the genesis of the major languages of the West? Further, could the formation of creoles provide, almost before our eyes (given their youth), a condensed image of the last evolutionary stages of language as the defining trait of *Homo sapiens*?

As seductive as this hypothesis may be, the situation is not nearly so simple; besides, the "new beginnings" theory subtly reduces creole speakers to a prehuman state. In its strictest form, it portrays them as a sort of lesser humanity of slaves presumably dispossessed of the power to speak their own languages, and humanizing themselves through the process of pidginization. The elucidation of this problem requires a precise understanding of the facts and careful theoretical reflection upon their necessary interconnection.

The Three Geneses

Linguistics has always been tempted by the model of the life sciences. In biology, the relation between phylogeny (the evolution of organisms) and ontogeny (the development of the embryo) has long been a subject of debate. It has often been asked if, in the history of species, phylogeny was actually the cause of ontogeny, or the preceding step, or the model reproduced; or whether in fact the opposite were true.[1]

In 1866, the scientific community witnessed the formulation of the famous biogenetic law by E. Haeckel, "whose impact upon the history of ideas compares with that of Darwin."[2] According to this law, the connection between phylogeny and the initial stages of ontogeny in living species "is not exterior or superficial, but profound, intrinsic, and causal."[3] Taken literally, this law would reflect[4] a strictly recapitulationist view of the stages of the individual embryo, each stage recreating one member in the complete series of adult ancestors. Thus ontogeny would be a brief history of the species itself. Biologists have not hesitated to criticize this simplified view of the facts, showing[5] that, for many species, the order of stages in embryonic development is a violation of evolutionary history as it has been reconstituted. But the principal weakness in Haeckel's thesis is the erroneous assignation of repetitive ontogenetic stages to the adult form of the ancestor. If there is a recapitulation, we must assume that it does not involve adult ancestors, but comparable stages in the development of immature phylogenetic precursors. Further, if recapitulation does in fact occur, it applies less to the embryo, which is globally conceived in complete correspondence with one ancestor, than to certain functional systems of its physiology. These systems have evolutionary sources distinguishing them from each other and providing independent evidence of various developmental schemas.[6] Thus rectified, Haeckel's recapitulationist model retains its interest and its value which, experts agree, are undeniable in biology.

This reference to biology is not merely ornamental. Powerful currents inspired by the life sciences in the nineteenth century attracted many linguists to the possibility of adapting biological models and terminology to the social sciences. Thus two fundamental processes could be treated as two manifestations, on different scales, of a single history—our history—that of the reciprocal development of man and of speech. One of these processes is the phylogeny of speech, its development in the human species from its "origins." The other is the ontogeny, or acquisition, of speech by the child in the form of a specific language. But the ideological consequences of such a mechanical application of the recapitulationist model to linguistics is immediately apparent. In simplest form, this approach eventually produces some rather worrisome equations: thus child language corresponds to the "childhood" of language; primitive languages are languages of "primitive" peoples; while more highly evolved languages are those of more "civilized" societies. A century or so ago, such equations seemed quite natural.[7] Contemporary scholars are more cautious.

Still, if an intermediate link existed in which the features of both phylogenetic and ontogenetic processes could be read, then perhaps the problem of the link which joins them could be reformulated: between phylogeny and ontogeny, we might define a third process, *cainoglossy*, the birth of a new language following presumed loss of another idiom. In a recent work which has been widely discussed in the English-language press,[8] D. Bickerton claims that this scenario of birth, strikingly illustrated by the development of pidgins and then of creoles, provides the missing link: "the equivalent of the Galapagos for Darwin!"

He undertakes to show that all creoles share certain syntactic and semantic characteristics, in particular the existence of three oppositions, which he considers fundamental (and which he emphasizes, strengthening the traditional view of discontinuity; see chapter 3): opposition of time, anterior and nonanterior; of mode, real and irreal; and of aspect, punctual and nonpunctual. He then concludes that, in order to explain the profound resemblances between these languages, we must recognize the cognitive processes ruling the passage from pidgin (an earlier stage defined by its rudimentary simplicity and economy) to creole as characteristic properties of languages. They would belong to what he calls a "bioprogram," genetically transmitted at birth and determined by the history of the species. But, as he points out, there is no reason that only creole-speaking children should possess the ability to create a language structured in this way. The same faculty must be present in children who learn any language; Bickerton undertakes to show this using research on language learning, particularly studies of creative errors and of the acquisition of grammatical categories. Extending this demonstration to the problem of the origin of the human speech faculty, the author claims that there must have existed in pre-hominid species a cognitive structure built upon distinctions similar to those found in creoles—and those which children, in every language, acquire before the others and in the most automatic way.

Although Haeckel is not mentioned, the method is clearly recapitulationist: the ontogeny of a creole and the acquisition of the native language duplicate the birth of speech itself. Creoles appear as the irrefutable image of child language learning: not in the sense which inspired the old linguistic racism of "baby talk," the infantile language of childish colored folk; but in the sense that creole speakers, like children, create speech because they are programmed to do so. Creoles thus open a broad avenue for research: they can solve the mystery of our linguistic origins.

The argument is a clever one. Accordingly, creole languages provide evidence not of a retrogade pantomime by underdeveloped actors, but of a fascinating revenge: the revenge of the humiliated, who had been reduced to subhumanity by the stubborn fantasies of slave traders anxious to absolve themselves by inventing this "justification." Now these supposed subhumans can, through their languages, help to establish (as Bickerton's dedication explicitly states) the identity of "real humanity." What is the value of this evidence, and of the author's use of it?

Substratum and Learning

As we have seen (chapter 1), the portion of the child's language learning which comes from the genetic code, i.e., from the neurological imprint of a universal cognitive schema, is already present and fully constituted at birth. This component could not, of course, reflect the stages through which the code was formed over hundreds of thousands of years of human history. Early humanity did not have the preexisting model that the child receives at birth, having acquired the basic framework while in the womb.

The creation of speech by the first users of pidgins is also unique. Assimilating it to the other two geneses betrays its special nature. Writing about the creole of Guyana (a former British possession), certain registers of which appear to be influenced by English, Bickerton claims that "decreolization" leads to greater and greater resemblance to English. Thus, just as the child's language tends to improve, creole speakers tend more and more toward the European language from which the creole derived. It follows that the author supports the notion of a *continuum* or uninterrupted line of progression between those registers closest to pidgin and those which most resemble English. This approach fails to take into account individual variation, and the image that individual speakers have of their language and culture. It obliterates the social aspect of discourse. The belief in the continuum coincides with the denial of the *substratum*, the lost language which occasionally reemerges. In the effort to prove the innateness of schemata which control similar manifestations in very different creoles, there is a great temptation to ignore—or at least to minimize—the role of the substratum. Inversely, those who believe only in the substratum pay little attention to the innateness argument. Yet, contrary to the most rigid theory of innateness, it is not true that the first pidgin speakers had no preexisting model at their disposal, no original language acting as a substratum for new languages—those of the colonists—which were acquired through imitation. The situation may instead be compared to what is known of much more recent pidgins. The end of the nineteenth and beginning of the twentieth centuries witnessed the constitution of vehicular pidgins, rudimentary means of communication between groups placed in contact but speaking different languages.

For these pidgins owed a great deal to the coexisting local languages. Thus in the pidgins of Melanesia, Australia, and the Vanuatu (Bislama), every transitive verb is obligatorily followed by a special marker -*im* or -*em*; in form, this suffix is a borrowing from English *him*, but in function, it directly reflects a vernacular syntactic constraint: in the Melanesian languages in question, transitive verbs are obligatorily followed by a transitive suffix. Similar cases could be cited in the domain of possession or in that of aspect and time. But this importance of the substratum in recently formed Melanesian pidgins is far from unique. The first African slaves,[9] torn from their homes and transported to foreign plantations, certainly ceased to speak their own languages; but this does not mean that those languages disappeared entirely. Certainly the slave traders, in an effort to uproot the prisoners, mixed individuals from different tribes in order to separate speakers of the same languages. But the most recent studies[10] call into question the notion of linguistic annihilation. Further, the masters' languages were grafted onto the structures of African languages which, although of distinct families, were closely related. Given this, the resemblance between the evolutionary stages of various creoles of African origin and European lexical base can be explained: the substrata are closely related, as are, for that matter, the genetically and typologically related European languages which were grafted onto them.

The Concept of Simplicity: Myth and Reality

Even if we overlook the substratum objection, other doubts arise with respect to the theory of three geneses. This is especially true for its characterization of pidgins. The creoles which succeeded most pidgins were formed rather quickly, and recently enough so that the process is more or less observable, as if in a natural language "factory." But the innateness theory conceives pidgins, later transformed by spontaneous process into creoles, as systems of communication destined to respond to emergencies—rudimentary codes with properties that are of no real interest except inasmuch as they permit us to characterize an *operational minimum* for discourse.

In order to define the properties of this type of code, a lexical test has been proposed:[11] for a "normal" language, the number of *hapax legomena* (words which appear only once) in a text of five or six hundred words represent 46 to 48 percent of the whole. If the percentages are considerably lower, the language cannot be normal. Such a criterion presupposes that a lexicon with sufficient entries to reduce the frequencies of the same words in a text constitutes a defining property for a language. This does not take into account the possibilities offered by juxtaposition of existing words, a natural way to create new meanings. A relatively short Chinese text could very well contain recurrent usages of the words *zhǎo,* "look for," and *dào,* "attain," not only to express each of these two meanings, but also in contiguity, since "find" is *zhǎodào.* In any case, the application of this criterion yields mixed results: the percentage is 42.94 percent for Motu (a New Guinean pidgin) and 31.5 percent for Sango (a pidginized variety of Ngbandi, in the Central African Republic).[12] Thus, the former would be close to a "real language," and the latter would not be. Yet both of them, widely used in their respective countries, have the status of primary national language. The "inauthenticity" imposed upon them by this lexical criterion does not seem to prevent them from fully playing their role.

The real issue here is the idea of simplicity, a notion loaded with psycho-cultural presumptions. Simplicity, which is often assumed to be ideally illustrated by pidgins, needs an objective definition. The communicative urgency of linguistically deprived situations has not, as is commonly believed, imposed an operational minimum. It does, however, explain the simultaneous presence of three fundamental tendencies in this type of languages: economy, analyticity, and motivation.

The tendency toward economy is manifested in the small number of sounds, of syllabic types, of prepositions, and of verbal tenses, as well as in the use of intonation as sole question marker (as in informal French, where *tu viens?* ("You're coming?") is more frequent than *viens-tu?* or *est-ce que tu viens?*). Economy is also manifested through invariability of form, and through its corollary, positional syntax: the nature of words, as well as the relationships between them, are a function of their position in the utterance. Thus, in Cameroons Pidgin English, the same word *dem* (from English *them*) appears both as a prenominal possessive, as in *dem hat*, "their hearts," and as a preverbal plural person marker, as in *dem kom*, "they come." Furthermore, discontinuous expressions, which require identification of each constituent and recovery of continuity, are absent: *bring him up* produces the verb *bringimapim* ("raise") in Bislama (Vanuatu) and in Melanesian pidgin. Here, the obligatory transitive marker *-im* (see above), is automatically suffixed, while in the English base it is already present between the verb and the particle *up*, here *ap*. Finally, pidgins resort almost exclusively to juxtaposition for the process of creation. The relation between two juxtaposed words results from their pure contiguity. This method is thus less onerous, in structural terms, than affixation (adjunction of prefix, suffix, etc.), composition with alteration of one or both components, internal modification through insertion or reduction, and accentual or tonal variation. Pidgins make extensive use of juxtaposition of two identical words, a process giving plural or intensive value (chapter 5).

The analytical tendency, i.e., the transparent association of units creating predictable meanings, clearly appears in the fixed succession of words whose sole position suffices to categorize them as either notion-words or function-words. Let us take a creole example which, on this particular point of syntax, resembles the evidence of pidgins: the French sentence *il m'a cueilli une noix de coco dont je me suis repu* ("he picked me a coconut with which I satisfied my hunger") appears in Haitian creole as: *I / fèk / sot / rivé / kéyi / ũ / kok / vin / bã / mwẽ / m / mãžé / vãt / mwẽ / vin / plẽ / plẽ,* literally "he / only does (= "has just") / leave / arrive / pick / a / coconut / come / give (from classical French *bailler*) / me / I / eat / belly / me / come / full / full." We see the action fragmented by a hyperanalytical and documentary perspective into a veritable kaleidoscope of microevents, as if the camera of discourse were linguistically filming the kinetics of the operation. The French *m'a cueilli*, which presumes a movement towards the goal and a return from it, corresponds in creole to a succession "leave-arrive-pick-come-give-me." African languages like Ewe (Togo), Yoruba (Nigeria), and Cameroons Pidgin English offer analytical structures of the same type, corroborating the substratum thesis.

The third tendency of pidgins, that of motivation, is logically linked to the other two. It illustrates a law of equilibrium, through which reduced burden on memory is balanced by additional impositions upon the encoding of structures. Indeed, a highly motivated lexicon abounds in descriptive paraphrases. It contains a greater number of combinations and, consequently, a smaller number of words than a lexicon with lower motivation. Neo-Melanesian pidgin contains a number of pairs like *gut / nogut*. The French and English equivalents, *bon / mauvais* and *good / bad* are not constructed upon the opposition between absence and presence of a negative prefix; but this economy of structure is counterbalanced by opacity, since learning them requires memorizing two terms, without the possibility of a deductive procedure applicable to a derivational relation.

The evolution from pidgin to creole illustrates in many cases the progression from the analytical to the synthetic, an essential part of one stage of the morphosemantic cycle (see chapter 10). Starting from the synthetic Latin form *cantabo* ("I shall sing") we find, in the Roman period, *cantar(e) avyo*, a form dislocated with respect to the original; in more classical Middle French, the two elements are reknit and an unstressed preposed element *je* is added to the suffixed personal marker, hence *je chanterai*. A new avatar appears in Haitian pidgin, according to a different evolutionary line grafting itself onto that of French: the verbal notion and future sense are separated, the preposition-adverb *après* expresses the future, hence *mo après chanter;* but in Haitian creole, the form is resynthesized by double elision, thus *m'ap-chanté*.

The tendencies toward economy, analyticity, and motivation which appear thus as characteristics of pidgins are the very tendencies also observed in the spoken style of languages possessing a separate literary tradition. French provides an example. *Tu vas où?* ("You're going where?"), *ça veut dire quoi?* ("That means what?"), *vous êtes combien?* ("You are how many?"), *il s'en va quand?* ("He's leaving when?"), illustrate the tendency toward invariability of sequences: the interrogative structure preserves the word order of the affirmative *tu vas à Paris* ("You're going to Paris"), *ça veut dire que non* ("That means no"), *vous êtes six* ("You are six" i.e., there are six of you), *il s'en va demain* ("He's leaving tomorrow"). Further, spoken French tends to use the same functional words with different intonational contours for interrogation and assertion, as in the causal sense of: *La maîtresse l'a puni.*

24

("The teacher punished him.")—*Parce que?* ("Because?")—*Parce qu'il bavardait.* ("Because he was talking.") Analytical comparatives and negatives are also preferred: the colloquial *mauvais / plus mauvais* and *pareil / pas pareil* are more strongly motivated pairs than the "correct" *mauvais / pire* ("bad / worse") and *pareil / différent* ("same / different"). Invariability also rules the irregular derivations employed on a large scale in the spoken French of pseudo-intellectuals and the technical French of certain scholars, perhaps in part under the influence of English: the verbs *lister* (from "list"), *visionner* (from "vision"), etc.

This resemblance of pidgins to the spoken registers of many languages provides several lessons. The three tendencies simultaneously attested in pidgins can be found dispersed through most major dialects. They reappear cyclically in the history of these languages under the pressure of spoken style. Characteristics which illustrate these tendencies can thus be considered dominant, as opposed to the recessive traits statistically characterized as such because of their declining frequency in the world's languages. This, then, is the sole objective criterion of simpicity. A language is simpler than another language if it contains more dominant traits, i.e. properties broadly diffused in most known languages. This large diffusion of dominant traits could correspond to a selective advantage for the users of a language. The situation would then be comparable to that of the notion of a dominant trait in neo-Darwinism, illustrated by the classic example of industrial melanism (black coloring) in geometrid moths: a dark form of the moth prevails over a light form which had been dominant during the period before the industrial revolution, but which is no longer adapted to the new conditions of life.[13] We are borrowing biological terminology here in order to emphasize the frequency parameter which can explain linguistic facts and provide us with a measure of simplicity. Languages of traditional societies living apart from the great centers of socio-economic exchange are most often those containing concentrations of recessive traits.

From the preceding we can see that pidgins, while economical, analytical, and motivated languages, are not, however, simple languages in the sense of rudimentary instruments responding to a need for minimal communication. Rather, they are languages rich in dominant traits. We cannot therefore summarily conclude that the development of creoles from pidgins is an argument in favor of a theory of creologenesis as an intermediate link between ontogeny and phylogeny of language. Creoles have developed in situations of community life imposed upon people with different languages. The effort to communicate in the absence of a common language naturally engenders codes. If these situations do not last, or if they are only intermittent, the codes thus created do not reach the creole stage and may even disappear. Thus Russnorsk, a Russo-Norwegian pidgin spoken from the second half of the eighteenth century until the Russian Revolution of 1917, was used only during the summer months between Russian merchants and Norwegian fishermen. When the socio-economic conditions favoring this commerce ceased to exist, Russnorsk disappeared. This historical example amply illustrates the role of situational factors.

There is, of course, no denying that the developers of creoles, given their circumstances, were predisposed by their genetic code to exercise cognitive faculties unique to the species. But neither is it reasonable to ignore the role of the substrata, those pre-existing languages which the plantation slaves had not so completely forgotten as has been claimed. The similarities between all of these African languages contributed crucially to the resemblances among the creoles of former Africans; moreover, the European languages of the masters—the immediately available models—were themselves quite closely related. These two elements, neither one attributable to innateness, played an essential role and help to explain the remarkable resemblance among creoles. Thus we cannot simply point to the predispositions of a bioprogram that commands linguistic destiny without regard for social factors. The creole laboratory is not a hermetically sealed autoclave.

3

Language Universals and Typological Differences

Amazing Diversity

Perhaps the most fascinating characteristic of the universe of languages is its diversity. And this diversity cannot be calculated by differences of aptitude. It is well known that, in many parts of the world, a single language is common to people of radically dissimilar lifestyles (such as the great economic and cultural differences in Brazilian and Saudian society); and that inversely, individuals with very similar characteristics (for example lawyers, writers, artists) cannot communicate from one nation or social structure to another, for lack of a common language. Neither is this state of affairs a reflection of morphological differences. If imaginary observers from another planet undertook to list human physical characteristics, and used the results to guess the number of languages according to variations within the species, they would arrive at an estimate of a half dozen, at most. Indeed, whether we use the number of races, the structure of the skeleton, or blood groups, current anthropological evaluations cluster around this number. Suppose our observers take into account divergences necessarily introduced by history; and variations which, in nature, normally link large identifiable units to each other. In that case, if they wished to be more precise, they might posit the existence of a dozen derived systems, corresponding to what are called dialects, whose kinship with each other and with the major languages would be close enough for human speakers themselves to have a clear awareness of the relations.[1]

In fact, the situation is entirely different. Estimates vary, of course, according to the criteria of status and classification adopted. Some scholars consider certain idioms (in the general sense) to be dialects of a single language, i.e., systems of communication identified as different, but not enough so to pose an obstacle to comprehension; others attribute to each of these idioms the status of a language; one may include or exclude some of the most prestigious dead languages from which certain living languages sprang, and from which they still borrow. But we may say that there are at least 4,500 to 6,000 languages spoken today on the earth, not counting the hundreds or thousands of others which have not been discovered. These are to be found in isolated regions, unknown or inaccessible to those who are not used to living or traveling there: the High Plateaus of New Guinea, the Brazilian and Peruvian Amazon, central and southwest Africa, the mountainous regions along the borders between the Soviet Union and China, or between India and Burma, and the large and small islands of the Indian Ocean and the south Pacific, from Sumatra and Borneo to the western Polynesian islands.

The extraordinary diversity of languages would thus seem even greater if we knew all those which elude our desire to know or our power to classify. And it would in fact be greater were it not equally true that many languages disappear with the last of their aged speakers. How can we explain this phenomenon, often observed by linguists? The hypothesis of inadaptation as a factor of degeneration, applicable to living species, is unsubstantiated in this case. In fact, languages that disappear are in no way ill-adapted to the needs of those who used them, nor are their lexicons or grammars so impoverished that they cease to be of practical use. The real reasons lie elsewhere. In those accessible areas where minority languages are still spoken but are rapidly losing their identity, increased interactions cause the irresistible diffusion of languages that convey money, technology, and ideology: on the world scale, American English; on that of the largest modern state, Russian in the Soviet Union. Minority ethnic languages, by which these three values are not communicated, are powerless to defend themselves: they

28

disappear one after another. But this is only the contemporary version of a process of extinction begun centuries ago. The history of mankind is characterized by the continuous annihilation of the most vulnerable cultures and languages; it is fair to recall, however, that this is balanced by the birth of new ones.

The outcome naturally depends upon the language's capacities for self-defense. In the case of Old Persian and classical Tibetan, we possess not only literary monuments preserved in writing (see chapter 4), but also brilliant descendants, living languages that sprang from these dead idioms. Such is not the case for indigenous languages which have disappeared (and continue to disappear) across North America under the pressure of English, which obliterates the Indian cultures; nor for those idioms which have been swallowed up or banished from the Amur and Kamchatka regions by the advance of Russian, which invades their vocabulary or their grammar. Among these languages of strictly oral tradition, those which die leave neither trace nor descendants. And yet it is true that the death of a language is a cultural, and not a biological, fact; and that consequently, resurrection (at least when the language was written) is theoretically possible. But in practice this does not often occur, the case of Hebrew being exceptional. The rebirth of the latter required stubborn determination, extremely favorable circumstances, and a kind of (un)conscious obsession. It is not often that any, let alone all, of these conditions are met.

However, despite the extinction of some languages and the inaccessibility of others, the inventory of languages remains immense. This supports the theory of diversity of origin (see chapter 1), as opposed to the notion of a single first language.

Such diversity inspires two opposite reactions. There are those who deplore it, either because they have no desire or ability to learn foreign languages, or because they see in this Babel the cause (as if there were not other more fundamental ones) of misunderstandings, or even of conflicts between nations. Or perhaps it is even because, while not opposed to fleeting peregrinations among different languages, they fear that extended visits could constitute a threat to the unity of thought. This is an old and sterile suspicion, echoes of which are found at all periods, as in this passage by Rivarol: "Leibniz sought a universal language. . . . This great man felt that the multitude of languages was fatal to genius, and consumed too much of the brevity of life. It is best not to clothe one's thought in too many ways; one should, so to speak, travel among languages and, after having savored the flavor of the greatest of them, settle down in one's own."[2] The second reaction welcomes diversity as nourishment for our curiosity about other cultures. But whether the profusion of languages is regretted or celebrated, almost all are struck by it, and very few remain indifferent. The situation does indeed have its extreme aspects. Languages often differ over very small distances, from one village to another, ten or fifteen kilometers apart, whether or not they are linked by genetic origin. Unless each group learns the other's language, their relationship remains a dialogue of the deaf.

But should we content ourselves with simply stating these facts? It can of course be said that, while linguistic diversity reflects no physical distinctions within the species, it often coincides with—or is profoundly linked to—the diversity of sensory universes and structurings of space and time among different social groups. But curiosity, the motivation for scientific research, seeks resemblances above and beyond differences. How is that goal to be achieved in this case?

The Dangers and Delights of Translation

There is a single human faculty for language (see chapter 1). The languages by which it is manifested thus necessarily reveal some degree of unity. It is by this fact that linguistics may study them as discernible objects. The mere fact of calling them languages posits universal features underlying their immense diversity. But these are definitional universals, general features that are proper to any language and figure in its definition. Those who go no further than this recognize as universals only those properties connected with the very notion of language. Moreover, the conception of this notion itself varies with theoretical goals. The features studied are either too formal or too general to apply to empirical language data. The latter case is illustrated by American structuralism of the early sixties, which posited as defining features only creativity, distancing in space and time, reception at the source, (metalinguistic) reflexivity, acquisition through learning, etc.[3] These are useful for distinguishing human languages from animal languages; they are not specific enough to characterize human languages themselves.

We need not quibble over definitional universals, however. Languages are such familiar objects that we may confine ourselves, at least for the present, to our everyday experience with them. A basic characterization is immediately available. It is implied by an activity as old as the most ancient of cultures, attested day after day, its constant necessity perpetually renewed despite its many presumed pitfalls: translation. Is translation in fact "the faded underside of a tapestry" (Cervantes), a "utopia" (Ortega y Gasset), or on the contrary "a rightful and determined quest for the horizons of the untranslatable" (Goethe)? Even those who seek to deny its value under the pretext that translation is always badly done, must admit that any text in a given language —for it is texts, not languages, that are translated—is, whether perfectly or approximately, translatable into a text of another language. However, if we confine ourselves to the system of signs, we know all too well the extent of variation between structures, and the impossibility for a sign in one language to occupy the same place as that of another by which we attempt to translate it. Yet despite this obstacle, each language possesses the singular property of being a "system of signs into which all other semiotic systems can be translated,"[4] beginning with other languages themselves.

The bold enterprise of translation may apply even to poetry, sometimes considered the most enigmatic of linguistic productions. The original version itself, invested with the expressivity peculiar to a specific voice, is frequently opaque. It is true that the translation of poetry imposes certain preconditions. Not only does it require, as does any translation, a perfect mastery of both languages and great attention to detail; the translator must actually be a poet and produce music that, although in another key, is as expressive as the original. Otherwise, of course, one can always resort to that most common of artifices: explaining everything that the translation is unable to convey in notes at the bottom of the printed page. Despite these difficulties, poetic texts continue to be translated. French, for example, is a more than acceptable vehicle for poetry, even from such distant languages as Hebrew, Arabic, Chinese, Japanese, Hungarian, Malagasy, and Persian. One need only satisfy the above requirements.

What then are the obstacles? They arise from two types of differences, in prose as well as in poetry. The first type is linked to physical and cultural conditions. Beyond the invariable base of unity of the species and of its lifestyle, these conditions produce quite different realities (human or otherwise). When we translate, we operate within the designated reality. The other type of difference concerns structures of sound, grammar, and vocabulary. Thus, when translating Verlaine into Japanese, it is impossible to evoke the melancholy of the nasal vowels in "les sanglots longs des violons" in the same way, since Japanese has no nasal vowels.[5] In the area of grammar, whether in poetry or prose, oral or written, it is impossible to translate class morphemes into those languages (such as French, English, or Spanish) which do not possess them. Class morphemes are elements obligatorily affixed, in many languages, either to the noun phrase (Chinese, Vietnamese, African Bantu idioms, etc.), or to the verb phrase (Athapaskan languages of northwestern America, idioms of New Guinea and Australia, etc.); these elements indicate the physical attributes of objects, positions in space, or ways of perceiving the world. Thus, the Chinese *yi-zhi-qianbi*, literally "an-object (stick-shaped)-pencil," can be translated only as "a pencil," with no equivalent for the morpheme *zhi*. We are also forced to sacrifice indications of social status which in many Far Eastern languages are integrated into personal pronouns (see chapter 11), in translating them by the single opposition between *tu* and *vous* in French or, worse yet, simply by English "you." Finally, we inevitably lose the trace of sexual and dialectal variants that are easily identified by readers of the original version. This is well illustrated in Kawabata's novel *Kyōto*, an already inexact translation of the Japanese title *Koto*, meaning "ancient capital"—another name for Kyoto that recalls its brilliant history. The author writes in the voice of the women of the city, a voice easily identifiable for Japanese readers because of certain (polite and other) forms which women use and which are less frequent among men in the Kansai region, cradle of Japan's civilization. These clues cannot be translated. *Languages differ not only in what they can or cannot express, but also in what must or need not be said.*

On the lexical level, finally, it has often enough been observed that each language imposes its own notional frame upon the objects of the world, such that any movement into another language is at best only a rough equivalent. What is central in one language is marginal in another. Procedures that are perfectly normal in the original are of limited use in the target language: English prefers "walk there" to "go there by foot," while in French we find the latter formula, *y aller à pied* instead of *marcher là*. Meaning can be poured into a variety of formal molds. "Meaning is everywhere. Translators, who know this from instinct or experience, choose a position to translate a form, or a form to translate a word."[6] As for plays on words, they are by definition untranslatable, except of course when the cultural contexts are close enough, and the contacts between them old enough—or the lexicons similar enough— for the equivalents to be interpretable. When these conditions cannot be met, the translations are in danger of remaining opaque. Those who do not know Hebrew cannot understand why, when the prophet says, "I see a rod of an almond tree," Yahwe answers, "Thou hast well seen: for I will hasten my word to perform it." (Jeremiah I:11–12). The Bible, here as in countless other passages, associates etymological meanings even when a formal distinction, for example between two vowels, produces two quite different words: "He who watches" is *shoked;* and the almond tree is called *shaked* ("vigilant") because, blooming before the other trees, it is believed to be the first to awaken from winter's sleep. In a quite different culture, the Malagasy Hain-teny use the same procedure: "If I have planted aviavy, I wanted you to come," says one couplet. What power does translation have in the face of the metalinguistic game which links the verb *avy*, "come," to the name of the fig tree whose black fruits fall to the ground when ripe? Even when the cultures are close, translation sometimes encounters the problem of works which exploit the latitudes of linguistic distortion to their extreme limits. James Joyce's *Finnegan's Wake* is no doubt the most astonishing illustration of this. If Lavergne's[7] recent attempt at translation may be considered a relative success, it is to the extent that he has reinvented Joyce's word games by furnishing French equivalents that, while far from the English text, provide comparable nourishment to the imagination.

All of these differences must be taken into account, and make the very ancient undertaking of translation a perilous one indeed. They nonetheless contribute, in an indirect way, to our file of language universals: they show what, in any case, cannot be included in it. But the most surprising thing is that we can always translate, even if imperfectly or only approximately. Languages must have profound similarities if the messages that they allow us to produce can travel in this way. Even those who minimize these resemblances still admit that they provide material for speculation about the minimum of features needed to constitute a language. Thus it is not true, as certain structuralists maintained thirty years ago, that we must accept the "American tradition (Boas) that languages could differ from each other without limit and in unpredictable ways."[8] The structuralists' training in anthropology made them sensitive to great divergence of social structures. But in the domain of language, it is precisely because the differences are predictable, and contained within certain limits, that a quest for universals is even conceivable.

The Search for Universals

It is clear that differences between languages are too pronounced for there to be much likelihood of substantive universals. Substantive universals are assertions about the actual linguistic material. For example, "the vowel *u* exists in every language." This is false for Japanese, where the vowel spelled *u* in Latin transcription is in fact pronounced with the lips open and not rounded as in English "too." Another example: "all languages have adverbs meaning 'always' and 'only.' " This is falsified by languages like Palauan (Micronesia) or Comox (British Columbia), where they are verbs, in structures of the type "he-always-past work," meaning "he always worked."[9] Again: "if adjectives of measure forming antonym pairs are derived from each other, it is 'small' which will be derived and 'large' which will be the base." This is often the case, but there are counterexamples, as in Bugis (Celebes, Indonesia), where "large" is expressed as "not small" *(teng-baiccu')*. Finally: "the noun 'man' and the verb 'see' are primary universals; in other words, given the importance and the generality of these concepts, they are simple irreducible words and not compounds or derivations." This assertion is contradicted by Diegueño (Mexico), in which "man" is *'isk*^{w} *-ič,* i.e., "he who is tall," and by Kalam (New Guinea), where "see" is "(with the) eyes-perceive." According to its most recent description,[10] Kalam, a hyperanalytical language, has only 95 verbs, 25 of which are in common use. This implies a very great number of combinations to convey the considerable number of states and actions which in English are most often expressed by different verbs.

If substantive universals are so clearly invalidated, must we then confine ourselves to formal ones? The present conception of formal universals remains distant from the reality of languages, as is clearly illustrated by generative grammar, a recent formalism that has in fact emerged periodically in the history of linguistics. According to this theory,[11] mechanisms linked to the formal constraints of a grammar are universals, and reflect the knowledge possessed by the ideal speaker-hearer of a language. This grammar involves certain types of categories, uses certain kinds of rules, and applies them in an ordered series and cyclically, in order to obtain all and only those sentences which can be produced by a speaker of the language. The deep structures from which arise the surface forms (the final product, i.e., what is said and heard) are obviously, as indicated by their name, inaccessible to direct observation. At this level of abstraction, deep structures are close to the notion of logical systems, and thus sufficiently general to go far beyond the specific features of individual languages. But the gulf between logical systems and their exploitation in languages is a vast one.

Languages are temporary compromises, in precarious balance because they are situated in time and subject to conflicting pressures. This explains the periodic replacement of logically justifiable meanings by new ones. The phenomenon is most frequent when the new meaning corresponds to a change in situation that linguistic expression, which evolves much more slowly (see chapter 11), has not been able to keep up with. There are many concrete illustrations. Among the simplest, directly related to the problem of the logic of linguistic expression, we may cite three cases: Puluwat (Micronesia) and Hindi, where a wife is "she of the house," even now that she may work in the village; and Wunambal (Australia) where "drink" is "go drink," even when no movement is involved, since the expression in its literal form originated during a period in which the partaking of a dry meal was followed by a walk to the stream for a drink. In these cases, the linguistic form has lost its motivation; it has taken on a meaning that no longer corresponds to its literal sense, a sense logically related to a former state of affairs.

Thus languages do not correspond to logical systems (see chapter 6). Formal universals, by virtue of their abstraction, are not of much use in analyzing actual languages. Formal universals are not, in fact, language universals, but, rather, general conditions of coherence for linguistics. They are epistemological requirements which can teach us something about logical systems, about methods to be used in the social sciences, and about the ingenuity of the people who develop them; they tell us little about actual languages as manifestations of the faculty of speech, or about the species characterized, at least in part, by those languages. We must not, simply because a linguistic theory requires certain methodological procedures, confound these procedures with the object to which they are applied, and consider them inherent to languages.

Limits to the Differences between Languages

General Tendencies. If neither substantive nor formal universals provide a promising avenue of research, what about general linguistic features deducible from the definition of a language? These features include the contradiction between the continuity of the physical and mental universe on the one hand, and the discontinuity of the distinctive oppositions of languages on the other. The latter, in fact, are often expressed as polar opposites: the French vowels / a /, low, and / i /, high; spatial indicators identifying objects as closer to or farther from the speaker; temporal and aspectual markers for complete / incomplete, real / irreal, punctual / durational, etc. In fact, this traditional version of discontinuity warrants rethinking. Languages organize their oppositions more freely than it may seem, and between the "extremes" we find a series of intermediate levels (see chapter 6). Another feature is the parallel variation affecting the form and meaning of words, reflected in a continual process of evolution responsible for the existence, on a scale varying among languages, of homonyms and synonyms. Discontinuity and parallel variation, while interesting (keeping in mind the limitations of the former), are not of much real use. They are simply general characteristics of languages. They cannot constitute a foundation for empirically verifiable hypotheses. Yet such hypotheses are certainly necessary for progress in our knowledge of languages and their users. A universal may be seen as a hypothesis based on the practical knowledge of a certain number of facts (whence its noncontradictory designation as "empirical hypothesis"), but which goes beyond the simple gathering of these facts to enter into a set of correlations among the properties of language. These hypotheses are then to be subjected to experimentation to verify their validity for a larger set of facts. Sources must be varied in order to avoid assigning the status of universal property to certain analogous facts that may be explained as well by common origin (genetic relation) or by continuous relations due to geographical proximity (areal relation).

We may neither invent formal universals a priori, nor be satisfied with simple inductions from accumulated facts, the latter remaining contingent. Available linguistic material does not necessarily exhaust the set of properties that a universalist perspective attaches to languages as theoretical objects. But we must accept that we can only work with the facts at our disposal. We will thus arrive at tendencies rather than laws, although we may use the term "law," since this more rigid formulation makes them more easily falsifiable. The facts very often provide counterexamples to our original hypotheses. If they are numerous enough, the study of these counterexamples can lead to progress in clarifying certain mysteries of languages as species-specific behavior. One such useful type of hypothesis is the *implicational tendency* of the form $A \equiv \rightarrow B$, meaning "if a language possesses feature A, it probably also possesses feature B." The theoretical framework and the experimental data available lead to the consideration that B is implied by A. The verification of such tendencies opens a vast field of research.

But before committing ourselves to this line of investigation, we must fix some limits. A brief technical detour is in order here. *Languages have problems to solve, all of which reduce to a single problem: how to associate sound with meaning.* But they do not form just any sound, they do not produce just any meaning, and they do not associate meanings and sounds in a random fashion. There are physiological constraints on sounds, reflecting the articulatory system that produces them and the ear that hears them. Further, languages do not exploit the same possibilities from among the set of those sounds which may be articulated. Each language is characterized by the number and nature of its phonemes (minimal sounds), and by the types of combinations permitted: French opposes / p / and / b /, Chinese and Danish, / p / and / ph /; Hindi, / p /, / ph /, / b /, / bh /; French has no words beginning with / tp- /, while Palauan (Micronesia) does. *Phonology* is the domain of linguistics concerned with the sound systems that distinguish words and the combinations of these sounds in speech.

As for the meaning (the signified) of these words, it is linked to the ways in which each language constructs its system of relations with respect to external objects, i.e., to the referent, which as an integral part of the creation of meaning is another factor in addition to the association of the signified with the signifier (see chapter 5). Words are the product of this construction: words or, in the case of those that are analyzable, parts of words. This constitutes the *lexicon.* The words of the lexicon are not a simple, undifferentiated or immutable list. Moreover—and to varying degrees in different languages—these words are subject to pressures that eventually place them in categories such as noun or verb, which can assume certain relations in a regular fashion. The study of these categories (the parts of speech) and of these relations is the domain of *syntax.* But beyond this, the differentiation of words into types is often accompanied by formal markers identifying those types. The study of such markers is *morphology,* and may be more or less developed depending upon the language. The four domains of phonology, lexicon, syntax, and morphology constitute the framework for assigning universal features.

Since diversity does not equal anarchy, and since languages cannot belong to any imaginable type, these features occur in the form of properties subject to variation within certain limits. The limits are predictable rather than arbitrary; for even if external pressures, arising from the history of societies, are contingent, the manner in which languages react to these pressures is not. However multifaceted the universe of languages, it clearly displays regulation of diversity. For any language, a relationship exists between certain functions and the structures that express them. Despite an appearance of extreme diversity, these structures vary over a finite field of possibilities.

Distinguishing Types against a Background of Universals. This is why the search for language universals is the basis for classification of languages into types, clearly a primary goal. "It is only through typology that linguistics rises to entirely general points of view and becomes a science."[12] It may seem paradoxical to seek universality in seemingly endless variation. But the diversity of types becomes visible only against a background of general features and abstract principles. Within the framework of the four domains we have defined, syntax displays the lowest degree of differentiation and morphology the highest, with phonology and lexicon falling somewhere in between.

The sentence is an important unit in syntax (but not the only one; see chapter 9). A nonelliptical sentence is organized into a core, called its "predicate," and a periphery. A simple example is the utterance *sa sœur est endormie* ("his sister is asleep"), which can be analyzed as the predicate *est endormie* and its nonpredicational periphery *sa sœur*. But beyond this minimal condition of expressibility, languages demonstrate great variety as to the degree of specialization of certain words in one or the other of these functions; or as to those functions which can be defined in relation to these two. The categories are not equally distributed: many languages have no adjectives; others have class morphemes (see the Chinese example given above); still others possess special nouns, used to express family relations, whose syntactic behavior is different from that of ordinary nouns. When two participants, agent and patient, are involved, phrase structures also vary.[13] So called ergative languages are distinguished from accusative and mixed languages (see chapter 10). There also exists a fourth type of language in which, even in the simplest structures involving only a single participant, with the verbs meaning "run," "fall," "work," etc., this argument may be marked with two different morphemes, or realized in two different declension classes, depending upon whether the action in question is carried out more or less voluntarily, or more or less consciously. Examples are Guarani (Paraguay) and Dakota (Oklahoma).

All languages can specify the circumstances of an action as well as its participants. But here again formal realizations are quite different. To take only one example, that of instrument or manner, we find in French *il coupe l'herbe avec un couteau* ("he cuts the grass with a knife"), while Poular (Senegal) does not use an independent word for the sense of "with", but rather an affix associated with the verb functioning as predicate: *tay-ir-ta paaka huḍo-ka* (cut-instrument-present knife grass-class morpheme).

In any language, it is possible to determine a word by means of another word, as French does with the element *de* in *le père de l'enfant* ("the father of the child"). But this is hardly the only possible strategy. Certain languages juxtapose the two terms, and it is the fixed order of succession, determined-determiner or determiner-determined, that indicates the nature of the relation. Declensional languages use genitive case (Latin), or another case governed by a preposition (German *von* + dative). Many other types of structures expressing this same relation are to be found: adjunction of an article to the postposed determiner, with possible modification of the determined (Arabic, Hebrew); change of accent (Fataluku on the Island of Timor) or of tone (see chapter 5) in the Bantu languages of southwest Cameroon; modification of the determiner (for example, in Celtic languages such as Breton and Irish, or in Gilyak of eastern Siberia—all idioms in which the initial consonants change); use of a determining "prop" such as "he / she / they of", agreeing with the determined (Berber, Hindi, Camalal in the Caucasus, Hausa in Nigeria); or, finally, recourse to a possessive, with the determiner appearing in apposition, as in Hungarian ("the child father-his") or in Palauan ("the father-of him the child"). A related case is that of possession expressed in an entire sentence (and not only in the determiner phrase). All known languages can convey the universal relation between possessor and possessed, but the corresponding sentence structures are quite varied. If X is the possessor and Y the possessed, the formulation may be equational:[14] "X is a Y-possessor," as in Quechua (Peru and Bolivia); attributive, as in the Australian languages that produce the structure "X is Y-ified;" existential, as in Jacaltec (Guatemala), where we find "Y of X exists;" situational, as in Russian and the Semitic and Cushitic languages of East Africa, where the formula is "Y belongs to (is for / with / in) X," or as in central African languages that, inversely, construct "X is with Y;" or, finally, active in those languages possessing a verb "have," like the Romance and Germanic languages, the principal Slavic languages other than Russian, and all those in which this verb is etymologically linked to words meaning "hold" or "hand" (idioms of the northwestern Caucasus, for example).

Lastly, a recursive procedure typical of syntax, the embedding of simple clauses producing complex subordinated structures, is also universal.[15] This is, however, realized in various ways. So called relative subordinate clauses pose many technical problems and have long been the basis of learned debate among grammarians, making them a favor-

39

ite subject for research into universals.[16] Limiting ourselves to subordinates other than relatives, we find that many languages indicate a hierarchical syntactic relation simply through intonation. Speakers know, without any need for conjunctions, that a string must be understood as part of a clause expressing a complement, an adjunct of time, cause, hypothesis, goal, etc., as if we had respectively "that," "when," "because," "if," or "in order to." In the absence of the intonational contour specific to independent complete sentences, the direction of the voice alone indicates a dependent clause. The same fact is attested in the oral registers of many Western languages, and apparently also in those whose written or formal registers use either conjunctions such as the above, or some special means of subordination (subjunctive, conjunctive), or a special pronoun or form (e.g., the Latin infinitive) in the clause subordinate to an assertive verb. Thus, in spoken French, the sentence *Il faisait un seul pas, il se faisait tuer* ("He took a single step, he got himself killed") has the same meaning as *S'il avait fait un seul pas, il se serait fait tuer* ("If he had taken a single step, he would have gotten himself killed.") Yet the former has a purely intonational marker of the hypothesis relation while the latter, closer to the written style, indicates this relation through a specific process of conjunction. We observe finally that, when conjunction is used, even its position is not universal. It is usually situated at the clause boundary, but not in all languages: Basque spoken in Labourd (southwest France, in contact with Spain), expresses the equivalent of "I say that he does this," with the structure *erran / dut / au / iten / due-la*,[17] word-for-word: "say / I it / this / does / he it has-that," where the conjunction *la* appears not between the two clauses but suffixed to the subordinate verb. The same is true of other languages like Guarani (Paraguay). These features are sufficient to demonstrate that languages, with their common base of organization for relations expressing roughly the same universal content, differ as to the structures used to represent that content.

The divergences are greater in phonology. It is true that the spatial and functional limitations of the speech and hearing organs impose universal limits upon the possible variations among sound systems. The sound chamber through which the production of meaning must pass in oral communication is certainly one of the defining features of the species. Beyond this common base, however, systems vary widely. Even the tendency toward more consonants than vowels is not absolute: Hawaiian, for example, has ten vowels for eight consonants, and other Polynesian languages have comparable ratios. Variety is also apparent within subgroups: many languages possess the three consonants articulated at three equidistant points, the lips (labials like / p /), the teeth (dentals like / t /), and the soft palate (velars like / k /). But others have only two: / p / and / t / in Tahitian, / p / and / k / in Hawaiian.[18] And / p / is absent, as a phoneme, in languages such as Palau and Arabic, although the latter has the corresponding voiced consonant / b /. The opposition of voiced and unvoiced consonants, characteristic of French and English (p / b, f / v, t / d, s / z, etc.) is attested in 37 percent of known languages. Consonants may also be aspirated or glottalized (involving closing, then reopening, of the glottis before or after actual articulation), and the combinations of these types result in great diversity. Additional subgroups of consonants include nasals (of which / m / and / n / are the most common) and liquids (especially / l / and / r /).

Vowel subgroups demonstrate a comparable variety. Beyond the three basic units / i / (high, front), / u / (high, back), and / a / (low), all sorts of intermediate articulations occur. There is vocalic lengthening or doubling (as in German where *bitten,* "beg," with short / i /, is distinguished from *bieten,* "offer," with long / i /); there are nasals, such as the three French vowels (written with a final *n*), illustrated by the three words *Ain, on,* and *an.* French is one of the known languages that possess nasal vowels, difficult to pronounce for adult native speakers of one of the majority of languages that have none. Vowels may also carry accents; and in many languages (Spanish, English, Russian, German, Israeli Hebrew, etc.), the position of these accents is sufficient to distinguish otherwise identical words. In most African languages, a quarter of the languages of Asia and North America, fifteen percent of those of Oceania and fourteen percent of those of South America, a similarly distinctive role is played by vowel tones (see chapter 5).

Not only is there variety in the systems and subsystems of sounds, but also in the combinations which may form words. Languages are quite diverse as to the admissible groupings of consonants and vowels in initial, median, and final position, and, consequently, as to the types of syllables found. We can nevertheless posit some implicational universals about certain occlusive, fricative, and liquid articulations and their combinations. Occlusives are consonants produced by the closing of a cavity (the mouth) followed by opening with a small explosion of escaping air: / p /, / t /, / k /, / b /, / d /, / g /, etc. Fricatives are articulated by friction of air through a narrowly opened passage: / f /, / v /, / s /, / z /, etc. If a language permits groups consisting of two occlusives or two fricatives, this implies that it also has occlusive-fricative combinations. Further, if a language combines an occlusive or a fricative with a nasal in at least one admissible consonant cluster, it must also allow at least one combination of occlusive or fricative with a liquid. French, which has fewer occlusive, fricative, or occlusive-fricative groups than German, provides examples like *aptitude* (occlusives / p / + / t /), *asphodèle* (fricatives / s / + / f /) and *aphteuse* (fricative / f / + occlusive / t /), or *jasmin* (fricative / s / + nasal / m /) and *frapper* (fricative / f / + liquid / r /). In other languages (Bengali, Berber, Bulgarian, Cambodian), this implication is verified on a wider scale.

Quantitative (and therefore structural) differences between lexicons exist even among individuals who speak a single language. One person may generally use a repertory of 1,200 words, while another commands 2,000 and a third, 2,500. Beyond these inequities—which might lead us to attribute three distinct languages to three "equally" fluent French speakers—languages confronting identical natural evidence do not set identical boundaries; they construct classes distinct in number and content. Chromatic vocabulary (five colors named in one language, only three in another) is a classic example, as are names of family relations: the Turkish word *kardes* cannot be equated with *brother* or *sister*, since it means "brother or sister." Objects familiar to the culture change with the environment, and so does the inventory of their names. The single English word *salmon* corresponds to at least ten different nouns among the Comox fishermen of Vancouver; the Lapps of Finland have about as many terms for *reindeer*. And we know of course that notions like "liberty," "conscience," and "honor," conceived according to the beliefs of different societies, create traps for the translator.

Not everyone is intimidated by such complexity. Certain Westerners have tried, since the seventeenth century at least, to posit a finite number of semantic variants for every lexicon in the world. Only the possible combinations would vary from one language to another. The vocabulary of each language would then simply be one of the possible sets of associations. If one is not overly rigorous, and has available some well-chosen examples from a small number of languages, one can almost be persuaded of the validity of this method. But the facts are not so simple. In response to a diversity of needs and situations, speaking man is continually creating and re-creating meaning. This suffices to disprove the invariants of an atomist point of view imposed a priori. Besides, the exterior world is undergoing constant transformation. Even such an "obvious" componential analysis (using minimal semantic features) as one segmenting "father" into "male parent" in every language is in danger of being contradicted since the development of sex-change operations: a man who has undergone such surgery and become a transsexual, having earlier sired a child, is indeed a father, but a female father.[19] In any case, what can this circular method reveal about the cardinal property of meaning itself? If we use words to represent the semantic primitives by which the lexicons of all languages are to be analyzed, we confront the problem of segmentation within words themselves. Of course, we can try to claim that these words are simply abstract symbols, metalinguistic primitives, methodological entities, and not the words of a real language. Whatever our pretensions, we cannot escape the fact that *linguistics is the only contemporary science whose object coincides with its discourse.*

General assertions that also imply analysis by minimal and invariable semantic features are not much more dependable. Two such well-known claims are that proper nouns must "be assigned to objects satisfying a condition of contiguity in space and time," and, further, that "artifacts are defined in terms of certain human goals, needs and functions instead of solely in terms of physical qualities."[20] This second claim goes back at least to Aristotle.[21] Chomsky adopts it with approval, as well as the first, which he borrows from Bertrand Russell[22] (although he notes one exception: the name of the United States, which violates the condition of spatio-temporal contiguity).[23] Chomsky declares that since there is no logical reason to forbid such "non-contiguous" nouns in languages,[24] those cases that confirm the assertion should lead us to consider this an innate property. However, a lack of logical necessity does not suffice to make a property innate. Besides, the second assertion is also contradicted, by such terms as *hardware* (the set of metallic furnishings for various machines, such as computers). *Hardware* does, in fact, designate a group of artificial objects whose features refer to physical properties, and not to their functions, which are extremely varied.

The difficulty of establishing lexical universals leads us to use general criteria, as in syntax. Such criteria are constituted by what may be called graduated scales: regular variations providing a common base for comparison between languages. We will examine five of these criteria or scales: synonymic extension, polysemic extension, arbitrariness, taxonomic precision, and extension of obligatory categories.

Languages have recourse in variable fashion to synonymy, whether the synonyms belong to the same register or are distinguished by stylistic level and by the circumstances in which each may be used. As for polysemy, or plurality of meanings for a single word, it is more developed in some languages than in others. Body parts, for example, may be used to form indicators of spatio-temporal relations, while still retaining their use as concrete nouns: "face" → "in front of," "belly" → "in," "back" → "behind," etc. This is frequent in Africa, Oceania, Central America. In fact it may well exist throughout the world, but during different historical periods, and for indicators whose nominal bases have disappeared from use.

Certain languages lend themselves to the analysis of complex words into simple elements. Their lexicons have a low level of arbitrariness. Thus, the German series *aufnehmen* ("take in"), *abnehmen* ("take away"), *mitnehmen*, ("take with"), whose meanings can be deduced by adding that of the prefix to that of the base verb *nehmen*, "take," is less arbitrary than the corresponding series of French verbs *relever, ôter, emporter*, which cannot be so obviously broken down. With the same criterion we can compare the Estonian series *kirjandus, kirjanik, kirjastaja* and that of the corresponding French *littérature, écrivain, éditeur* (similarly, English "literature," "writer," "editor")—opaque in the absence of a common root like the Estonian *kir-*. In certain languages, descriptive compounds whose meanings are predictable from their components are very numerous; hence, a vocabulary that is "poor" because highly motivated. Such is the case of the African, Oceanian, and Tibeto-Burmese languages in which "skull" is expressed by "bone of the head," "dust" by "flour of the earth," "heel" by "eye of the foot," and "moustache" by "hair of the mouth."

Depending upon its relationship to its surroundings, a language may have a larger or smaller assortment of terms for classifying objects. In the languages of industrial societies, technical subsets of the lexicon are already highly developed in physics, biology, and various industries, and continue to grow. More generally, certain domains corresponding to essential activities or to those of cultural importance produce a particular abundance of designations. This is just as true of nonindustrial societies, as we saw with the Lapp names for reindeer and the Comox words for salmon. *Hyperonymy*, the use of a generic term to dominate the set of specific ones, may also be absent. This phenomenon, while not exclusive to nonindustrial societies, has still inspired hasty racial inferences about the "primitive mentality" that is unable to rise to abstract generalization. But it is a universal and perfectly logical practice for languages to name what is basic to the needs of everyday life, needs that vary greatly among societies. Moreover, the ease with which speakers of lexically-specific languages acquire languages with generic terms suffices to lay to rest these extrapolations on the mentality of the races.

Finally, categories such as gender (masculine, feminine, neuter, rational, inanimate, etc.), number (singular, dual, plural, etc.), class (phys-

ical, functional, etc.), position in space, and others, are present in varying degrees in different languages. They may not be immediately visible,
showing up through compatibilities between words. Thus, one cannot
normally say *il feuilletait son gant* ("he leafed through his glove")
because of the type of action and the type of object referred to here by
feuilleter and *gant*. We may consider the differences in distribution of
required linguistic categories as a particular case of a general principle
of evident typological interest: the *division of labor between the lexicon and the grammar*. What is obligatory in some languages is taken
care of by the lexicon in others.[25] Naturally, these different distribu-
tions contribute to the dangers and delights of translation.

Morphology, the last domain of our search for universals, is the one
which yields the smallest harvest. But for this very reason, perhaps, it
may be the one that has the most to teach us. Morphology is the field
of greater differentiation. Like living species, languages resemble each
other in the functions invested in them, and in the place they occupy
between man who uses them and the universe of which they speak;
but there is no reason to assume homology of form. It is sufficient to
posit the basic need for words that carry meaning, and that can be
analyzed into sound units. We need not imply that the structure of
those words must be uniform. In the nineteenth century, and at the
beginning of the twentieth, the goals of typology and the search for
universals were not linked in the way we have suggested here. A
typological classification of languages, first sketched by the brothers F.
and A.-W. Schlegel (1808 and 1818) and still used today by many linguists and non-linguists, was made famous through research by von
Humboldt, Bopp, Pott, Schleicher, Steinthal, Misteli, Finck, de la Gras-
serie, and Sapir, during the period between 1833 and 1921.[26] According
to this system, languages are divided into the categories of inflectional,
agglutinative, and isolating.

Inflectional languages are those whose words are made up of combinations of radicals and affixes, with fusion at the boundaries between
them, for nouns (declensions) as well as for verbs (conjugations): in
Latin we have *tempus* "time", but *temporis* "of time;" French opposes
savons "(we) know" and *sais* "(I / you) know." Agglutinative languages
are those in which words result from pure juxtaposition of radicals and
affixes, without modification at the boundaries: French *des maisons*
"of the houses" corresponds to Turkish *ev-ler-in*, literally "house-plu-
ral-genitive." Isolating languages have invariable and unanalyzable words
(although composition and derivation do exist), and the relations between these words are indicated by position. Thus in Mandarin Chinese

gěi means "give" or "to" and *yòng* "use" or "by means of," depending on their position in the sentence. Words in isolating languages tend, moreover, toward monosyllabism, in contrast with other types of idioms. Finally, certain authors like Pott (pursuing a proposal made by the Franco-American scholar Du Ponceau in 1819), have added a fourth type of language, called "polysynthetic." This type is well illustrated by the Amerindian languages in which certain affixes with concrete as well as grammatical meaning are synthesized upon a single radical base, in particular through a process called *incorporation*. The result is a frequent coincidence of word with sentence.

We can easily see that this typology, while based principally on morphology, also takes syntax into account. Implicitly evolutionist, it represents inflectional languages as the summit of development. In fact, however, change is cyclic; isolating languages such as Chinese were very probably once inflectional. Finally, such a theory suggests that each language fits a type, when the evidence is much less simple: most languages possess features of several types. Yet in spite of its deficiencies, this trilogy (or quadrilogy) has at least the merit of demonstrating the variety of word-types among languages. Morphology has little place for universals; we find ourselves at the point of extreme variation. If, beyond this defined threshold, limits are imposed upon theoretically possible diversity, it is only because all languages fulfill a common set of functions, calling upon formal structures that are not likely to vary in a totally anarchic manner.

According to rationalist theory, universals are innate. In considering them here as empirically verifiable hypotheses about the degree of difference among languages with respect to general properties, we leave aside the question of innateness. These are universals neither of form nor of substance. The innateness debate, however, is far from trivial. But why must universals be the uniform result of genetically inherited properties of the human mind? Why should they not be analogous responses, in all languages, to situations encountered by the species in discourse? Innateness theories do not take language use into sufficient account. Their object of study is the faculty of speech, not actual languages. But, even in this domain, innateness hypotheses remain questionable. A well-known experiment provides indirect confirmation for an intuitive observation. The aptitude for social life has probably been written into the code of the species in the course of an evolution spanning hundreds of thousands of years (see chapter 1). This social aptitude—and the accompanying aptitude for speech—necessarily suppose a group of individuals. The experiment is that of wild children who, when they have been taken from their natural state, must be painstakingly taught to become social beings. Thus the language faculty matures into communication only if social life is present. Of course, speech has functions other than communication. But although we can characterize it as an autonomous faculty, the species itself is defined only by the group. The designation of oneself and of others in the act of discourse is universal, whether expressed by a personal pronoun, a verb form or by any other means. If humans have this aptitude, it is because an "I" says "you" to another "I," and hears "you" in return. If universals exist, their purpose together with their explanation lie in the universality of discourse.

4

Writing and Speaking

Letter Lovers and Sound Lovers

How is it that some people become enamored of the written word, while others are interested only in speech? The destiny of languages and the destiny of humanity have been closely linked through the ages, each helping to shape the other; in gradually establishing our own identity, we have continually perfected our language systems. An amazing phenomenon has drastically altered linguistic destiny, and, with it, the destiny of the species, or at least that of a large part of it: the phenomenon of writing. This was an initiative whose results were so slow to appear, and whose continuing evolution involves so many different and complex factors, that we may well wonder if the word "invention" (legitimized as it is by tradition and by the titles of so many books) is really appropriate to describe it.

Suppose we take speech as a given which, unlike writing, has always been basic to language. There would then be no point in discussing antecedence. Yet the relationship of speech to writing has, in fact, been the subject of unceasing controversy. Many modern linguists of the structuralist school would no doubt ridicule these lines by Fabre d'Olivet, which are, however, characteristic of a current of thought by no means limited to the early nineteenth century:

> The books of universal principles called *King* by the Chinese, the books of divine science called *Veda* or *Beda* by the Hindus, the Sepher of Moses—it is these writings that have brought lasting greatness to Chinese, Sanskrit, and Hebrew. Although Oighoury Tatar is one of the primitive languages of Asia, I have not included it among those that must be studied by anyone who wishes to return to the principle of the word; for an idiom without a sacred literature could in no way approach that principle. How could the Tatars have had literature, sacred or profane, when they were not even familiar with written characters? According to historians, the famous Genghis Khan, with his immense empire, could not find among his Moguls a single man capable of writing his dispatches. Timur-Lenk, who later ruled a part of Asia, could neither read nor write. This absence of written characters and of literature, leaving the Tatar dialects in a state of continual fluctuation quite similar to that of the formless dialects of the American savages, makes their study useless in etymological terms; their flickering and false light can only mislead us.[1]

The primacy of writing is not the only point of this text. Its corollary contends that languages without written traditions are fluctuating and formless. This prejudice was strengthened by the sketchy stories of missionaries who had no linguistic competence, and who were incapable of perceiving the complexity and historic continuity of many oral languages. Thus the notion of the primacy of writing, under various guises, has been dominant in the West since at least the Renaissance. The invention of printing naturally played a decisive role.

At the dawn of the classical period in France, de Vigenère and Duret went so far as to state[2] that writing precedes speech just as the "male principle" dominates the female side of language. In their view, a natural form of writing must have existed at the time of creation; this system of writing was used by Adam to find names for all the creeping and flying beasts as they were led before him by God. This point of view is far from extinct in the twentieth century. In his classic *Histoire de l'écriture*,[3] Février devoted three pages to refuting the theories of

Van Ginneken, who claimed[4] that the appearance of writing preceded that of spoken language and that the first pictograms were only the graphic representations of hand gestures, themselves the primary source of all language.

As to this last point, while we have no proof of it, we can certainly speculate about the original role of gestures. But as for the hypothesis of a direct graphic representation of gestures, it is contradicted by what we see in the most ancient of known writing systems. These consist of drawings, soon stylized, of objects—not of gestures miming them. Further, even if we maintain that "real" writing is extremely old, its existence in no way precludes that of spoken language, and nothing proves that the beginnings of the two were not simultaneous. One famous defender of writing seems to agree, assigning primacy neither to speech nor to writing: "Philosophers have mistakenly believed that speech was born first, and writing later; on the contrary, they are twins who have always developed together."[5] And Derrida, in a work honoring writing (taken in the broadest sense), still notes that "the term 'original' writing does not imply a real chronological order."[6]

Meanwhile, those in the other camp, for whom speech is the primary value, attack the "terrible bookish amnesia"[7] resulting from the development of printing in the West:

> Writers, and later printers and those of the printing and paper industry have committed the same crime against the faculty of memory. They have made our memories lazy; today even the most talented can hardly retain the names of their most intimate friends. This is not due to degeneration, but simply to the decline of a faculty that, given our arsenal of letters and books, has become almost superfluous.[8]

To the champions of the spoken word, the writing down of texts such as the traditional teachings of the great religions does not appear to constitute a serious editorial activity; it is simply a tool at the service of "oral transmission," the inevitably incomplete adjunct to living speech:

> Oral teaching has almost always preceded written teaching, and . . . the former has been used alone for very long periods. . . . In a general sense, traditional writing (for example the Hebrew recounting of the Creation) is . . . only the relatively recent version of a lesson that was first transmitted orally; thus, even when we are certain of possessing the original

manuscript, we must also know how long the previous period of oral transmission lasted.[9]

Not only does the living voice precede the written word; in certain civilizations, writing is forbidden, guaranteeing the oral transmission of knowledge. Many texts of the Talmud illustrate this taboo: "He who writes down legends [*aggadot*, traditional Jewish narratives] will have no share in the afterlife."[10] Also: "Whoever commits to writing the *halakot* [Jewish rules of practical behavior] is like one who throws the Torah into the flames."[11] Such texts are related to the way in which Jewishness is experienced by certain authors, for example Jabès, tormented by the difficulty of being Jewish, "which merges with the difficulty of writing; for Judaism and writing involve the same hope, the same expectation, the same ordeal."[12] Even an agnostic reading of this text should not prevent one from seeing that this expectation must be experienced by the faithful as the absence of the Word itself in the promised land; thus all writing, even that of the Cabala (which analyzes even individual letters of words) is the behavior of exile, removed from the living exchange of words.

Writing: Invention and Dreaming

The term "writing" can be interpreted in various ways. It may, for example, include the hunting scenes represented in cave drawings of the upper Paleolithic. But in its usual sense, that of a technique for reproducing speech through traces left on a permanent surface, we may call writing an invention (in the broadest sense). We may, although rather approximately, assign this invention to a historical period. It was a decisive development for those humans who were able to profit from it; a development comparable in importance to that, at a much earlier epoch, of the discovery of fire. With the advent of writing, the species had available a lasting means of fixing speech; it became possible to preserve human history, a history that even thousands of years of oral tradition could not always preserve from the abyss of oblivion.

Thus, for the most ancient of known civilizations, the birth of writing constituted the birth of history, carrying with it all the ambiguity of any revolutionary innovation. Written texts, deferred narrations without protagonists, are unlike the speech they reproduce: they are lifeless furrows, long-distance dialogues without the direct relation of mouths, ears, and eyes. Yet, and for that very reason, writing produces an object available to any reader, lending permanence and density to reported events. Through its extension in space, writing allows all possible combinations, inversions, and permutations; for absent objects, and for the continually evolving flow of speech, writing substitutes fixed traces of words, each of which can be contemplated alone. Thus, writing has the power of inspiring reflection, and perhaps also of encouraging the development of the faculties of analysis and abstraction. Peoples of oral cultures are certainly not without these faculties, but they develop them through other means, perhaps less easily available to all. Further, at least one of the intellectual activities of man is inconceivable without writing: numbering according to position, which assumes an alphabet of numerals and an order of written succession, as studied in arithmetic.

In prehistoric times, the new human species defined itself gradually over hundreds of thousands of years through its capacity for social life and its faculty for language. On the other hand, as far as we can presently ascertain, writing appeared in a very small number of societies. And, in any case, it appears to be directly linked to a particular complexity of human relations and to a finely woven network of hierarchies characteristic of settled societies with highly structured economies. This, then, is not a development of nature, and even less a defining property of speciation.

In order to grasp the implications of this development, and the destiny in which writing engaged mankind, we must make a technical digression. The three centers of civilization where the phenomenon appeared were old agricultural societies, partially urbanized, with large populations and well-developed systems of exchange. Sumer and ancient Egypt, in the Middle East, invented writing within two hundred years of each other: Sumer around 3300 B.C. (the Ur inscriptions), Egypt around 3100 B.C.—and we cannot be sure whether one was a model for the other. The relations between the two civilizations were certainly close; but the difference in writing techniques makes any direct influence between them uncertain.

In Sumer, an alluvial region in lower Mesopotamia, the writing surface was a tablet of fresh clay. Straight segments were printed with the reed of a stylus, and wedge-shaped points with its tip—whence the name *cuneiform writing* (Latin *cuneus*, "wedge"). Through increasing stylization, this system soon abolished all resemblance to the objects that were directly represented in the initial pictographic stage. Cuneiform passed through the two classic stages of pictogram or drawing, then to ideogram or schema of the idea corresponding to a word in the language. This progression, ancient as it may be, becomes familiar when we see the degree to which the modern world has rediscovered the value of ideograms: tourist guides, public parks, road signs, all sorts of advertising, cases and packages on which unambiguous schemata indicate top, bottom, fragility, humidity, etc.[13] In Sumer, in any case, phonograms appeared only after pictograms.[14] A phonogram is a written sign representing a word whose pronunciation contains a certain sound or combination of sounds; eventually, the phonogram becomes the character representing this sound in any word or syllable containing it.

Egyptian scribes, for their part, chewed the ends of reeds into fine brushes which they dipped in black ink. They wrote upon papyrus, made from a type of cypress then abundant on the banks of the Nile. The stem was cut into strips which were glued together, dried, smoothed, and assembled into a strong and flexible roll.[15] This is not the only difference between Egyptian and Sumerian writing techniques. Another is fundamental: even the very earliest samples of Egyptian writing are of a highly sophisticated form. Not only are the hieroglyphics the oldest known texts already consisting of a blending of pictograms and ideograms; we also find a complete system of phonograms functioning like those of cuneiform, on a rebus principle. These texts even contain a series of special hieroglyphic signs called determinants: placed next to signs corresponding to consonantal homonyms (only consonants were written), they resolved ambiguities by specifying the semantic or syntactic category of the word—much like the keys of homophonic Chinese characters.

Considering its antiquity, the refinement of this writing has long been underestimated. Its interpretation has occasioned many errors of judgment, such as this one by Rousseau:

> The more primitive the writing, the older the language. The first writing was not the painting of sounds, but that of objects themselves, whether literally, as in the Mexican system, or in allegorical figures, as in the Egyptian. This state of affairs reflects passionate language, and already assumes a society with needs inspired by the passions. ... Object-painting is appropriate to savage peoples.[16]

In 1822, Champollion deciphered the hieroglyphics. Yet, six years later, Nodier still writes: "The spoken names of objects were the imitation of their sounds; and the written names of objects were the imitation of their form. Onomatopoeia is thus the classic form of spoken languages, as are hieroglyphics of written languages."[17]

Nodier, whose name is associated with the *conte fantastique* and with illuminism, was seeking the key to the mystery of languages at the height of the vogue of comparative grammar. The relation he sketches here between hieroglyphics and onomatopeia is consistent with the following passage from his *Notions élémentaires de linguistique:* "The names of the creatures were . . . their real names in the language of Adam . . . [who] . . . chose them according to his perceptions, that is according to the most saliant aspect that appeared to him."[18]

These charming romantic visions, of course, fail to recognize the complexity of the cultures that invented cuneiform and hieroglyphics. Despite the differences noted above, the birth of writing in both Sumer and Egypt seems to have been linked to the development of an increasingly prominent accountancy system, necessary for the management of accumulated wealth. Just as money is a substitution of symbols for real objects, so was writing, in the Middle East, an invention of merchants. Hermes, the Greek god of trickery, thieves, and commerce, corresponds in Egyptian mythology to Thoth, god of science and technology, but also of writing (Plato attributes its invention to him at the end of the *Phaedra*). And according to all evidence, it was peripheral users of writing—foreigners, travelers, and merchants of regions neighboring the two great central empires—who were responsible for the next stage of its development: stylization, the first step on the path to true writing detached from the pictographic representation of objects. This, in turn, led to the development, and later to the systematization, of phonetic syllables. Indeed, the extreme specialization required for the profession of scribe, which demanded long study and hence financial means, had made knowledge of writing a privilege. There is no proof, by the way, that writing was actually invented by the scribes, who were invested with official functions, or by the priests who appropriated this knowledge. Perhaps, seizing upon a system of notation first conceived communally, they diverted it for their own purposes. For writing is an instrument of power, permitting the writer to send orders to faraway provinces and to set down the law by which he will prevail. And when writing is mysterious, it is even more powerful. We might suppose that "esoterism, far from being the original form of knowledge, is, in fact, merely its perversion."[19] This, of course, is sheer hypothesis. But Egypt is not the only case in which a privileged group was anxious to preserve its advantages and reluctant to share them. To give only one other example, in an entirely different geographical and cultural context: the learning of Aztec writing, also a mixed and complex system, was limited to priests and nobles. "Midway between picture-writing and phonetics, with elements of ideography, Aztec writing remained esoteric, like all knowledge in a highly stratified society."[20]

But contact with other societies involves exchanges that can overturn an established order. In Sumer, by the first half of the third millenium B.C., the Semitic language coexisting in Mesopotamia with Sumerian was written in cuneiform. The many Sumerian words borrowed from Semitic, and foreign names like those of neighboring Semites, were also recorded in cuneiform[21] (similar to the procedure in Japanese of using a special syllabary, the *katakana*). This situation had two essential consequences. First, in Akkadian (official language of the Akkad Empire by 2340 B.C.), and therefore in Sumerian itself, phonetic writing flourished at the expense of ideograms[22] after a period of mixed notation. This led to a system that records language itself, representing unit by unit the signifiers of its characters as speakers pronounce them. Secondly, this situation resulted in a major invention—that of the alphabet. In spite of the many contacts between the Egyptians and the Semites who created it, (inhabitants of the Ugarit Kingdom, now Ras Shamra in Syria), the alphabet was first recorded around 1500 B.C., in cuneiform and not in hieroglyphics.

This invention, although decisive, was doomed to imperfection: we observe in all languages a progressive modification of pronunciation that, sooner or later, renders an initially precise graphic representation obsolete. Such change helps to explain the difficulty of modern French spelling, and the agony associated with learning it. Still, even if the problems of alphabetic notation, which retains traces of former pronunciations, increase in direct proportion to phonetic changes, this notation may also be a stabilizing factor. Thus, in French, the final -r of the -ir infinitives, which had disappeared, was reinstated by analogy with the forms of the infinitives of the first group, in which the fall of ("mute") e had left a final written -r.[23] Inversely, widespread ignorance of the alphabet can favor and even accelerate change. French underwent its most extensive phonetic changes in the Middle Ages, before the invention of printing, during a period of widespread illiteracy.

When the alphabet was created, in any case, its advantages were probably more apparent than its drawbacks. Very soon, it was used to record many Semitic and non-Semitic languages.[24] Another more recently attested alphabet, the linear system of the Phoenician traders (in present-day Lebanon), was to have a brilliant destiny. This alphabet passed through various stages, including the addition of vowels by the

Greeks (since, previously, only consonants were written). And it is a form of the Phoenician system that has come down to us in the West. It is not by chance that the inventors of the alphabet were speakers of Semitic languages. *Writing is a linguistic analysis at varying levels of perception.* In the languages spoken by the Semites, segmentation could not stop at the word level the way it does with Chinese ideograms, which record a monosyllabic language of invariable words. For in Semitic languages, many words consist of several syllables, and the change (alternance) of consonant or vowel plays a grammatical role. Alternance serves, for example, to oppose singular and plural nouns, or the different forms of a verb. It is the more or less clear awareness of phonemes, associated with this type of language, which favored the development of the alphabet. Reciprocally, alphabetic writing fostered a kind of semiotic reflection unique to the West. For letters transcribe—however imperfectly, given phonetic changes—the constitutive sounds of words. Thus, for linguists of the Greek and Latin tradition, the meanings expressed phonically by these letters were linked to that phonetic realization by a unique reciprocal relation. This is not at all the case for ideogrammatic notation, as seen today in Chinese writing or in the Chinese component of Japanese writing (the rest of which consists of syllabaries). Ideogrammatic writing sketches the profile of meaning distinct from its relation to sound; meaning is thus conceived outside of the correspondence (institutionalized in all languages) between phonetic structure and semantic content. Such a system does not favor the notion of a one-to-one correspondence between signifier and signified.

Still, Sumer and Egypt, the prealphabetic centers of writing, should be studied in themselves and not in purely historical terms. Since the Middle East and the West are the seats of alphabetic civilizations, scholars have tended to arbitrarily assume that the alphabet was the inevitable destiny of previous writing systems. Egyptian writing proves that this evolution was in no way necessary. An "ancient Eurocentric obsession" makes us seek in the stages of the history of writing a solution to the "problem of the origin of alphabetic writing," when we should in fact be concerned with "the reciprocal role of sign and signifier."[25]

The third major type of writing may help to clarify matters. Chinese characters do have some features in common with Sumerian and Egyptian writing. The first is their antiquity, although there is no real consensus about the date of their appearance (perhaps the end of the second millenium,[26] perhaps 4000 B.C.).[27] Another shared feature is diffusion over a broad geographical and cultural area. Chinese characters were employed in Vietnam until the seventeenth century; they are still used in Japan, where they are associated with syllabary symbols, and on a smaller scale, in Korea, where the primary system is a highly precise semialphabetic code.[28]

However, the resemblance between Chinese writing and that of the Sumerian and Egyptian civiizations ends there. The origin of Chinese writing appears to have been mystic and religious rather than commercial and economic. Moreover, although pictograms did undergo some process of stylization, traces of direct representation of the world are still visible today in certain characters. But above all, the introduction of the phonetic principle in the majority of characters, creating combined notations of sound and meaning or *ideophonograms*, never resulted in syllabic writing. This is especially true since the rebus principle of the script was never systematized. There exist no characters of fixed phonetic value that can be extended to any phonetically identical element; also, when the phonetic principle appears, it usually notes only certain features, not the exact pronunciation of the corresponding word. Further, since the pronunciation of any language changes over time, the inaccuracy of the system tended to increase. In any case, the nonphonetic part of the ideophonograms represented only meaning, not sound; thus Chinese characters give no indication of the important phonetic changes that characterize the history of Chinese.

It is this system of pictograms and ideophonograms which, in more or less fixed form, has been preserved from ancient times to the present day. One of the most interesting aspects of this script is its power over the imagination of Westerners. It has inspired philosophers and poets, who are both masters and slaves of speech, in their recurring attempt to break through a wall of words. Chinese characters seem to provide an alternative.

In the eighteenth century, certain great thinkers were seduced by the mythical quest for a *pasigraphy*, a universal writing system that would be understandable to those of every nation or language. Leibniz admired Chinese writing, finding it more philosophical than the Egyptian, and proposed using it as a model to be developed and improved. The goal was "a kind of universal writing having the advantage of Chinese script, for each of us would understand it in our own language; but it would be infinitely superior to the Chinese system in that it could be learned in a few weeks, having characters closely linked to the order and connection of objects."[29] In fact, the information then available on Chinese writing, which had been provided by Jesuit missionnaries, was partly erroneous. Only in 1836 did Du Ponceau, a researcher in both Chinese and American linguistics,[30] show that these characters represented the Chinese language and not a universal system of ideas. In the meantime, speculation was nourished by ignorance. Sixty years before Leibniz, Kircher was fascinated by hieroglyphics. Yet he eschewed any attempt to decipher them, content to observe "a much more excellent, more sublime, and more abstract form of writing, which, through an ingenious sequence of symbols, or its equivalent, simultaneously grants the scholar access to complex reasoning, higher notions, or unseen mysteries hidden in the breast of nature or of the Divinity."[31]

As for the poets, many were fascinated by Chinese writing, which expresses meaning without encasing it in a material shell of words.[32] Ideographic reverie[33] breaks the bonds of language and seeks the harmony of lost worlds in characters that record both history and prehistory. For however we may try to imagine the articulations of early human speech, the cave walls provide only the anthropological evidence of drawings like mythograms, ancient ancestors of pictograms. Voices left no fossils.

This sanctification of nonalphabetic writing that does not record actual words can only detract from speech. It is significant that the contemplation of speech, reflected in centuries of study and finally becoming one of the major preoccupations of contemporary linguistics, is the work of Westerners accustomed to reading sound-based script:

> Since, in China, writing never resulted in the phonetic analysis of speech, it was never seen as a more or less faithful transcription of the spoken word. This is why the graph, unique symbol of a unique reality, has retained much of its original prestige. There is no reason to believe that speech in China was not as effective as writing; but its power was in part eclipsed by that of the written text. On the contrary, in civilizations in which writing evolved rather quickly towards the syllabary or the alphabet, words were able to concentrate all of their power, all of their religious and magical creation, in definitive written form. And, in fact, it is remarkable that we do not find in China this astonishing glorification of speech, of words, of syllables, or of vowels attested in all of the ancient civilizations from the Mediterranean basin to India.[34]

And yet, even if alphabetic writing seems closer to speech and to real pronunciation, we shall see that the distance between written and oral activity—and between the cultural attitudes and linguistic conceptions underlying them—remains enormous.

Lessons from the Oral Tradition

According to Plato (*Phaedra* 275e), a written utterance separated from the natural conditions in which it was spoken "is not strong enough to defend or sustain itself," since it is the frail "idol" of "living and animate discourse," and "deprived of the assistance of its father." And in his Seventh Letter, Plato declares that it is hardly a sign of seriousness to treat serious problems in written form.[35] Only natural oral communication can carry all of the original meaning. This meaning occurs at multiple levels. The essential phenomenon of intonation, reflected in no writing system, illustrates the point. In ancient times, grammarians and certain philosophers had observed that certain Latin texts can result in contradictions (a question taken for an assertion, etc.) or absurdities because of the absence of intonation. Quintilian and Saint Augustine give revealing examples.[36] Intonation often stratifies oral discourse into a hierarchical structure in which the principal message is not spoken in the same register as the interpolations, which may be embedded within each other. A graphic reproduction which, while otherwise exact, does not record intonation, can seem almost unintelligible, while the spoken form is perfectly clear for both speaker and hearer.

The invention of writing, then, while essential to the destiny of men (at least of those who participated in it), tended to obscure living speech. Pictograms, ideograms, phonograms, syllabaries, and alphabets remain lifeless and inadequate graphic projections of articulatory gestures and other meaningful features such as facial expressions. But in many oral civilizations, movements of the larynx and mouth, supported by the rhythm of respiration, are deeply established in gestural memory and become the elements of an *oral style.* Jousse's work of this title, which appeared in 1925, had an explosive effect. Some hundred articles in the press of the period, as well as all sorts of academic work, applied this discovery of the laws governing ritual discourse to various little-known societies. The notion of oral style must be distinguished from that of spoken style; the latter is applied to ordinary usage, more or less distinct from writing, in everyday discourse. Oral style is a true literary genre. It is a cultural tradition which may justify the creation of a precise term, *orature*, corresponding to French *écriture* ("writing"), understood here as literature (often excluding the oral tradition, which is certainly equally literary, in the sense that it preserves cultural monuments, but leaves no material trace).

Civilizations which have cultivated the oral style are not necessarily purely oral. Contrary to Western expectations, such civilizations may reserve graphic representation for nonliterary uses. Thus, as we have seen, the writing that appeared in Mesopotamia and Egypt was not necessarily associated with literary pursuits. As a phenomenon linked to a certain type of social structure, it was a practical instrument (for writing laws, codes, and public and private contracts), an economic tool (for accounting), and a formula for political or religious power: "The Sumerians, it appears, long resisted the use of writing for purely intellectual purposes; it is only several centuries after its invention that a few literary texts appear in clay."[37] Oral style makes use of various kinds of gestural and articulatory symbolism to ensure a remarkable mnemonic efficiency: refrains, initial syllables, interjections, connectors, inductive expressions, a profusion of quasi-synonyms, assonance, rhyme, alliteration, and other semantic and phonic echos, lexical and grammatical parallelism, meaning pairs, and rhythm produced by gestures and by movements of the mouth. The general procedure underlying these techniques is repetition. Repetition may be related to lateralization, a defining feature of the human race, by which certain organic functions are controlled by one or the other of the cerebral hemispheres. Proverbs around the world illustrate repetition in their symmetric formulas (such as *tel père tel fils*, "like father, like son"), well-known examples of echo structures. Repetition, a much more efficient instrument of iconic cohesion than the written formulas "etc." or "and others," is primary to oral style. Such discourse is not a visual script over which the eye can range at will, but an actual sound wave that may fade from memory as the flow of speech moves on.

In living speech, repetition techniques facilitate the perpetuation of ethnographic, legendary, and historical narratives by African griots, Biblical prophets, Berber, Malagasy, Senegalese and West Indian poets, and storytellers the world over, who constitute the living memory of man. The following proverb, attributed to the Malian scholar H. Hampaté Ba, has often been quoted: "In Africa, when an old man dies, a library burns." It has even been reported[38] that among the Ashantis of Ghana, any man admitted into the caste of reciters, or royal historians, was punished by death at the slightest error that might mutilate the authorized version. This is obviously exceptional; in fact, the most gifted African storytellers are often, on the contrary, those who can

60

improvise upon a schema transmitted by tradition. Still, the Ashanti custom reflects the high stakes of *orature*. In oral societies, moreover, when writing was used for literary ends, it was mainly as a memory aid. But once the written poetic form becomes a genre, it adapts certain procedures of oral style, in particular rhythm and, if possible, rhyme, stripping them of their mnemonic and didactic purpose. This purpose is well known in oral civilizations, but is also present to some degree in other civilizations. One very obvious manifestation is the teaching of grammar to children[39] using litanies, riddles, rhymes, and poems, abounding in formulas exploiting the possibilities of insertion and inversion of syllables, or tonguetwisters like *un chasseur sachant chasser sait chasser sans son chien* (cf. the English "she sells seashells by the seashore").[40]

Writing as an End in Itself

Despite the virtues of speech, it has been difficult to resist the primal temptation to use writing to try to burst the bonds of nature, matter, and existence. The opposition between spoken and written language can be developed quite extensively. In Chinese, for example, it resulted very early in an elliptical language in which most words can play quite different roles depending upon context. This language, known as *Wen-yan*, appears never to have been used orally,[41] aside from the fact that Chinese writing was used only for ritual and magic purposes for nearly a thousand years. It is, however, true that the resistance of the Chinese language to Roman script cannot be entirely explained by tradition. For only characters could distinguish between homophones, of which Chinese has a rare abundance. In any case, Chinese is an extreme example, since Wenyan constitutes a type of third register in addition to the written/oral opposition already present in most languages that possess any form of writing.

For these languages, the written / oral opposition does not simply separate two systems representing equivalent meaningful content. The division implies a divergence between two registers, one more spontaneous and less concerted, the other more prestigious and powerful. For, from the moment we begin to write, even if we are addressing ourselves to a single reader with whom we are on familiar terms, our message takes on a more solemn tone and we become concerned with its appearance. It has often been observed that within a given language, the written and spoken styles do not exploit the same resources. In English, for example, written texts contain a greater number of nominalizations, participles, and qualifying adjectives than do oral texts.[42] In certain cases, the prestige of writing derives from an archaic period of the language, quite distant from contemporary usage, acting as a phrasal repertory and a source for borrowing, independently of its continued liturgical use. This is the situation of Latin, Sanskrit, Old Slavic, Pali, classical Arabic, Guèze, and classical Mongolian, compared, respectively, with the Romance and Indo-Aryan languages, Bulgarian, Burmese, modern Arabic, Amharic, and contemporary Mongolian. Nevertheless, the use of an ancient religious language is not unknown in oral societies. Hawaii provides an example, although on a rather limited scale.

The autonomy of writing has tended to make it an end in itself. In written civilizations, literary pleasure is first and foremost that of style. Everything contributes to the creation of a written "voice." Above all, the autonomy of writing abolishes linearity, inescapable for oral language, which was for so long the focus of all considerations about speech. Set out in a visual medium, writing can take advantage of all possible directional combinations: vertical, horizontal, rightward, or leftward (*boustrophedon* combines these last two). Hieroglyphics provide examples of counterpoint. But this escape from linearity is not only a procedure of ancient Egypt. Manifestations of it are found in all places and periods. *Palindromes* can only be conceived in written form, since they are words or phrases that can be read identically from left to right or from right to left. So called concrete poetry and contemporary spatial poetry are not emprisoned, like oral poetry, within the constraints of a single dimension: calligrams, iconosyntax, toposyntax, and all the techniques originating in Mallarmé's *Coup de dés*, lend a physical contour to the text that reflects its content.

Still other procedures contribute to the autonomous destiny of writing. Through typography in particular, speech abandons the confines of time to enter those of space: paragraphs, spacing, chapters, capitals, titles, subtitles. Language becomes a two-dimensional object on the page and a three-dimensional one in volume.[43] Typographical techniques, while they only imperfectly transpose the rhythm of respiration, also contribute elements of their own. The very interpretation (reading) of alphabetic writing, which assumes highly complex cerebral mechanisms,[44] does not necessarily involve deciphering the phonemes represented, although it is true that this analytical writing represents them with considerable exactitude. If phonemes were essential to reading, educated deaf-mutes would be able to read only those words that they have learned to articulate. In fact, however, they read and write much more. And when their knowledge *is* limited by their actual speech, this is due to faulty training, founded on the illusion that a direct relation between written words and their referents would be impossible. Such a notion ignores the relative autonomy of the written code with respect to language.

It does not follow, however, that writing is also autonomous with respect to culture. Japanese writing is a complex combination of two syllabaries with at least 850 Chinese characters; further, there may be one (and often two) Sino-Japanese interpretations of these characters in addition to the Japanese one. This script is rather ill-adapted to the type of language it records. Yet, the ideograms which, when borrowed from China in the fourth century A.D., permitted the notation of a hitherto unwritten language, have been profoundly integrated into Japanese civilization. They are also an artistic manifestation; and attempts to increase the use of the syllabaries have succeeded only in fixing a limit to the number of officially recognized characters. As for Arabic writing, it had close ties with Islam and recorded its philosophical, religious, and political thought. Aware of the abundance of these terms in the Turkish lexicon, and anxious to de-Islamize Turkey, Mustapha Kemâl adopted the Latin alphabet in 1928. From his point of view, this was not a simple orthographic reform, but a cultural revolution.

But if writing is not entirely independent of culture, it is certainly rather free in relation to the spoken language. Writing has the amazing power to transform meaning into an object. It thus tends to become what its nature has always implied: an esthetic system. Egyptian hieroglyphics very soon became part of the decor, and their arrangement reflects a sheer love of the written sign. Chinese calligraphy is intimately related to poetry and painting, always accompanying them and, in fact, playing a constituent role. Certain complex Chinese characters, made up of combinations of several simple ones, permit graphic games: by juxtaposing the compound with its components, it is sometimes possible to create interpretable sentences.[45] Stone arabesques transmit esthetic messages along with verses of the Koran. Systems derived from the Brāhmī script, including the (deva)nagari and the many Asian syllabaries, offer myriad designs and patterns to the eye.

Beyond its formal intention, writing reveals its magical one. However stylized it may be, most notably in the abstraction of the letters of the alphabet (Roman, Hebrew, or Arab, for example),[46] it retains some historical relation with the originally representational image. This may explain the fact that so many linguists are indifferent to writing, which is never as completely arbitrary as the signs that it records are presumed to be. This quasi-magical bond between writing-image and reality is confirmed in certain Egyptian funeral chambers, where we find that "signs representing animals, or potentially hostile beings, are modified—mutilated, or pierced with knives—to keep those that they represent from troubling the deceased."[47] Thus, a consubstantial link joins the hieroglyph to the being it symbolizes. The ideological content of writing can even violate Egyptian syntax. For example, in this language in which determined nouns preceded determiner nouns, "scribe (of the) king" was said *sš nsw* (same order); but it was sometimes written *nsw sš*, preposing the sign corresponding to the more prestigious element.[48] Thus, even when writing is such a clearly codified system (as it seems to be in Egypt, as far back as we find it) that it is not merely plastic, but true notation of language, the temptation to remotivate its graphic representation is already a powerful one.

The result is comparable to that often produced orally through intonation or body language: the counterpoint of a second message with which the writer complements or even subverts the first, adding graphic meaning to the graphic representation of meaning. The *ateji* of Japanese writing illustrate the point. Taking advantage of the fortuitous coincidence between certain Japanese words and the Sino-Japanese pronunciation of certain Chinese characters, the meaning of the latter is added to that of the former. Thus, on many garbage cans in Japan we see the Japanese name *gomibako*, literally "garbage can," written not with the syllabary for Japanese words *(hiragana)*, but with two specific Chinese characters representing the syllables *go* and *mi*. In Sino-Japanese pronunciation, they are indeed read *go-mi*, but in Chinese they correspond to words signifying "protect" and "beauty," respectively. The garbage can is a "can to protect beauty!"

Similarly, in some ancient Egyptian inscriptions, the original phonetic representation (itself arising from a rebus principle) is replaced with a character corresponding to the same sound, and which has the added particularity of referring to a divinity from whom the writer seeks protection. Sometimes, in fact, the temptation produced by writing is to create a secret message that may be deciphered only by certain readers. The eighth-century *Book of the zealot's frantic desire to learn the enigmas of ancient writing*, by Abu Bakr Ahmad ben Ali ben Washiyya An-Nabati, gives formulas for the composition and interpretation of the mysterious alphabets that were used in ritual practices, as well as in the secret correspondence between sovereigns and their ambassadors, or between military leaders. But these are private codes, invented for specific ends in precise historical contexts. The esoteric nature of the message carried by the hieroglyphics was that of a national script, even though it was not widely diffused among the populace. Such writing remains unique in its coherence and intention, and in its symphonic value. Egyptian texts are invested with propitiatory co-texts; they are messages upon or within which apostrophic formulas (defenses against evil spells, as well as invocations to the gods) are inserted in a rebus chain. This writing constitutes a final product. It immediately appeared in its most sophisticated form of multi-layered message; it could evolve no further. It was not, in fact, an anonymous copy of vocal articulations, as are alphabetic writing systems. Egyptian writing reflected a contrapuntal relation between the writer and his desire.

Speech, Writing, and Society

Why do so many nations, especially in Africa, adopt the alphabet to record their hitherto purely oral languages? Does this reflect a need to participate in the economic structures of the modern world? Is it simply another consequence of colonialism? Or is it the pressure of the media, which assigns a negative connotation to illiteracy? Surely we need not resurrect the notions of Rousseau in defense of illiteracy. It is not obvious that writing necessarily constitutes an instrument of oppression by allowing the transmission of precise orders and leaving a trace to verify their execution. Law is not oppression, and we must wonder if the chief of the Nambikwara was indeed abandoned by his people merely because he sought to confirm his authority through a pretense of writing.[49] Still, the introduction of writing into an oral society requires certain precautions. It is a conscious transfer, not a spontaneous development. There is a very real cultural difference between societies that write and those that do not. The latter have long developed, based on oral practice, their own models of expression, their systems of exchange and balance, and their memory. To avoid a dangerous eruption of writing into the oral milieu, these societies must be allowed to find their own route to the conveniences of written notation. For these conveniences are undeniable.[50] But, in oral societies, the notion of illiteracy, like that of languages "without" writing, does not carry the condescending, pitying, and Eurocentrist weight that it does in those parts of the world where languages have long been written.[51] The historical records of oral societies are their sages and their poets.

This intrusion of writing is a danger not only for the societies into which it enters, but for the languages themselves. The recent history of certain creole languages may serve as an illustration. For a creole with a French lexical base, like that of Haiti, access to written form has long been the concern of cultivated speakers, writers, and teachers. But the written representation of a previously oral language is not a simple exercise in transcription. A written language is not a transcribed oral language. It is a new linguistic and cultural phenomenon. The recurring temptation, in this case, is to introduce subordinating conjunctions that do not exist in creole but are borrowed from written French: *que* "that," *lorsque* "when," *parce que* "because," *si* "if," *bien que* "although," *de sorte que* "so that," etc. I say written French, since in certain registers of oral French, as in many other languages, syntactic links between clauses are marked by various intonational curves, veritable prosodic morphemes (see chapter 3). Such is the case for Haitian creole. The only solution, if we wish to avoid deforming the language by "Frenchifying" it with the substitution of nonprosodic markers for intonational ones, is to represent intonation by means of a precise and diversified system of punctuation marks. Those used currently in Latin writing are, in fact, the imperfect and vague symbols of vocal inflections, the pauses and curves that constitute intonation. Is it unrealistic to hope to enrich this system by adding other graphic signs that more faithfully reflect the melodies of speech? Yes, to the extent that no contemporary writing records intonation precisely: commas, question marks, exclamation points, etc., are poor approximations. No, to the extent that one of the principal reasons for this weakness is the historical ignorance of intonational phenomena. These phenomena are now the object of extensive research. Oral languages acceding to writing should be the first to take advantage of that fact.

The link between punctuation and intonation, which thus remains to be exploited, is indirectly confirmed by the study of certain literary texts. Written texts that use little or no punctuation are also those that make the most of lexical and grammatical procedures for connecting words, groups of words, clauses, and sentences. In *orature* discourse, intonation corresponds to these procedures, which are characteristic of a certain form of hermetic poetry, or artistic prose, that defies graphic conventions. At the same time, the simple versified disposition of even the most classical poetry can suffice to make punctuation unnecessary, as long as each line corresponds to a syntactic group, or even to a single sentence. In the absence of enjambments and of long phrases projected over several lines, the division of meaning follows that of the meter. We find examples of this in creole poetry.[52]

"Writing veils language: it is not clothing, but disguise," wrote Saussure.[53] And, long before him, Rousseau stated that "Languages are made to be spoken; writing serves only as a supplement to speech."[54] Derrida, who exalts writing, reproaches these two famous "scriptophobes" for their prejudice.[55] Worshipping spoken discourse, they ignore its written trace. But is this written representation that men have invented for their greater power assured of such a brilliant future, that those who are "deprived" of writing should so covet it? Several decades of technical developments have seriously eroded the power of writing. Its reign is threatened. From politicians to advertisers, from poets to journalists, in more and more professions, no communicative act—whether to inform, to please, or to convince—can be carried out through a written text alone; it must also include speech. The tape recorder, the computer (scribe of the twenty-first century), the videocassette recorder may overturn—may, in fact, already be overturning—the relationship between speech and graphic symbols. This relationship has no particular influence upon the essence of language; it does, however, exercise a powerful negative influence upon writing. Is this not enough to convince us that, despite the essential role still played by writing, despite all its remaining prestige, it is inevitably external to language?

The invention and dissemination of means for conserving speech may be pertinent to linguistic reflection. Long ago, it was no doubt the invention of alphabetic writing that gave a decisive impetus to grammatical research. For when we use a single symbol to represent the innumerable regional or individual variations of / p /, or / a /, or / r /, we become aware of a surprising phenomenon: the immensity of these differences does not prevent the members of a single linguistic community from understanding each other. Constants must therefore exist. And what is linguistics, if not the search for these constants, in the domain of sounds as well as in the domains of lexicon and syntax? If in fact a revolution appears imminent, it is because machines that record speech do the opposite of what the linguist does: they retain only the variations. Linguistics cannot remain indifferent to this technical development. In fact, linguistic research has already made some use of it. Of course, variation was studied long before machines could so faithfully reproduce it. But sound recording has provided a new stimulus for this movement. Linguistics, born of the recognition of constants, is in large part becoming a study of variation against a background of invariants; a science that no longer contemplates constants in and of themselves, but subsumes them under the thousand faces of their variants. In other words, linguistics is becoming sociolinguistics.

PART TWO

Applications

OR

Universe, Discourse, and Society

5

The Territory of the Sign

The Meaning of Sounds: the Indivisible Pair

Words are an institution. Most of the world's languages have a term for the notion "word," or a close approximation thereof. But the only unit that can shed real light upon language is the one known as the *sign:* the smallest unit resulting from analysis, the final product of all dissection. In many cases, sign and word coincide. The French word *jardin* ("garden"), which has two syllables, cannot be broken down, nor can the three-syllable *élégant.* These are signs. At this level, the matter appears quite simple. But many other cases arise, even with words of the highest frequency, in which the language rebels against any effort to define it. Thus, the verbs *est* or *a* in the sentences *il est élégant* ("he is elegant") or *il a un jardin* ("he has a garden") are single syllables, single vowels in fact, phonetically represented as [ɛ] and [a], respectively. Yet neither can be reduced to a single sign. To take the case of *est:* if, in the first sentence, we undertake an analysis by successive variations of a single meaning, we obtain a different sign with each operation. If tense is the variable, and we modify nothing else, we will arrive, for example, at *il était* ("was") *élégant*. If we modify the verb itself, we can produce *il devient* ("becomes") *élégant*. If we change neither tense nor verb, but only person, and then only number, excluding tense, verb, and person, we obtain two other sentences, *tu es* ("you are") *élégant*, and *ils sont* ("they are") *élégants*. In this fashion, the context established by the first and third words remains the same, except for liaisons, which in any case are not consistently made in all styles of modern spoken French. The conclusion, familiar to linguists, appears as troubling as it is inevitable: *est*, this most common French word, indivisible in form and in fact reduced to a single vowel, contains no less than four signs.

The method illustrated here is not a pure linguistic invention. The operations are carried out upon observable facts. Communication through language assumes that meaning is produced and perceived. The particular meaning of a word results from the elimination of the meanings of all other words that could appear in the same context. Consequently, for any meaning that can be distinguished, we must posit a sign, even though the sounds corresponding to any sign are dissolved in an unanalyzable compound. Thus the basic definition of the sign: it is the smallest association of meaning (expressed, from Saint Augustine to Saussure, as the *signified*) with a sound segment known as the *signifier*. The latter is usually identifiable, as in the case of *élégant*, which, resulting from the analysis of the above sentence, is itself a sound unit that can be subdivided into five phonemes, or sounds serving to distinguish between signs: /e/ + /l/ + /e/ + /g/ + /ã/ (a nasal vowel written here as -*ant*). But in more complex cases, like the fusion illustrated above with *est*, the signifier may result from several operations and may not be obvious.

The mysterious process by which languages invest sound with meaning, or make meaning arise from sound, is the primary characteristic of the sign: signifier and signified are absolutely indissociable and cannot be conceived separately. Many ancient (and not so ancient) linguistic puzzles result from a misunderstanding of this elementary fact. In the interest of brevity, we will note here only one among many of its practical consequences. *Taboos* (the term was borrowed from one of the Polynesian languages at the end of the eighteenth century) have been used at one time or another all over the world. These verbal avoidance strategies are aimed not at the tabooed object itself, but at the signified, automatically invoked by the mere use of the signifier. When the sounds of the tabooed word are forbidden, its meaning and all of its connotations are also repressed. Thus, for any given sign, its signifier (of whatever form) and its signified (in whatever domain), through the effects of the structure of the language in question, constitute two sides of a single reality:

> The linguistic entity exists only through the association of signifier and signified . . . ; it vanishes if one of these elements is withdrawn. . . . A series of sounds is linguistic only if it conveys an idea; taken in itself, it is only an object of physiological study. The same is true of the signified, once separated from its signifier. Concepts such as "house," "white," "see," etc., considered in themselves, belong to the field of psychology; they become linguistic entities only by association with acoustic images.[1]

Classic as they now seem, these lines have not lost their clarity with respect to the notion of the sign, a notion dutifully accepted by some and hotly debated in the rhetoric of others. Let us merely emphasize that there is no equivalence between signifier and word on the one hand, or signified and object on the other. The sign, its two faces as indivisible as those of a coin, refers to objects and to notions—to what linguists call "the world." Language exists in its own realm. The utterances that may be produced by language speak of the world. They are not the world. They are the manifestation of the human aptitude to signify.

Sign and Difference

The aptitude to signify is to be distinguished from the simple aptitude to symbolize. Other human activities, essentially artistic ones, involve symbolization. The procedures of speech are, quite literally, *sign-ifying*, i.e., they produce signs. Textbooks always emphasize this point. The sign, unlike the symbol, is not linked to the referent (the world of objects and notions) by any rational or justifiable bond. The sign presumes simple consensus. It is acquired as a convention, through a sure and rapid learning process without parallel in any symbolic system. The acquisition of signs by human children maintains a relation of reciprocal influence with the development of intelligence and the invention of the world. With speech acting as a mediator, the child acquires mastery of the world through representation of the world.

The linguistic sign functions on the level of conceptual intelligence.

73

Beneath this level we perceive two others that are apparently not exclusive to the human species. Chimpanzees possess sensorimotor intelligence, allowing them to recognize external objects and to adapt their behavior to those objects. With training, they may also acquire representative intelligence, which is the use of symbols for deferred notation of objects in absentia.[2] But conceptual intelligence, linked to arbitrary signs and not to symbols, appears to be limited to humans.

If the sign thus characterized entertains any relation of necessity, it can only be to other signs within a single language. Further, linguistic signs have the cardinal property of being autoreferential. This is the foundation of all discourse upon language; it also demonstrates the perils of such discourse. A differential relation exists among the signs of a given system. This relation is guaranteed by the indivisibility of the two sides of the sign. If the concept of difference can be applied to linguistic data at all, it is to the extent that phonemes, the nature and combination of which compose the signifier of every sign, are themselves distinct. This is the simple truth to be found in the phonological tables provided in any good description of a language. Such tables demonstrate the architecture elaborated by each idiom to organize its universe of signs along the sound continuum. Obviously, two signs may sometimes have the same signifier: these are cases of polysemy, as in the French word *chemise,* a word having several meanings ("shirt," "folder," etc.); and homonyns, such as *louer,* which has two distinct meanings originating from two Latin sources, *locare* ("rent") and *laudare* ("praise"), converging by chance through the process of phonetic evolution. But in these cases the signified are sufficient to distinguish the signs. The signified of any sign is first defined by the fact that it is not the signified of any other sign—which gives us only an indirect definition.

And yet this principle, the keystone of Saussure's theory, is challenged by a strange and fundamental phenomenon: synonymy, that magnetization between meanings that makes dictionaries possible. Synonymy is not easy to integrate into a theoretical system. Long before Saussure, Aristotle (*Metaphysics,* 10006 [b] 5) posited a singularity forbidding the coincidence of two signs for a single meaning: "not to signify a unique object is to signify nothing at all." And later, Du Marsais condemned perfect synonyms to eternal exile, for there could not be "two languages within a single language."[3] But we need only look beyond the familiar Indo-European languages to see that paraphrase and explanation (the only homologies of meaning accepted by Western linguists) do not exhaust the properties of languages. The borrowing of learned or archaic vocabulary, in many languages, creates extensive areas of perfect synonymy between the borrowed terms and those of the native base. Such is the situation in Hindi-Urdu for the Arab and Persian terms that doubled those of the Indo-Aryan stock. Similarly in Japan, Chinese terms were introduced alongside the Nipponese base toward the end of the fourth century. In fact, a single Chinese character was used to transcribe both members of the pair produced by each of these borrowings. Of course, it can always be argued that there is a difference in register.

Even so, the probable existence of authentic synonyms does not prevent any language from organizing the signified of its vocabulary on the basis of differences. For a change in signifier suffices to produce a change in sign. Of course, this indirect characterization cannot alone serve as the foundation for a theory of meaning, even if several decades of Saussurian teaching have softened the edges of the paradox. Establishing the signified of the sign is only one aspect of meaning (see chapter 10), despite the structuralist tradition and its prolongation in the form of generative grammar. The indirect definition remains a useful foundation, however, and by underestimating it, we lose sight of an essential characteristic of languages as systems of signification. The history of lexicons amply illustrates that the content of a sign within a language is largely determined by that of other signs, primarily those belonging to the same semantic field. A single change in signified can suffice to entail that of a whole series of neighboring signifieds. These adventures in semantics are extensive enough to have inspired much learned research.[4]

Besides, linguistics is not the only science that resorts to the concept of opposition. Among the humanities, consider the case of child psychology. Wallon writes,

> Thought exists only through the structures it imposes upon objects. . . . There is no punctual thought, but rather dualism or doubling from the beginning. . . . As a general rule, every expression, every notion is intimately linked to its opposite, so that one cannot be conceived without the other. . . . The simplest and most striking demarcation is opposition. An idea is defined first and most simply by its opposite. The link between yes-no, white-black, father-mother, becomes automatic, so that they sometimes seem to reach the lips at the same time and one must make a choice, rejecting the inappropriate member of the pair.[5]

75

A similar view is found in other scientific fields. According to Schro-dinger,[6] in physics and biology, "the differences between properties are in fact discrete," and "their differential character is the fundamental concept." Bell[7] observes that in the topological approach to mathematics, "it is not objects that are important, but rather the relations betwen them." And Braque is said to have suggested, "Let us forget about objects and consider only the relations between them" (*Cahiers*, Gallimard, 1952, p. 40)—a perfect summary of pictorial art.

Signs, Apes and Communication

Keeping in mind the distinction between human semiotics and animal symbolism, we may still wonder if the differential nature of the linguistic sign might not be found in the codes taught to the "near" relatives of man. During the sixties, experiments were conducted on chimpanzees in California.[8] What can these ethological experiments teach us about human speech? American Sign Language was taught to a female chimpanzee named Washoe. Sarah learned a code based on metal tokens displayed on a magnetic board. And it is true that she acquired the meaning of the units of this code only through the oppositions between them. Here, then, we do not find the boundary (in synchronic terms, of course, since the history of species involves a continuum) between the signs of human language and elements of a code acquired by higher primates. The frontier lies elsewhere, in an apparently trivial fact with profound significance: human languages are *both* systems of signs and means of communication.[9] Each of these properties is fully realized, and each reinforces the other.

Thus the two may not be conceived separately. For, in our daily use of speech, it becomes so familiar, and its messages so accessible, that we are no longer aware of the difference between the two properties. The unified phenomenon of speech, associating sign and communication, masks its duality. Here, as in other fields of research, the study of the "normal" can gain precious insights by considering the deviant. Glossolalia, languages invented in the context of mystic or religious inspiration, are generally relegated to the misty peripheries of normal language use.[10] Yet they display a strange symbiosis: communication occurs without semiotics. Communication does indeed take place, yet in the absence or quasi-absence of signs. This communication is that of an expressive or metaphysical message, something like the playful or esthetic messages of Khlebnikov's transmental poetry (*za-um*, literally,

76

in Russian), studied by Jakobson.[11] Other examples are the jargons devised by Rabelais, Joyce, Michaux or, more recently, Eco, who places a similar potpourri of words in the mouth of the monk Salvatore in *The Name of the Rose*.[12] But in glossolalia we do not find linguistic signs as entities that can be identified by the stability of the relation between signifier and signified, and by the consensus of a community that authorizes them through use.

These abnormal forms of speech reveal a startling sort of divergence: a constitutive relation between two properties associated in the norm is dissolved. In such marginal linguistic behavior, a kind of communication is established, but is not mediated by signs. If the audience, reader, or decoder can understand these "pathological" utterances that communicate without signifying, it is probably because they call upon only one of these "two faculties of the mind" considered distinct by Benveniste: that of recognizing and that of understanding, "that of perceiving the identity between past and present, on the one hand, and that of perceiving the meaning of a new utterance, on the other."[13]

The speech of apes, like paranormal human speech, possesses only one of these two properties. And it remains quite rudimentary in form. The way in which the two chimpanzees Washoe and Sarah seem, during their training, to master the code they are learning, indicates that they are capable of symbolization, and that they can even use symbols in the absence of their corresponding physical objects. Better still, they can isolate features through analysis. As long as symbols rather than arbitrary signs are involved, the chimpanzees can use them to abstract, i.e., to classify different objects according to some common feature: for example, apple and banana, a series from which they can abstract the symbol for "fruit;" or inversely, red and round, a series from which they infer "apple." Above all, these apes are capable of assimilating abstract structures corresponding to simple human sentences; and when constitutive elements are arranged in nonrandom sequences, each one may be replaced by others belonging to the same set. Thus, Sarah is able to combine units into a single structure, to obtain utterances such as *Mary + give + apple*. Sarah can even teach the code to other apes.

And yet, despite appearances, all of this does not suffice. Language, and even the generalized speech faculty, are not defined by the unilateral perception of messages, as in the case of the apes who were taught how to react to utterances made up of symbols that they were first trained to interpret individually. There must first be conceptual intelligence fashioning pure signs; and then an initiative by each of the individuals of the emitter-receiver pair toward a systematic interaction between them, the receiver assuming in turn the full functions of the emitter.

For, in addition to assertion, there are two essential modalities of communication that are characteristic of language use in human societies, and that almost never appear in the apes' use of codes. These are interrogation and injunction. Gardner does point out the single case of a message addressed by Washoe to a companion who was unaware of an approaching danger. The message consisted of the sequence of symbols "come" + "hurry up." But this occurrence remains isolated and fortuitous. That does not mean, however, that it should be ignored. The case suffices to demonstrate that the "only" thing distinguishing human languages from the codes taught to the higher apes is some two million years during which the human species developed an increasingly complex social life and ever more efficient tools.

The example cited above also reminds us that, despite the difficulty of inventing a reliable and realistic experimental method, it is not entirely impossible to reveal the continuity between human and animal communication. This experiment in acquisition, fascinating in its hypothesis and goal, remains an entirely reasonable enterprise. And yet, the exceptional nature of injunction and the total absence of interrogation (so far, at least) among the trained apes show clearly that different types of communication must be distinguished. In fact, the notions of speech and of communication coincide only in the richest acceptation of the latter concept, according to which a single channel establishes communication between two individuals united by a close network of social relations. Given their actual complexity and scope, these relations must necessarily be the product of a long period of living in coherent groups sharing the diverse needs resulting from their symbiosis. And this history is that of humanity alone.

Thus the issues involved are not those supposed by Premack. The question is not whether Sarah does or does not confirm Chomsky's universals concerning the interrogative transformation, or the existence of a verb "be" with equative meaning, or the manipulation of conjunctions such as "and." This is an endlessly circular argument, seeking in the chimpanzee certain linguistic universals whose outlines are already presupposed by a biological faculty of speech. A more fertile area of research, highly pertinent to the study of human languages, is suggested by the following question: how and to what extent do chimpanzees communicate? The answer is clear: in comparison with human primates, we find only the aptitude, perhaps genetic, for a very rudimentary social life in small groups. We see no development even comparable to that observed in the archeological vestiges of *Homo habilis* to *Homo erectus*, not to mention the subsequent stages. If chimpanzees do not "speak," it is because their "social" life does not place them in the situation of having much to say to each other. And if they do learn to "speak," after an extended period of training during which the instructor's impatience is allayed by his curiosity, it is because the rewards (bananas, chocolates, candies) provided at each training session create needs that the learners must satisfy.

But what the chimpanzees are able to "say" shows that they cannot pass a certain, genetically fixed, limit, the equivalent of which is found only at the dawn of human prehistory. This limitation is equally demonstrated by the poverty of the "social" relations artificially established between an animal, isolated or in small groups, and an experimenter operating by a system of rewards for correct responses. Surely this is not sufficient to bridge the temporal gap. Perhaps, since the reward is always expected, this is only *training* in the strictest sense. Highly complex training, of course, but in no way related to real linguistic acquisition, the illusion of which may however be created since the researcher practices, in a human language, the dangerous exercise of paraphrase, or establishes English equivalents for messages made up of conventional signs.

In any case, another essential characteristic of human linguistic production is entirely absent here: humans can speak of the non-existent—words without known referants, sentences contradicting actual experience. The human receivers may not appreciate this type of misleading communication. But no one remains indifferent to it; it elicits many types of reactions, verbal or otherwise. Among the animals trained to "speak," there have been no messages involving the non-existent (although chimpanzees can "lie" through ruse).

These experiments, then, provide indirect confirmation that man, alone in the living world, is able to signify and to communicate in the full sense of each of these notions. Man uses a continually evolving repertory of signs, organized into coherent structures, to transmit and interpret messages presupposing a highly complex social relation of interaction and dialogue. These are messages that assert, interrogate, command, and express states. And it is because human languages are the only systems invested simultaneously with this dual property that they must be recognized as unique. This singularity—that of being a duality—is reflected in *one* science of linguistics, not two, contrary to the proposals of some who, while clearly perceiving the double nature of languages, have not accepted the idea of a single model.[14]

The Animation of Signs

In every science, certain truths have difficulty gaining acceptance. Is this because the power of the mass media in the late twentieth century has created an audience in search of myths? Is it because the slow, stubborn work of reason must continually struggle against the temptations of fantasy and the attraction of the irrational? Whatever the reason, one essential truth concerning speech has been resisted by the layman; indeed, it was long ignored even by professional linguists. It is simply this: although for every sign of a language, an indissoluble bond links its meaning and the sounds that compose it—the two faces of the sign, acquired together—this link nevertheless has no real motivation, no character of necessity. We often have evidence of this in the fact that so many languages associate different signifiers with signifieds that can be quite readily translated. And yet, as far as the ordinary speaker is concerned, his language says things as they ought to be said.

This speaker will be even more reluctant to admit that there is no motivational link between the sounds of words and the objects to which they refer, that is between signifier and referent. Even if we could assume that all objects in the universe (not to mention abstract notions) produce or evoke sounds that can be reflected in human languages, the signifier does not mimic the referent. In other words, the signifier of the sign is unmotivated, and has no formal bond with the reality that it translates into language.[15] This inescapable fact, while normally taught in any introduction to linguistics, is not universally accepted. Does the quest for universal harmony fulfill some deep need in the human spirit? A few scholars, at least, do realize that this quest is only a dream. In his famous letter to Père Mersenne (1629), Descartes observed that it is theoretically possible to fashion a truly philosophical language, one in which words would be direct symbols for objects. But he expressed grave doubts that such a language could ever come into common usage; as for Mersenne,[16] despite his desire to realize a language conceived so "naturally" that it would not even have to be learned, he recognized that the arbitrariness underlying all real human languages rendered the project largely utopic.

But this has not sufficed to lay to rest the myth of motivation.

Theories of the symbolism or mimesis of language sounds have long been popular, although they have never been corroborated by any irrefutable demonstration—on the contrary, innumerable counter-examples are available to any bilingual, and even to the attentive monolingual. The notion is not limited to medieval doctors, certain of whom saw in grammar the key to the sciences, since if one understands words and their laws, one should then understand the universe that words express through sound. Such theories have also flourished when so-called rationalism failed to separate convention and power: on the one hand, the conventional nature of the sign, substituted by implicit agreement for the designated object; and, on the other, that sign's very power of designation, issuing from its relation with the referent. It is this second aspect which interested Court de Gébelin, who marveled at the relation between words and objects:

> How could anyone have believed that words have no power of their own? That their only value is bestowed by arbitrary convention? That the name of the lamb could have been that of the wolf and the name of vice that of virtue? That man was mute, and for long centuries communicated only with simple cries? That is was only after many fruitless and painful efforts that he managed to stammer a few words, and much later that he learned that these words could be linked together? [17]

Since the Middle Ages, one language in particular, Hebrew, had fascinated those who interpreted the story of Babel as a divine judgment. A penalty for human excess,[18] this exemplary punishment demotivated the sign, thus reducing it to a product of pure convention and triggering the proliferation of languages. Only Hebrew still seemed to bear the traces of the original affinity between sign and referent. The once-famous esoteric Fabre d'Olivet devoted to this language his work *La langue hébraique restituée,* published in Paris in 1816–1817. In it, he attempts to show that in Hebrew, thanks to the "prodigious fertility of events," "there is not a single word of more than one syllable that is not a compound derived from an original root" (part 1, "Hebrew Roots," p. 1). This refers to the rich system of derivation characteristic of Semitic morphology.

Fabre believed that this system could not be arbitrary. Apparently confusing phonetic motivation (sounds evoking or imitating the designated object) and morphological motivation (derived words with regularly predictable form and meaning), he naturally drew upon the work

81

of Court de Gébelin. Fabre, of course, contrasts this approach to that of Hobbes, a well-known defender of the arbitrariness of the sign:

> Only a mind obsessed with systems . . . and, further, singularly ignorant of the primary elements of speech, could maintain with Hobbes (for it is from him that all our modern scholars have derived this idea) that the institution of speech is wholly arbitrary: a very strange paradox indeed, and worthy of the man who . . . advised that one should not conclude from experience that a thing is to be called just or unjust . . . , claiming that truth and falsehood exist only . . . in the application of terms.

The same inspiration is clear in the posthumous work of de Maistre, *Les soirées de Saint-Pétersbourg* (1821), where we read: "Let us never speak of chance, nor of arbitrary signs."[19] (This same de Maistre cites in all seriousness the remotivating "etymologies" of Isidore of Sevilla, such as that of *cadaver*, which would supposedly come from *caro data vermibus*, "flesh given to the worms.") According to this line of thought, there is a connection between the motivation of signs and a system of ethics; in the other camp, the connection is between arbitrariness and a nominalist conception of words as the pure instruments of unjustifiable designations. This nominalism, with its sacrilegious flavor, characterized the English philosophy of Hobbes, as it still does that of Russell and Austin.

But upon what precise criteria could the antinominalists base their position? Quite simply, they used well-chosen examples to illustrate a supposedly natural link between the sounds of words and the objects of the world. Quoting again from Court de Gébelin, "the labials, the simplest sounds to produce, the gentlest, the most gracious, were used to designate the first beings that man knew, those that surrounded him and to whom he owed everything;" while "the teeth are as hard as the lips are mobile and flexible; the intonations coming from the teeth are strong, sonorous, loud."[20] Rousseau would later echo these speculations, finding in the roughness of consonants and the softness of vowels the ancient reflection of what they quite "naturally" expressed at the dawn of humanity.[21]

These are only a few examples from a rather vast body of literature. It is simple enough to provide counter-examples. The quest for motivation within real languages is not qualitatively different from the long history of fantasies about ideal languages. For thinkers like Wilkins, Cyrano de Bergerac, Vairasse, Foigny, and Brissot,[22] the goal has always been the invention of languages in explicit harmony with nature. "The advantage of this way of speaking," said Foigny of his "Austral" language, "is that one becomes a philosopher by learning to pronounce the first words, and no object in this country can be named without explaining its nature at the same time; this would seem miraculous, if we did not know the secret of their alphabet and of the composition of their words."[23]

More serious research, since time immemorial, has been devoted to onomatopoeia. De Brosses, a contemporary of Court de Gébelin, defined these etymologically as forms by which one can "make the same sound, with the voice, as is made by the object one is naming."[24] But those who have studied languages know, and most others accept, that even in the clearest cases the resemblance is limited; the articulatory habits and phonological systems of each language give a different form to words which, if they resulted from a purely mimetic process, would be identical. The crow of the rooster, an oft-cited example, provides a pertinent illustration: doubtlessly the same animal is involved, and very probably an identical human hearing faculty; yet different languages give distinct versions: English *cock-a-doodle-doo*, French *cocorico*, Dutch *kukeleku*, Japanese *kokekokkoo*.

This being the case, perhaps we should not seek the mystical powers of language in the elementary and illusory reproduction of the sounds around us. Merleau-Ponty's phenomenological goal, although slightly archaic in formulation, may help to illuminate the issue: "Phonemes are so many ways of singing the world . . . and are destined to represent objects—not, as suggested by the naive theory of onomatopoeia, through an objective resemblance with those objects; but because they extract and, in the literal sense, express their emotional essence."[25]

But this suggestive statement must be rigorously aligned with the facts. It is not the phonemes themselves, but rather the degree of force of articulation, the degree of clarity or harshnesss of the voice, the rhythm of speech, that reflect emotional categories. This results from a general property of the species, the relation between muscular tension and psychic state, which explains why repulsion, uneasiness, disgust, scorn, and hatred can always be marked by a contraction of the pharyngeal muscles. However, this is not a necessary relation. Even the most iconic of articulatory phenomena, intonation (the melodic curve accompanying the emission of a word, a group of words, or a sentence), is not constant among all languages. Only such a constant as this could argue for a real motivational link with extra-linguistic factors. Certain theories attribute only a marginal role to intonation in the definition of a language. The reason is clear: like articulatory energy and the lengthening of consonants and vowels, the melody of intonation is necessarily present in oral communication. It is thus considered less remarkable, and more characteristic of speech *(langage)* than of languages *(langues)*.

The best-known experiments on the interpretation of intonational melodies have yielded uncertain results. On the one hand, languages as genetically, typologically and geographically distant as Huastec (Mexico), Japanese, Swedish, and Kunimaipa (New Guinea) assign more or less similar melodic curves (from a physical point of view) to more or less similar meanings relating to roughly equivalent situations: surprise, strong rejection, polite request, questions expressing denial or assertions of obvious truth or absurdity (as, in English, "Do animals have languages?").[26] But, on the other hand, it is not always possible to establish for a given language an intonational content so clearly iconic that the same curve is identically interpreted by all subjects. If we submit intonational curves alone, isolated from the rest of their utterances, to a group of French-speaking subjects with equal linguistic competence, we find that sadness, fear, admiration, and joy are recognized at a rate of 80, 70, 50, and 30 percent, respectively.[27] Sadness and fear are thus widely identified by the subjects, but the figures for admiration and joy are low enough to suggest that intonation does not constitute a dependable clue to content. A spatial projection of laryngeal imitation, intonation is no doubt a melodic gesture partially written into our muscular physiology. And yet, in language, intonation is moderated through integration with words. It becomes only one of the many elements that contribute to the production of meaning, and consequently it, too, is subject to the encoding process in which they all collaborate.

The same is true for other phenomena of prosody, as for example, the expressive lengthening of vowels which often translates superlatives or insistance. It can also express various other emotions, such as tenderness in speech addressed to children, or in dialogue between lovers. Similarly, the lengthening of consonants is not always a sign of aggression, but sometimes of stupor or admiration. In a more general fashion, the primary (and partially iconic) value of such expressive procedures is intensity, whatever the exact nature of the phenomenon being reinforced in this way. Moreover, and above all, many languages possess double consonants or vowels that are simply ordinary phonemes, and do not correspond to any signified bearing the phonetic feature of quantity. There are others, it is true, like Karok, Wiyot, and Yourok (of the North American Algonquin family), in which certain double consonants have the occasional function, independently of their participation in the signifier of a sign, of referring to certain physical features of the interlocutor.[28] But this example of phonic symbolism remains quite rare among known languages.

The feature that most closely relates phonemes with prosody (in many languages of Africa, Southeast Asia, America, and Oceania) is tone, a vocal melody distinguished as even, rising, falling, or bidirectional, which suffices to distinguish otherwise identical vowels or syllables. Of course, we do find cases of correlation between tone and content. Thus, in certain African languages, the highest tone, corresponding in acoustical terms to the highest frequency, replaces the lexical or original tone (perhaps already high) to mark a strong assertion, in particular to emphasize or focalize an important piece of information; the lowest tone, by contrast, is substituted for one of the vowels of a word bearing older or less important information. This is true for Toura, Wob (Ivory Coast), and Efik (Nigeria).[29] But aside from these languages, and a few others illustrating a comparable phenomenon, the informational role of tone remains statistically rare. This fact is not difficult to understand: tones are encoded in languages as a means of distinguishing segments. Their primary status, in the lexicon and sometimes in the grammar of these languages, is that of distinctive features of these segments. Like position (vowels articulated in the front or back of the mouth), aperture (open vowels like / a /, close vowels like / i /), rounding (rounded vowels, like / u /, nonrounded vowels like / i /), tones participate in the identification of segments, usually vowels.

It is not easy, then, to confirm any symbolic value of the melodies of speech. And since, logically, it would be even more difficult to do so for elements of sound not directly linked to melodic gesture, such as consonants and vowels themselves, it might seem that the latter would not give rise to symbolic speculation. But even here, many are not willing to abandon the ancient belief in the mystic nature of language, that vast cave in which the sounds of the universe are heard to resonate. This belief has flourished since very early times. Admittedly, the very form of the speech organs, and the movements of which they are capable, appear to provide some foundation for the argument. De Brosses, already cited, emphasized the possible resemblance: "The sound resulting from the form and natural movement of the organ . . . becomes the name of the object."[30] The abbé Copineau, a contemporary of de Brosses, judged that "the impression made upon the eye by the color red, which is bright, rapid, and hard, is very well rendered by the sound R which makes a similar impression upon the ear."[31] Even more specifically, the same / r / which, when rolled, implies tension and vibration of the tongue, would be perceived as an erectile sound,[32]—for, we are assured, "the tongue and the penis are the only muscular structures attached to a single bone. The form and color of the tongue confirm the analogy."[33] This symbolism appears to be confirmed by various facts: the frequency of r in poetic texts with themes of imperious virility or masculine sexual drive;[34] or the shame and confusion of the young Chukchee (Northeast Siberia) girl put to the blush when encountering in a language class a text containing rolled / r /, a consonant that in Chukchee occurs only in the speech of men and is replaced in feminine speech by the alveolar fricative / š / ("sh" in English orthography).[35]

As for the movement of the tongue toward the center of the palate, this is believed to imitate closeness, and consequently all that the imagination associates with it: intimacy, gentleness, tenderness, smallness. It has often been stated, in particular, that the palatal vowel / i / appears almost universally in words meaning "little" or in words of the same semantic field. It has also been noted that other sounds articulated in the palatal and alveolar region, the fricative / š /, the vowel / ü /, appear in the affectionate or gentle speech that adults address, for example, to household pets. The sensation of tickling the front of the palate with the tongue during the production of certain palatal consonants has resulted in attributing to them the property of evoking erotic gestures. More generally, the semiconscious rapprochement is made between the oral cavity and the female sex organs; the vocabulary of many languages invites this analogy, as seen by the French word *lèvres* (similarly, English "lips"). Describing the pleasure felt by one of his patients in caressing his palate with his tongue, Abraham wrote of "oral masturbation."[36] It has become commonplace to emphasize the link between *mytacism* (a tendency to repeat the sound / m /) and the longing for the mother's breast, for kisses given and received, and for sexual relations.

The objection that can be raised against all of these associations, classic in the literature devoted to the motivation of linguistic sounds, is not that they are false, but that they tell only a part of the truth. The substantive "universals" suggested by certain striking examples lose all validity when the investigation is broadened. Thus, there are many counterexamples to the supposed link between / i / and the notion of smallness: over a set of some 750 languages, 58 percent confirm it, 42 percent do not.[37] Some of these contradictions are quite well known: English *big*, similarly Arabic *kabīr*; in Hungarian we find *kicsi*, "small," but also *apró*, "very small." True, the imagery of languages does not necessarily correspond to the imagination of their users. An interesting experiment[38] reveals that even Korean subjects, whose language figures among the counterexamples (many words with open vowel / a / have signifiers involving smallness), associate smallness with / i / and largeness with / a / on a questionnaire of invented words. This is one case (of which there are relatively few) where representations do not arise from linguistic forms, but from sensory reactions.

At any rate, contradictions of the theory of motivation of linguistic sounds are so numerous that we must seriously question the validity of such a notion. Of course, in our earliest prehistory, a natural bond may have linked certain meanings to certain sounds. This bond survives in the evocative power attached to those sounds, often exaggerated in the interpretations of certain schools of thought inspired by psychoanalysis. But any extension of this tendency is excluded in advance by one unavoidable fact: the immense chasm between the infinity of expressable meanings and the very limited number of sounds that can be articulated by the species. Thus it is not possible for one of these sounds to specialize, in any regular and unanimously recognizable fashion, in the linguistic translation of a single domain. Contrary to the passage by Rousseau cited above, the opposition between consonants and vowels, one of the major distinctive elements possessed by languages, cannot be, in addition to that, the reflection of a specific opposition (roughness / softness) between real objects, even if it was invested with this role in the early days of humanity—whether in the "unique" language implied by this vision, or simultaneously in the languages that appeared in different parts of the world. The signifying component of the sign is made up of phonemes, which are sound units distinguishing between words but not corresponding to any specific signified. If phonemes did possess signifieds, how could they simultaneously accomplish both tasks—that of signifying, and that of differentiating words? Especially since the small number of phonemes and, more generally, the modest formal means available to languages in the face of the immensity of thought, are already so conducive to the creation of homonyms?

One consequence of all this, although not immediately obvious, is that the conventional and the motivated are not mutually exclusive, despite what is commonly believed. It is possible to demonstrate correspondences suggested by the anatomy of the vocal organs and the physiology of speech. In so doing, we should not lose sight of the fact that languages must exploit as fully as possible the modest means of distinction provided by nature. Consequently, convention is written into the destiny of languages. This is why, beyond certain specific articulations, generalizations about the relative human character of various sounds is sheer speculation, except to consider these generalizations in function of their fields of application. In an 1893 lecture entitled "Humanization of language,"[39] Baudouin de Courtenay mentioned two oppositions, "that between the larynx and the oral cavity in general, " and "that observed, in the oral cavity, between the anterior and posterior organs." He continues,

> We find a universal decline of the activity of the larynx in favor of that of the oral cavity; the former may simply disappear, or may be partially replaced by the latter. Thus, the ancient Indo-European aspirated consonants / ph /, / th /, / kh /, / bh /, / dh /, / gh /, which were pronounced with a puff of air from the larynx, have been greatly reduced in modern languages of this family: in the Slavic, Baltic (Lithuanian, Latvian), Celtic, and Iranian branches, aspiration has disappeared without a trace; in others (Germanic languages, Greek, etc.), this distinctive sign, while maintained, has passed from the larynx to the oral cavity. In this transition of speech activity from the profound and hidden regions to the upper and frontal organs—in this "Excelsior!" which, like a suspended verdict upon the life of language, determines the historical development of its sound component— I see a manifestation of the progressive humanization of language. This ascension of speech activity from the depths to the surface, to the proximity of the face, is perfectly compatible with the physical position of a biped who holds himself upright and observes boldly from these heights the world around him.

Upright stature, the liberation of the forelimbs, and the carriage of the head have of course played an essential role in the destiny of the human race, and the development of the cranium is closely linked to these phenomena. But, in this case, the chronology is a bit confused, for the linguistic evolution traced here is historic and not prehistoric. According to Baudouin de Courtenay, a language rich in posterior articulations, like Arabic, is the language of a primitive society! In fact, the author proposes a type of evolution, which he believes to be linear, as a general characteristic of the species. But even in Indo-European languages, to which this essay could apply, this feature represents only part of a cycle, not a straight line (see chapters 2 and 10). Thus laryngeal articulations are not necessarily linked to a lesser degree of humanization. Here, too—and even when we start from a purely factual base—the quest for sound symbolism leads us astray.

Do nouns result from some naturally-based rule of naming, or do they arise from pure convention in each society? The eternal question that tormented Cratylus was also present, and at almost the same period, in a distant region: Confucian philosophy. At the general level, this debate may concern speech; it does not concern languages. As Hermogenes maintained against Cratylus, different names correspond to the same natural referent in different languages. In a given language, sound systems are continuously evolving; thus the name of an object changes without ceasing to designate that object (and without that object changing at the same rate). Finally, the sounds that one associates with an object are also found in the signifiers of unrelated signs.

But there is more. The natural referents of language cannot exercise direct control over phonemes, since the latter are defined by the relation that links any phoneme in a word to each occurrence of the same phoneme in another word. In addition, within the systems characterizing the phonology of each language, each phoneme participates in a network of relations with other phonemes. This independence of phonic representation with respect to the element represented is clearly visible in the direction of the changes affecting phonological systems of languages, although it is true that the causes of these evolutions are largely fortuitous. Phonological systems—and, on a larger scale, the representational structures of languages themselves—are constructed upon an external relation with the referent. The signifier is indissolubly linked, not to the referent, but to a sort of deferred referent: the signified. There exists a clear witness of the status of the latter: signifieds also belong to relational networks which constitute the lexical structure of each language. This does not prevent the referent from participating in the construction and interpretation of meaning. But the intimate association of the two faces of the sign guarantee their linguistic status—and the sign's autonomy.

Motivationist theories, then, succeed only in demonstrating the evocative power of certain sounds and combinations of sounds in specific situations. But although this power does constitute an expressive terrain, it is, once again, compatible with the conventional nature of sounds. Conventional, that is, rather than arbitrary (Saussure's term): for arbitrariness implies pure chance as much as free choice. We have seen that sporadic motivations argue against the exclusive role of chance;

89

meanwhile, our ignorance of the dawn of language leaves the importance of free will in this context open to speculation. The evocative power of sounds is illustrated by *ideophones,* a type of onomatopoeia widespread in African and Asian languages. Ideophones employ phonic articulations or combinations, expressive by virtue of their relative rarity, to express particular sensory or mental impressions linked to certain objects, movements or situations.

But, contrary to what we might expect, and despite the expressive fantasy of their use by the most gifted storytellers, ideophones are strictly coded entries in a lexicon of conventional associations betwen sounds and meanings, recognized by all users of a given linguistic community. Korean, for example, is remarkable for the regularity of the parallel between alternance of initial consonants in "doubling" ideophones, and very precise variations of relative meanings within an organized semantic structure. Thus, *golong golong* (initial voiced / g /) translates the sound of a liquid in a partially filled vessel, or that of a person hesitating; *kolong kolong* (initial unvoiced / k /), a more intense sound, in a restricted space; *kholong kholong* (initial aspirated / kh /), the sound of a liquid in an almost empty vessel.

In addition to this precise encoding, the sounds of ideophones are not necessarily absent from the rest of the vocabulary of the languages in question, once again because the poverty of means of phonic distinction results in multiple uses for each of them. Therefore, in the case of ideophones and other kinds of onomatopoeia, we cannot speak of phonosymbolism in any literal sense. The symbol is not as conventional as the linguistic sign. It conserves a more easily identifiable, although sometimes rudimentary, link with the object symbolized. The conventional nature of linguistic signs leaves only a relatively limited field for symbolic activity, even in cases of apparent mimesis.

Grammar and Icon

In the absence of strict *phonosymbolism,* do languages at least possess *morphosymbolism,* the symbolism of the structure of words divided into syllables? Do the structures of words, groups of words, and phrases sometimes represent designated objects? The possibility is suggested by a universal phenomenon, widely attested in ideophones themselves. This is the phenomenon of multiplication, the most frequent case being that of doubling. Doubling is iconic in that the repetition of one, two, or several syllables of a word, or of the word itself, is a kind of photograph of plurality, duration, intensity, progression, or effort. The vocabularies, and even the grammars, of many languages employ this procedure: plural or intensive of nouns; iterative, progressive, or durative forms of verbs. But even here, the change inherent to speech gradually obliterates the initially apparent link, eventually demotivating the structures. The perfect tense of ancient Greek and Latin illustrates the point: *tango*, "I touch," becomes *tetigi*, "I have touched," through a process of purely grammatical marking with little remaining trace of expressive value. Many other examples could be given.

Can the domain of morphosyntax provide more convincing cases of iconicity? A parallel between reality and language has often been observed in the expression of more or less inalienable possession, more or less direct causality, more or less powerful effect of an action, and more or less immediate succession. These relations, despite their diversity, may be grouped under the notional headings of continuity and discontinuity, and correspond in many languages to two distinct structures. The discontinuous relation is expressed through the insertion, as if in imitation of reality, of supplementary linguistic material in the form of a grammatical word materializing the mediation; in the other structure, linked elements are contiguous.

Thus, in Israeli Hebrew, Palauan[40] (Micronesia), and the Mande languages (West Africa), inalienable possession (that of body parts, or immediate relatives) is marked by an affix or by simple juxtaposition, while alienable possession (that of objects or notions not constitutive of the possessor) is marked by an independent morpheme. In Amharic (Ethiopia), Mixtec (Mexico), and Japanese, the morpheme marking indirect causality is longer and more complex than the one used for direct causality.[41] The case of French is similar, if we concede that *je lui ai fait apprendre sa récitation*, ("I made him learn his recitation") with *lui* in the oblique case sometimes called "indirect," implies a lesser initiative on the part of *je* than in the alternative construction *je l'ai fait apprendre sa récitation*, with *l'* a direct object. In Tongan (Polynesia), Kabardian (Caucasus), and Palauan, transitive verbs have two structures—one with, one without, a morpheme symbolizing the distance between the action of the verb and its result, depending on whether this action is more or less complete or affects its object more or less profoundly.[42]

In French, this oposition is apparent in the pairs *fouiller ses poches / fouiller dans ses poches*, ("search (in) his pockets"), *pénétrer un objet / pénétrer dans un object* ("penetrate (into) an object"), *toucher quelque chose / toucher à quelque chose* ("touch (upon) something").[43] Finally, in Fefe (Cameroon), Mooré (Burkina Faso), and many other African and Asian languages, we find so called verbal series in which two verbs may form an immediate chain, or be separated by a coordinating element, depending upon whether the events to which they correspond are concomitant or successive, or whether they are in simple chronological succession or in a purpose relation. Thus Fefe opposes the following structures: *à kà sá' n-za wúza* (literally, "he past come and-eat food"), i.e., "he came and ate;" and on the other hand *à kà sá' za wúza*, "he came to eat."

There are other examples of such linguistic painting of events, such as the curious case of Hua (New Guinea). In this language, reciprocity is marked by paradoxically associating a verb at the end of an utterance with the suffix which has the specific function of indicating that the verb is not final, and that another one must follow; the effect is thus to force a return to the beginning of the utterance. This linguistic structure can only be interpreted through the same circular movement implied by reciprocal action.[44] Certainly, in this case as in the others we have seen, grammar seems to imitate a feature of a real-world phenomenon. But these are frequent cases and not universal laws. Besides, they are not iconic properties of words, but of phrase structure, and therefore much more abstract.

Language as Magic

Having explored the animation of signs and iconic grammatical structures, can we justify the use of the term "magic" in referring to the motivation of linguistic facts, that is to say the immediately transparent link sometimes observed between meaning and sound? Magical mediators replace action with imitation. They exercise the power to create or to reinvent action. The more or less conscious initiative that tends, throughout the history of language, to reduce the territory of convention, appears as the projection into sound of these magical mediators. Eventually, however, they are broken up on the rock of convention. Yet they often succeed in fracturing its surface, and this slim success is enough to encourage others. Thus there is a permanent tendency toward remotivation that periodically challenges arbitrary forms.

In this way, users of a language leave their signature upon its history. Everything would be so simple without this tension between the two poles of motivated signs and conventional signs! Remotivation is the product of a regressive tendency of speech and of the expressive need to renew forms by making them more like their referents—making them live by the world and its sounds. Thus, passing from convention to convention through intermediate stages of motivation, human languages follow an unending series of cycles. If we find, however, that convention dominates, it is because these cycles apply only to a part of the lexicon or grammar. By and large, the linguistic sign, by inevitable evolution, abolishes the corporal substance from which it springs, and which rooted it in the universe: this is a necessary act of self-obliteration.

Necessary, because otherwise, communication would become impossible, or be reduced to extremely rudimentary form. The sign could not be a purely semiotic element with the property of producing meaning through sound. Language only becomes possible when the sign breaks away from what it represents to become a purely conventional means of representation. Languages ensure our discursive possession of the world by evacuating it. If they contained as many different forms as there are notions, objects, and relationships in the exterior world, they would be useless because of the enormous burden they would place upon memory. And indeed, no such language has ever been discovered. Thus, human societies, through properties of their own, have made languages paradoxical systems. Although they are found everywhere and are continually evolving through history, they are systems beyond time and space, whose successive manifestations can however be identified in time and space. This double nature, resolved in the very existence of languages, has made them excellent instruments of abstraction.

Such a destiny is quite instructive. For if languages, which are not themselves knowledge systems, are constructed in this way, what are we to make of an opinion widespread today in the mass media, namely, that the rational and the symbolic are being reconciled in scientific research at the end of the twentieth century? We are assured that, from physics to biology, the sciences resort increasingly to procedures and concepts (genetic field, interaction, inseparability, etc.) related to mythological and magical thought. It is true that certain metaphorical formulas, today as always, have evocative power; but the sciences are by no means abandoning their defining principle, that of the rational study of the universe and its laws. The history of human languages amply illustrates the way in which the mind simultaneously clings to and rejects its ancestral myths.

This oscillation is endless. The dialogic species is homesick for the universe. Not that we are mad enough to hope that the finite number of words could ever suffice to represent the infinite number of objects in the world. The impossibility of such a situation has been recognized since Aristotle at least. But we simply cannot resign ourselves to ridding our language of all traces of the material world. This is why the dialectic between convention and motivation has something to teach us about this dialogic species, an object of endless contemplation. Periodically inspired to reattach ourselves to the world of objects, we are always sidetracked somehow. The phonological systems that we unconsciously construct for our language, and whose cohesion reacts to many external factors of disorder, are unaffected by the expressive elements we graft onto them. They remain essentially safe from the noise of the world. Thus the order of abstraction is dominant, and we create taxonomies. But we don't give up nature entirely. Our procedure is a rational one, but our instinct sometimes inclines toward magic.

6

Language, Reality, and Logic

Language and World

The universe exists for us only to the extent that our languages can assign names to what our senses and our machines may perceive. Objects themselves have little need for names. But the species living in the midst of those objects has a great need to name them. We find this same basic truth, in another context but as clearly expressed as in any theoretical study, in the most linguistic of fictional works, *Alice in Wonderland:*

> "Of course [insects] answer to their names?" the Gnat remarked carelessly.
> "I never knew them do it."
> "What's the use of their having names," the Gnat said, "if they won't answer to them?"
> "No use to *them*," said Alice; "but it's useful to the

people that name them, I suppose. If not, why do things have names at all?"[1]

And yet, naming is an activity not of re-creation, but of classification. When we give names to things, we do not attach labels to them. When we construct or interpret utterances, we do not take, or contemplate, photographs of objects. If words were only images of objects, thought would be impossible. The universe does not exude thought. Still, man can think — and talk — about it. Therefore words, and more precisely *signs* (see chapter 5) are not simple labels, the sum of which would constitute the inventory of a language. They are not countable members of a classification. They are sources of concepts. Through them, the universe is ordered into conceptual categories. These categories, then, are in no way inherent to the nature of objects. Language reconstructs for its own ends the objects and notions of the outside world (which, as we have seen, constitute what linguists call the "referent"). And this construction itself undergoes modifications, since usage in discourse is always variable, as are the ideological models employed.

Thus languages reinvent the world by speaking about it. They order objects and notions according to what may be called a *principle of dual structuring.*

The first structuring creates categories through abstraction, and establishes a hierarchy among them. The world does not contain objects representing plurality, singularity, duality, animateness, humanness, quality, quantity, possession, determination, agent, patient, transitivity, color, or relation. But these categories are universally present in language: they may not all occur with the same formal structures in every language, but they constitute a set of possible formal elements.

The second structuring is an internal one which organizes languages at several levels into networks of units. The signifier of a sign, within a lexicon and especially within a semantic domain, is defined by difference (see chapter 5). The phonological and grammatical systems of each language are linked, both historically and synchronically, in an interactive relation that corresponds to nothing in external reality. The two systems, in opposition to that reality, assure the autonomy of languages as models of meaning production. In this way, they function as conceptual reservoirs or principles of classification. It is this function that draws the epistemological line between linguistics and the natural sciences, even though languages may be considered natural entities.

The linguist, unlike the physicist or biologist, does not study the elements of the perceptible world. Of course, the basic explanatory theories of both physics and biology involve ordering concepts that do not correspond to real objects. But these concepts are drawn from the direct observation of physical phenomena, and serve as underlying principles to explain these same phenomena. Moreover, they are abandoned as soon as a new theoretical model is found that can account for a greater number of observable facts.

On the contrary, the concepts created by the signs of human languages are not temporary models of knowledge that can be easily disposed of in favor of more adequate ones, even if they do in some ways constitute an interpretive network. They are the very fabric of languages. Only the evolution of these concepts—a process as natural as their very structure, and just as difficult to control—can disturb the network. Thus, while the natural sciences create the concepts and categories they need in order to describe and explain the phenomena of the perceptible world, linguistics, resembling in this the other humanities, finds these categories and concepts already constituted in languages. The opposition made by structuralist linguists between phonetics and phonology provides an illustration. Phonetics is related to the natural sciences in that it seeks to establish, on an articulatory and acoustic basis, the categories of sounds that may be produced from the lips to the larynx and perceived by the ear. Phonology, on the other hand, examines the phonemes, or classes of sounds already constituted in a given language and used as discriminants of signs. Of course, since phonemes are continually evolving, they cannot be faithfully rendered by fixed alphabetic spellings. But speakers may also have a certain awareness of phonemes. Phonologists can use this awareness to establish phonemes as functional units that are not always immediately manifest.

Any string authorized by the grammar of a language is a possible utterance, whether or not listeners are prepared to understand and accept it. A topical example is the linguistic distinction between the human and the nonhuman. If it seems incongruous in French to say that *une maison de retraite héberge du vieillard* ("a retirement home houses 'some' old man"), it is because we do not customarily perceive human beings as masses of noncountable matter. Yet the language in no way forbids it. The controversial status of such an utterance is precisely the fact that it exploits the (admittedly marginal) possibility of using the partitive to designate "some" humanity. The same is true for any association that intentionally violates accepted compatibilities, such as *Paul se répand partout* ("Paul is spread all over"). These are called semantic restrictions, but are semantic only if the term applies to meaning as a mere reflection of reality. "It isn't etiquette to cut any one you've been introduced to," cries the queen when Alice begins to slice the leg of mutton to which she had, indeed, been ceremoniously introduced.[2] In this way the queen bestows human status on the mutton, since in this context "introduction" can only apply to human beings.

The relative independence of language with respect to the world is also illustrated by the case of personal pronouns. As we have seen, names are not simple labels. They filter reality, allowing us to think and speak about it. But, through this filtering process, they preserve content. On the contrary, a striking property of personal pronouns is that they have no fixed referent beyond a specific discourse context. In those languages requiring personal pronouns with verbs, "I" and "you" have no meaning until they are proffered by the participants in a conversation. Their referents then become, respectively, the person saying "I" and the one saying "you." But these individuals vary infinitely with situations in time and space; the personal indices can have no invariable content. They are—by definition—signs without corresponding objects.

The Noun-Verb Polarity

The relation between noun and verb most clearly illustrates the way in which languages manipulate the universe. An ancient antagonism exists between those who assign priority to the verb and those who assign it to the noun. For thousands of years, grammarians and linguists the world over have carried on this debate, which may be considered a central issue in the study of language.

There are two main lines to the discussion. The first is based on logic. Logicians have argued for the priority of the noun on the basis of several observations. First, they note that when a word itself is cited in a so-called metalinguistic context, it is impossible (in French, English, and the languages known to Western philosophers) to use it in any way other than as an autonym, i.e., a term that designates itself. This is true whatever the grammatical category to which the word otherwise belongs. In French, for example, even adverbs or prepositions must be nominalized in this context. Thus we find *le "avec" du français a produit en japonais un mot, "abekku," signifiant "l'amoureux, ou couple d'amoureux"* ("the *avec* ['with'] of French produces in Japanese a word, *abekku*, meaning 'lover, or pair of lovers' "). In addition, we

98

may observe that nouns possess intrinsic features, resulting precisely from the way in which they filter designated reality: object, animate being, possibly masculine or feminine, human, adult, etc.; as for verb features, they are not intrinsic but depend upon the context in which the verb appears. Finally, as a corollary to this second observation, it is noted that from the morphosyntactic point of view, it is the noun that governs agreement of the verb (in languages that possess this agreement feature). Traditional grammars express this fact by the rule, "the verb agrees in gender and number with its subject."

If we now pursue a chronological, rather than logical, line of argument, the problem is presented in terms of the history of languages and even of human speech. This debate originated in very ancient times. According to Arab and ancient Indian grammarians, as well as the Greeks and most of the Latins, the verb must have preceded the noun. This conviction survived through various periods of grammatical thought, emerging stronger than ever at the beginning of the twentieth century. The German linguist Schuchardt quite simply stated that the elementary sentence consisted originally of a single member—a verb.[3] The opposite point of view, attributing chronological precedence to the noun, was supported by some of the Latins, including Varron and Saint Augustine, and later by the medieval nominalists. Leibniz,[4] in the classical period, Muller,[5] in the modern, and, Wundt[6] more recently, have all taken this latter view.

We can easily see the futility of this discussion. The terms noun and verb designate parts of speech, which are elements of utterances that cannot, by definition, be conceived in themselves, but only in relation to each other. Bréal[7] made the rather surprising claim that discourse was originally composed only of pronouns, a universal category of human languages, so essential that it is difficult to conceive of any stage of language without them. Of course, one might imagine that there were, at a very early period, deictic elements accompanying the mimed designation of oneself and others, which constituted the essential part of early gestural speech (see chapter 1). But it is difficult to see how this justifies claiming that a *part of speech* called "pronoun" existed prior to all others. Discussion of chronological anteriority is even more surprising when applied to noun and verb in an endlessly circular argument. Why insist that nouns existed before verbs, or that verbs predate nouns, when each is defined only in terms of the other? The reasoning is quite simple. We can speak of nouns only insofar as there exists a category of verbs, and vice versa. The theory of relativity must be applied to syntax. Those who argue for a chronological ordering might then appear as amiable dilettantes. Yet they are for the most part serious scholars. Apparently, then, this pointless debate is fueled not by the errors of incompetence, but by certain deeply rooted misunderstandings.

The assigning of opposing content to nouns and verbs is so ancient that we have come to believe that the distinction between the two reflects a difference in the order of nature. There has naturally been much speculation about this opposition. Certain facts appear at first glance to confirm the tradition. Let us consider two types of such evidence and show, for each case, the error underlying its interpretation. The first type involves child language learning; the second, the famous problem of the so-called nominal phrase.

Among French-speaking children, an important event signals the end of the babbling stage and the beginning of true language acquisition. This event is the production of minimal utterances in which we can recognize—although we must carefully avoid the pitfall of "translation" into adult language—a noun followed by a verb, or a verb followed by a noun (word order is not always pertinent). Now, it is well known that this decisive stage, occurring between the ages of 18 months and 2 years, is generally simultaneous with the first perceptual dichotomies. At the same time that children realize the opposition between events and objects, they also begin to distinguish two sorts of words that seem to respond to these two categories of perception. It is thus very tempting to conclude that the noun-verb opposition is quite simply the reflection of our experience of the perceptible world. The process by which the child acquires language would then become clearer, facilitated as it would be by this correspondence between word types and the universe. However, such a conception ignores one of the fundamental components of the process: children's imitation of the adults in their environment. Above all, this equation between perception and language acquisition is not consistent with the hierarchy of learners' needs. In order to construct a linguistic utterance, we must have the necessary tools: the various parts of speech.

Despite these difficulties, the conviction remains strong that the opposition between noun and verb corresponds to a dichotomy in the phenomenological world. This conviction is further reinforced by traditional notions of the so-called nominal clause, generally defined as a clause in which the predicate is represented by a noun or adjective instead of a verb. It is supposed that this type of structure best illustrates the essential feature of the noun, which is the expression of substance, entity, notion, object, or constancy. Verbs, meanwhile, are presumed to express events according to the modalities of the action, the state, behavior, circumstances, or changes. The nominal clause is believed to assert "a truth presented as such, without respect to time, person, or circumstance."[8] This would distinguish it from verbal clauses, including those containing the copula "be." Yet, even in the most frequently cited languages, such as ancient Greek (particularly Homeric and Pindaric), we find numerous examples that contradict the predictions of these traditional principles: verbal clauses expressing general truths and nominal clauses referring to particular situations, or even to the results of actions.[9]

Nor may we assume that nominal predicates do not reflect tense, person or circumstance, unless we make the circular claim that only clauses characterized by these negative features will be called nominal. Tense is perfectly compatible with nominal predicates, as attested in various languages of North and South America. Comox and other languages of British Columbia, as well as idioms like those of the Uto-Aztecan family (southern California), say roughly "this-one chief-past" in the sense of "this one was chief."[10] Meanwhile, many languages associate person with a nominal predicate. This was the case of Akkadian, and is still true for Samoyed (central Siberia), Bugis (Celebes), and Aymara (Bolivia). As for circumstance, certain languages "conjugate" complements: in Bugis, for example, we find "my father he-in house," treating the locative as a verb "to (be) in house." This verb carries the person feature: *ri-barúga-i padaworoané-ku* = in-(meeting)house-he father-mine, or "my father is in the (meeting)house."[11]

The conclusion is obvious. The noun functioning as predicate in a nominal clause receives no particular status determined by the supposed property of nouns to express substance, notion, or object as opposed to action or change. Such nominal predicates can bear the same features as verbs. Another conclusion: what has traditionally been called the noun-verb opposition actually extends to a wider range of phenomena. In certain types of languages the difference between noun and verb is very marked—the verb asserts and the noun implies. In others, however, this distinction is less obvious: Nootka (British Columbia) is a known example. Consequently, even if the distinction between entity and behavior is of interest in itself, and may have philosophical importance, its manifestation in the form of the noun-verb opposition in language is not regular enough to be confirmed.

The confusion that has long characterized this debate is reflected in its very name. Noun and verb are names for parts of speech, categorial terms supposed to reflect in some way the external world—not functional notions. And yet, the organization of an utterance is not governed by categories (which vary among languages), but by functions or relations between terms. The basic relation, upon which every utterance crucially depends, is that between a determined element, the predicate (see chapter 3), and the rest, i.e., the determinant. This relation is essential because in order for a message to be recognized as complete, a clear hierarchy must exist between a center (the determined element or prediate) and a periphery (the determining elements or non-predicate). This is true whatever the formal manifestation of the predicate; segmental (consonants and vowels), intonational, even gestural or situational. Thus a relation of necessity arises between predicate and nonpredicate, not between verb and noun. The primary notions are thus *functions*, and not parts of speech.

The emergence of a noun-verb opposition may then be understood. Indeed, certain elements have progressively become specialized in the nonpredicate function, because their referents in the outside world are participants in a process. The process itself is represented by the element in the predicate function, which provides connections between these participants. Further, the participants, by nature, are mentioned more often than the relation, both in the utterance (when it is not strictly mininal) and in any text consisting of a series of utterances. As we might expect, there are fewer linking words than elements linked. Consequently, the terms in the nonpredicate function are the first to acquire marks to distinguish them from each other. These marks limit the confusion that could result from their semantic or functional diversity. For the nonpredicate is a set of heterogeneous elements which must necessarily be differentiated, either by position, or by special morphemes, such as declensions combined with linking words like prepositions or postpositions. The latter case is illustrated by Latin, German, Russian, and Classical Arabic, all languages in which a clear distinction is made between a nominative subject and an oblique object, whether it be patient, goal, instrument, or benefactive.

It is only after this differentiation is accomplished that the category specialized in the predicative function acquires its own markers, at least in languages where there is a formal distinction between the two. This identification occurs later because the predicate is the center of determination; it does not behave like the periphery, which must distinguish itself with respect to its nucleus. But once it becomes necessary for the predicate to acquire markers, where will it seek them? Clearly, in the available material: the markers already acquired by the nonpredicative elements. It is in this way, in many cases at least, that the category "verb" gradually becomes specified. But while the noun is multi-functional, the verb (excluding here its nominal forms) can have only a predicate function. This morphogenetic summary is of course not universal. But it suggests the evolutionary process of those languages for which we have at least some historical evidence. It also explains the striking formal parallels between noun determiners and verb determiners in certain families, such as Uralic and Austronesian.

It appears, then, that the principle of divergence is the syntactic role in its subtle relationship with meaning, and not grammatical class in itself. Noun and verb are like the two poles of a magnetic field within which categories oscillate, attracted by one or the other. These phenomena are better represented by the notion of polarity than by that of a true opposition. We shall use the term *nominants*[12] for those that depend upon the noun, and *verbants* for those that are linked to the verb's field of attraction. These morphemes are linked by a relation we shall call *intercurrence*, the best known example being the type of grammatical agreement which, in French, associates *-es* and *-ment* in the utterance *les enfants dorment* ("the children sleep"). As for "adjectives" and "adverbs," where their existence can be clearly established at all, they constitute two classes that, by their nature, lean either in the direction of the verb or in that of the noun—or, in many languages, toward both at once. Finally, verbal nouns (infinitives in many languages; gerunds in English) preserve some of the features basic to the verb: the possibility of *combination* with other kinds of words, and the role of *government* or dominance with respect to complements (elements *governed* by the verb).[13]

The noun-verb polarity suggests a continuum. This implies that we must give up the traditional notion of discrete categories (separated by a clear boundary with no possible transition) and binary features ("plus or minus X," or disjunctive relations like "either A or B") in favor of a model based upon a flexible scale of transition between degrees. The progression from noun to verb, passing through all other kinds of words, is fluid. We may go even further: since language evolution is cyclic, it is possible that we may at some time (and to some degree, depending upon the type and family of language) return to an original stage of indistinction between noun and verb.

In any case, the present state of the noun-verb polarity is the product of a distinctly linguistic fashioning of the represented world, and not the pure reflection of the world's phenomena. This polarity thus clearly reveals the way in which languages appropriate reality in order to make it "say-able." But there is more. A language does not simply mime phenomena; it orders them according to linguistic classes, reinvents them, evokes them *in absentia*, exercising a profound influence on each community's conception of reality. The term "influence" suggests the difficulty of demonstrating a direct causal link. Yet the so-called "Sapir-Whorf" hypothesis, named for two twentieth-century linguists, assumes just such a relation. "It is quite an illusion," claimed Sapir, "to imagine that one adjusts to reality essentially without the use of language and that language is merely an incidental means of solving specific problems of communication or reflection. The fact of the matter is that the "real world" is to a large extent unconsciously built up on the language habits of the group."[14] Whorf, a student of Sapir, wrote:

> We cut nature up, organize it into concepts, and ascribe significances as we do, largely because we are parties to an agreement to organize it in this way—an agreement that holds throughout our speech community and is codified in the patterns of our language ... No individual is free to describe nature with absolute impartiality, but is constrained to certain modes of interpretation even while he thinks himself most free.[15]

Whorf added that the Hopi, an Indian community living on the desert plateaux of northern Arizona, are unable to imagine the heaven or hell of Christian missionaries.

The Jesuit fathers must have faced similar difficulties in China. At the end of a work relating and interpreting this impasse,[16] the author recalls an article, famous among linguists, in which it was suggested that Aristotle's ten categories were closely related to the distinctions in parts of speech constructed in classical Greek on the basis of a strong noun-verb opposition:

> What Aristotle presents as a table of general and permanent conditions is nothing other than the conceptual projection of a given linguistic state ... Beyond the Aristotelian terms, above this categorization, the notion of "be" is all-enveloping. ... Greek not only has a verb "be" (which is by no means a necessity in all languages), but it makes quite singular use of this verb. ... This language ... has made "be" an objectifiable notion that can be manipulated in philosophical reflection, analyzed, and situated like any other concept.[17]

The importance of essentialist philosophies in Western thought is probably related to that of the verb "be," and it is instructive to observe the way in which various languages treat the notion of "being" (when they, in fact, have forms corresponding to this notion).[18] But the debate extends to other notions. The most famous Jesuit missionary in China, Father Matteo Ricci, attempted to explain to the Chinese the scholastic reasoning underlying the doctrine of the "Master of Heaven," the translation used to assimilate the concept of "God." To show the difficulty of this undertaking, Gernet emphasizes the links that exist, in China and elsewhere, between language and thought:

> Since Chinese is non-inflectional, the sentence must, with a very limited number of particles, be deciphered through rapprochement of terms with related meanings, opposition of terms with different meanings, rhythm and parallelism, the position of "words" or semantic units, and the types of relations between them. . . . At every level, meaning arises through combination. This no doubt explains the predominant role in Chinese thought of pairs of complementary antonyms and correspondences, and in particular its fundamental relativism. . . . Chinese thought . . . does not deal with yes and no, being and nothingness, but rather with opposites functioning in sequences and combinations. . . . The manipulation of the Chinese language involves mental mechanisms and develops aptitudes different from those accepted in the West.[19]

The influence of linguistic structures on modes of thought appears in other domains. In addition to the noun-verb opposition, languages of western Europe oppose noun and adjective, parallel to the distinction between substance and accident.

> Here also, no doubt, language helps us to conceive of the existence of permanent and ideal realities, independent of the unstable diversity of perception. But for the Chinese, whose language has no inflection, the abstract notion of substance could not have the same character of logical necessity as it did for the European missionaries of the seventeenth and eighteenth centuries, who were speakers of languages that regularly distinguished adjective from noun and heirs of a long scholastic tradition. To express the notions of substance and accident necessary to the demonstration of

Christian truths, and without which the missionaries considered all correct thinking impossible, Matteo Ricci had to resort to circumlocutions, translating *substance* as "that which is established by itself" *(zìlìzhě)* and *accident* as "that which depends upon something else" *(yīlàizhě)*. From the Chinese point of view, this distinction was completely gratuitous and artificial, since their language suggested nothing of the sort.

According to the famous paradox of Gongsun Long (320–250 B.C.), *bái* ("white") has the same status as *mǎ* ("horse") in *báimǎ* ("white horse"): "the horse that is not bound to white is the horse. The white that is not bound to the horse is white."[20]

We must nevertheless remember that the interchangeability illustrated by this paradox is a property of *wényán*, the classical written language (see chapter 4), which has apparently always been quite distinct from the spoken language. In contemporary Chinese, words like *bái* are subject to entirely different constraints than are words like *mǎ*. Further, whatever the obstacles to translation, we have seen (chapter 3) that it is always possible, the prerequisite being a careful analysis of the way in which each language organizes the expressible. Finally, it can be *demonstrated* that a relation of determination exists between linguistic structures and thought systems. "Influence" is a prudent term for this relation. If even this seems too strong, we might limit ourselves to the concept of correlation. Language remains a mechanism of socialization. Children learn what they can or cannot say, according to their language. The world they then discover is already organized by that language into categories; the signs are jointly established. To this degree, language shapes representation. Each of us gives less consideration to what our language does not name.

But we must maintain some distance with respect to such philosophies of causal continuity as expressed in these lines of Nietzsche:

> The strange family resemblance between Hindu, Greek, and German thought is all too easily explained. When languages are related, it is inevitable that a common philosophy of grammar ... predisposes thought to produce phiosophical systems that develop in a similar way. ... There is every reason to believe that the philosophies of the Ural-Altaic linguistic region (where the notion of subject is least developed) view the world in a different way and take different paths from the Indo-Europeans or the Muslims.[21]

In point of fact, a grammatical influence upon philosophical models would not imply that thought is entirely subjugated to grammar. It is clear that mental objects are perceived as indivisible entities, while language divides up the representation of the world so that it may be expressed in discontinuous units, i.e., grammatical categories. But it is nevertheless true that the parallelism between language structure and thought patterns in very different cultures is regular enough to be striking. The appropriation of the world by languages, and the restructuring of reality by (linguistically-influenced) thought, are no doubt the two phases of a single cycle of phenomena.

The Logic of Languages

Can languages be interpreted, wholly or in part, in terms of logical systems, or are they totally independent? Linguists are divided on the question. Some remain skeptical, and even ignorant. Others have known the temptation of logical analysis, which recurs cyclically in the history of grammar. In the nineteenth century (the period during which the term "linguistics" first appeared), Grimm rejected logic. Steinthal, Baudouin de Courtenay, and others later agreed.[22] But from the time of Aristotle, through the grammars of Port-Royal, and now in the work of Chomsky, an opposing view has arisen from the axiom of a parallelism between grammar and logic. More than fifty years ago, a much-read work denounced the negative consequences of this axiom for the explanation of linguistic phenomena as well as for logic itself:

> For one thing, science is not served by the grammatical values attached by speech to the expression of our ideas. For another, speech, a material tool, has not been able to keep pace with scientific progress; in order to do so, it would have had to be infinitely malleable, both phonetically and grammatically. Language is a combinatory system that plays with words and the relations between them; it is subject to rules that, subtle as they may be, are not rules of thought. . . . As long as logic seemed to reduce to subordination and identity, it was possible to entertain the notion of its direct correspondence with grammar. . . . We were not sufficiently aware of the effects of discourse upon thought. . . . The traditional error, rejected here, is still that of a theory of grammatical logicality, like that expressed by Sicard (*Grammaire génér-*

ale, Paris, 1808, p. 306): "Everything in speech, even the greatest irregularity, is easily subsumed in the general system. . . . Logical grammar is the grammar of reason." If there are some very general attitudes common to all languages in the world, they reflect the mental definition of the human species, and belong to the realm of psychology. . . . Speech, by the nature of things, has become indifferent to its own philosophy; and on many points it has broken its mold. Similarly, sociology considers the utility of social institutions without concern for the prejudices that gave rise to them.[23]

While rather dated on several points, this text clearly defines the terms of the discussion.

Many have tried to design a language consistent with the forms of rational knowledge, a system that would be free of the paralogisms abundant in so called natural languages (a term used with a mixture of condescendence and respect by logicians and by creators of artificial languages). One of the best-known attempts of this century is that of the Polish school of Tarski,[24] founder of a "semantic theory of models": this theory posits a set of rules permitting "the formation of scientific propositions, and their tautological transformation into other equivalent propositions that may be submitted to the test of the facts by virtue of rules of correspondence between our systems of symbols and the real experiences they symbolize."

All such attempts are belied by the originality of languages, which associate representations of our emotions and drives with purely cognitive processes. If languages were reduced to methods of abstraction, or to mere metasemiotics (i.e. the interpretation of one system of signs by another), communicative interaction—and with it, all social life—would be impossible. Externalizing through words and sentences is a process of liberation without which affectivity has no outlet beside gestural mimicry. The individual then remains imprisoned in inhibitions that threaten his own equilibrium, as well as the harmony of his relations with others. Logic is a production of reason, and languages are not necesarily the conscious or semiconscious model of rational processes.

Languages do not merely reinvent the world by ordering it according to their own conceptual categories. They do not even require that reality coexist with discourse. Languages quite literally re-present the world. Speech, by translating objects into words, makes their appearance unnecessary; thus it also abolishes both time and space, appropriating them by the mere fact that it mentions them in its own spacetime. Unlike the messages of the apes trained to "speak," true speech can express the unreal. *Unicorn,* the name of a mythical animal, has long inspired the imaginations of linguists and logicians fascinated by this aptitude of languages for naming the nonexistent. Speech provides the same free access to the "impossible." We can say *he died tomorrow,* or *his widow served him a sumptuous meal,* whether in the context of poetic license, dream representation, play, or sheer provocation. And while they may seem absurd or shocking, there is no fundamental distinction between such sentences and the bizarre results authorized by oppositions of time in grammar. Thus a French journalist, writing about a mother's struggle to save her comatose son, uses the narrative future to refer to an event in the past: *Et pour ce fils, elle se rendra en mars dernier à New York à l'International Coma Recovery Institute* ("And for this son, she will go last March to the International Coma Recovery Institute in New York").[25]

These features may help to explain a familiar but often misunderstood characteristic of languages: they are not tools for revealing truth. For individuals and for societies, they serve as an available means of expression. Languages, then, are perfectly capable of lying. One need only respect certain structural rules, which do not necessarily reflect the order of the world; one may then construct any utterance inspired not by the desire to speak the truth, but by a given user's need for expression in a particular instance. This user may, for example, want to say, "It's a chicken that barks," or "He was drawing circular squares." Some of these "lies" are one day transformed into obvious truths, as a result of inventions or discoveries. The history of languages follows that of societies (although with a certain time lag). The sentence "He flew to Vienna," inappropriate before the development of flight, surprises no one today.

Equally familiar is the reverse phenomenon: since languages successively encode different systems of representations, and a continuing series of knowledge states, they may quite naturally associate elements from different periods that are incompatible with each other. Yet an astrophysicist is not troubled by (or, perhaps, even aware of) the fact that the common expression "the setting sun" arises from an archaic, pre-Copernican notion. Only logicians dream of languages that behave as they "ought to." In speaking about the world, languages also create the world about which they speak.

As long as they serve the needs of those who use them, the "living museums" constituted by languages need no scientific updating. When such updating does however seem to occur, it is in fact because the languages, continuously recording successive states of knowledge, have simply incorporated the latest available material. Yet language function is not improved by such evolution. This reflects a fundamental property of language, as often misunderstood as its role as an outlet for affectivity. If we remain on a level of pure deduction, we are likely to forget this property entirely; for it is a historic one: languages exist in time, always subject to change and ready to incorporate useful innovations (without necessarily ridding themselves of outdated material). Languages, then, accumulate disparate knowledge. This makes them valuable historical records. Rousseau claimed that the history of liberty and of slavery could be read in languages; [26] and Michaelis believed that they contained a record of human beliefs, prejudices and superstitions.[27] Foucault, citing both authors, quotes from Michaelis: "the single word δόξα tells us that the Greeks identified glory with fame; and the expression *das liebe Gewitter* shows that the Germans believed in the creative power of storms."[28]

Still, there is a "natural logic" to languages. But it may not be reduced to pure logic, and does not constitute a coherent system of constraints. "All grammars leak," Sapir is said to have observed. We may speak of a *linguistic fluidity principle*, or, in a more specific domain, of *grammatical strabismus*. Examples are abundant. One of the best known is the opposition, frequently observed by linguists of all schools, between markedness and nonmarkedness. The linguistic system is not bound by the logico-mathematical principle of distinction between positive and negative terms, but instead conforms to a participation mechanism consistent with the fluidity principle. This mechanism is based not on the pair A / not A, but on the opposition between the presence of A (marked case) and the presence or absence of A (unmarked case). It has even been suggested that this phenomenon represents the linguistic residue of a prelogical mentality.[29]

Illustrations of this fact are to be found in such varied domains as, for most Slavic languages, the opposition between perfective and imperfective aspect, or between phrase structures with genitive or accusative complements after negation. Many languages with declensions develop functional complementarities, which are complex realizations of the same principle: these include directive / attributive / goal-patient, or agent-instrument / agent-beneficiary. Similarly, in French we find *par* in *le livre d'art a été acheté par Pierre* ("the art book was bought by Pierre") and *Jean a fait acquérir le livre d'art par Pierre à un très bon prix* ("Jean had the art book acquired by Pierre at a very good price").[30]

As for linguistic negation, it is not simply the abolition of the negated element. By the very nature of languages, every element of an utterance corresponds to a representation. Therefore, negation denies only what it simultaneously postulates. Languages display the same autonomy with respect to logical premises in the sentences that they allow the speaker to construct. If logic ruled the art of speech, many familiar expressions would seem to be pure tautologies lacking any informational value. Yet they are common enough in discourse. Thus in French we find *je suis comme je suis* ("I am what I am"), and various proverbs: *(il) faut ce qu'i(l) faut* ("it will take what it takes"); *les affaires sont les affaires* ("business is business"); and *ce qui est dit est dit* ("what has been said has been said"); the latter also occurs in Dutch as *gezegd is gezegd.* In Spanish, we find *lo dado, dado, y lo prestado, prestado* ("What is given is given, and what is lent is lent"); *lo que no debe ser, no debe ser* ("What must not be, must not be"); and in Portuguese, *o que está feito, está feito* ("What is done is done") and *negócio é negócio.*[31]

Any analysis of these formulae in terms of propositional logic cannot fail to note their inanity, due to the identity of content in each clause. Yet these expressions are far from innocuous in discourse; they forcefully emphasize one aspect of a precise situation to which they are linked by *referential attachment,* that is, by a connection to punctual circumstances of discourse in which a very clear sense arises from formulae whose tautological appearance is in fact misleading. But proverbs are not the only examples. The *pas très* of *Pierre n'est pas très malin* ("Pierre is not very smart") does not correspond to the logician's interpretration of "not very;" it means, in fact, "not at all." In French, the sentences *le libraire a vendu un livre aux parents pour leur fils* ("the bookseller sold a book to the parents for their son") and *les parents ont acheté un livre au libraire pour leur fils* ("the parents bought a book from the bookseller for their son") are equivalent in logical terms, but the two are not interchangeable in a discourse situation: each posits a distinct agent of the act. One can even say *il fait froid, donc il ne fait pas froid* ("It's cold, therefore it's not cold") if one wishes to suggest to one's interlocutor that he is known to deny the obvious.

Two words or expressions which are opposites out of context may in certain cases refer to the same situation—but to a different aspect or stage of it. Thus, in French, we have *c'est un accident dont on imagine la gravité* ("one can imagine the seriousness of this accident") as well as *c'est un accident dont on n'imagine pas la gravité* ("one cannot imagine the seriousness of this accident"). In both cases, the accident is serious; but to say so, we can suggest either that it is conceivable through reflection, or that it goes beyond what one can imagine. Similarly, we find a superlative meaning behind the apparent opposites *un avantage appréciable* and *un avantage inappréciable*. The two expressions refer to two different senses of the verb *apprécier:* "enjoy" and "evaluate." In the former sense, the advantage is great enough to be enjoyed; in the latter, the advantage is too great to be precisely evaluated. *Réduire au maximum* and *réduire au minimum* both imply an extreme reduction: *maximum* applies to the process of reduction, and *minimum* to its result.

Finally, in certain languages, there are words that seem to have two opposite meanings. Confronted with a *Janus bifrons* of this sort, and confounded by its complete ambiguity, should we conclude that languages ignore the principle of non-contradiction? Many an amateur has attempted to explain such phenomena: a famous case is that of Abel's *Über den Gegensinn der Urworte.* [32] No doubt inspired by Bain's theory [33] on the essential relativity of knowledge and the duality of all experience (which, in language, would be reflected by double meanings for all words), Abel offers various "evidence" in support of the claim that primitive languages contain many words with two opposite meanings. Freud was seduced by this notion, which seemed to provide valuable linguistic support for his theory of dreams as the expression of archaic and alogical thought.[34] But a precise and detailed study [35] has since shown that none of Abel's arguments withstand close scrutiny. Of course, a theory is not disproved by refuting its individual arguments. But the real problem lies elsewhere. What we really see is not *enantiosemy* (co-presence of two opposite meanings), but the including of two meanings under one global heading. Languages are able to subsume multiples under flexible and extensible classifications, whose very vagueness allows them to better capture reality while contributing to the dynamic of vocabularies. Classical Arabic is known to contain a certain number of words that express a relation, however asymmetrical, between two terms: *bāᶜa* once had the meaning "buy" as well as "sell;" and while other languages present the two processes as opposites, we need not assume those categories to be universal. It is possible to designate only the operation of exchange, without expressing its asymmetry. Notice that in most languages, prepositions, postpositions, and other "relators" [36] express the relation itself, which explains their use in apparently contradictory contexts, as in French: *la passion qu'elle éprouve envers lui* ("the passion that she feels toward him") and *la répulsion qu'elle éprouve envers lui* ("the repulsion that she feels toward him").

Arabic also possesses certain neutral words found in ancient poetry, whose double value is often assumed by translators to be a contradiction: *tahānafa,* "to be disturbed by a powerful movement of the soul," whence, according to the context, either "burst into tears," or "burst into laughter." In the same vein, *taġašmara,* "to act according to one's own judgment," which, depending upon the situation, means "to be just" or "to be unjust."[37] We also find cases of structural enantiosemy that permit us to characterize language in contrast with the closure of logical systems. The prolific derivation of verbs from nouns (a common feature of Semitic), added to the principle of linguistic fluidity proposed above, produces cases like that of *'aṣrada,* "to reach one's goal" or "to miss it"; *'ashana,* "to sheathe" or "to unsheathe"; and *ta'aṭṭama,* "to sin" or "to abstain from sin." In fact, if the language considers relevant to these verbs (derived from nouns) only the general sense of "to do something related to what the noun designates," these verbs will naturally be able to contain meanings considered opposites by pure logic. The same is true in Amharic (Ethiopia), where a form of doubling can result in either an intensification or an attenuation: *sababbara,* "to break into pieces," or "to break slightly."[38] Only the notion of fracture is retained here as relevant to the smallest signified (semanteme), irrespective of the role of context.

In none of these cases does language actually contradict itself. Rather, generalization is facilitated by the ordering of opposing elements under the heading of their common features. There *would* be a contradiction if a single element were asserted and denied within the same utterance: if "to say yes" and "to say no" were not in opposition. But no known language contains such phenomena.

Even with all of these reservations, it is nevertheless true that languages share with logical systems one essential feature: both express relation. Of course, the operations reflected in certain linguistic instruments (whatever their grammatical category in various languages) cannot be reduced to those of formal logic: universal and existential quantifiers "all" and "some," as well as the terms meaning "and," "but," "without," "if," "thus," "or," etc. But instruments of relation play an essential role. All languages of the world possess at least two types of units that linguists call lexemes and morphemes, and which correspond more or less to what Chinese grammatical tradition designated as "full words" and "empty words."[39] The former provide linguistic categorization for objects and notions; the latter are tool-words, like prepositions or conjunctions in English. This distinction is not as simple as it may appear, however. One might suppose that the two frontiers of the noun-verb polarity, the categories noun and verb themselves, would together represent only full words, since they are clearly more referential than tool-words. But, in fact, inasmuch as they command the organization of the sentence, verbs are centers of connection, and thus relational elements as well as lexemes. That is why they may be associated with tool-words, like prepositions in those languages that have them.

Bertrand Russell claimed to have legitimized verbs *and* prepositions, which bring words into relation. The link between verbs on the one hand, and prepositions or "relators" in general on the other, is not only a logical one; it is strictly genetic in many languages in which prepositions have developed historically from verbs, languages such as Chinese and other Southeast Asian languages, in which "go," "concern," and "be located," have yielded respectively "toward," "as for," and "in."[40] The substantialist tradition, originating with Aristotle and including the nominalists, had always given precedence to nouns and adjectives, which express substance and attribute, respectively. "This omission [of verbs and prepositions]," notes Russell, "has had a very great effect upon philosophy; it is hardly too much to say that most metaphysics, since Spinoza, has been largely determined by it."[41]

Gertrude Stein, a patron and devotee of analytical cubism, was also possessed of a similar passion for linguistic restructuring that made her reject nouns, finding them hopelessly bogged down in referentiality: a noun is "unfortunately so completely unfortunately the name of something;"[42] similarly, adjectives are obliged to express the properties of this something. She was delighted, on the other hand, by verbs and— above all—by conjunctions and prepositions; she attempted to draw poetic effects from these words, linking-words, patient workers that do much more than simply designate. Stein apparently forgot that their very referential "vacuity," (which is in fact quite relative) condemns them to redundancy when relations have been made explicit through context or situation. It is at the intersection of the zones of relation and content that the mystery of meaning is realized, independently of the external elements involved. Phonology versus phonetics, and in a comparable way lexicon versus the referential world—these are no doubt relational grids at each level. But these grids are interdependent with the material they realize. This is why language, while it is indeed the seat of differential relations, must also be more; it is not only a system of signs but a system of meaning production as well. For language is not a body of knowledge, but a practice. And even if, in the sciences dealing with the universe, "the recognition of relation, a logical act, has precedence over the individual consciousness of objects,"[43] the former can be no substitute for the latter. In the history of another, more fluid, means of expression—painting—the notion of focusing on the relationships between objects was only conceivable, in the early twentieth century, in continuity with a long tradition of saturating matter through precision of drawing and luxury of color.[44]

Situated at the communicative juncture of content and relation, languages also maintain a precarious balance between the rational and the irrational. On the one hand, they are reservoirs of imagination with little concern for the demands of logic, at least in its classical form. The oppositions instituted by languages are not always resolved; they leave behind a residue of interference, and domains of infiltration through which all kinds of "impurities" may enter. But, on the other hand, there is certainly a logic to languages, even if it is entirely distinct from what we generally call "logic." Languages impose various constraints upon sound; they link sound and meaning through complex rules of correspondence; they organize signs and sentences into a hierarchy; in sum, languages demonstrate the human aptitude for ordering the continuum and for defining class boundaries despite the opacity of objects.

But what, in the final analysis, are we to make of such an aptitude? It is perfectly conceivable as a defining feature of our species; it may, in other words, be visualized independently of its discourse relations. And yet, because this capacity is realized in discourse, it is refined and adapted according to the needs of constant communication. This is why linguistics, by establishing the position of language with respect to the world and the domain of logic, teaches us something essential about ourselves: by creating linguistic systems of representation, we produce meaning, and make of it a means of social exchange. The production of meaning, even when it seems entirely gratuitous, or of strictly internal or therapeutic use, is by its nature oriented toward discourse—that is, toward social life.

7

Word Order and World Order

The Natural Order Controversy

Is there a natural, and therefore universally justifiable, order of words in a sentence? Languages do analyze world experience into linearly ordered signs. The subject is of interest for two reasons: first, for what it may reveal about certain properties of the species, and second, for the way in which it has been treated in the history of linguistic thought. On this question, the linguist must become a historian. As a prerequisite to studying the links between categories of thought and word order, we must retrace the historical steps of these relations. If we fail to consider this evolution, word order remains a purely formal constraint; and we overlook the social (and even political) assumptions involved. Of course, by retracing the history of word order, we do not arrive at an explanation of it; nor do we provide any real theory of interpretation. We are simply unfurling the scroll of language evolution in the hope of better deciphering its complexities. In addition, a lesson is learned. Beyond the specific question of word order, we perceive a general truth, one that may perhaps be applied to the other human sciences in this era of methodological doubt: linguistics cannot be separated from the history of linguistics.

Studying the sequence by which words are ordered into sentences may appear to be a task for the specialist, an area of research with merely grammatical implications, or a debate of interest only to language scholars. We have only to look as far as Greco-Latin antiquity, however, to find the question treated as a philosophical as well as a linguistic matter. Dionysius of Halicarnassus (first century B.C.) believed that the noun, which expresses substance, must be placed before the verb, which designates only the circumstantial; and that the verb itself must precede the adverb, since action, by its nature, is anterior to circumstances of place, time, manner, etc. Further, the adjective should follow the noun, and the indicative clause should precede clauses in other modes. Cautiously proposed by its own author, and rejected by Quintilian (who found it too complicated and, besides, had little difficulty finding evidence to refute it), this doctrine would, however, exercise its influence for centuries. Perhaps it was simply that the prejudices on which it was based were powerful enough to inspire succeeding generations of supporters. It was probably the Greek rhetorician Demetrios Ixion (Alexandrian era), in his principal work known under the Latin title *De elocutione,* who first used the expression "natural order" *(physikê taxis)* for the sequence outlined by Dionysius of Halicarnassus. Demetrios himself agreed that this order was entirely proper.

The natural order doctrine was ideally suited to sixteenth-century apologists for the French language, or *sermo vulgaris,* as distinct from Latin. At the dawn of the classical period (the mid-seventeenth century), this doctrine was supported by the prestigious edifice of Cartesian rationalism. The disciples of Descartes considered linguistic categories to be the universal components of innate reason. Consequently, the natural order, which arranges them in a descending hierarchy, was presumed to be the order of reason itself. Taking this order as a reference point, any construction deviating from it was called *inversion.* Such constructions were imputed to imagination and, more generally, to the passions (which, arising from the flesh, were necessarily imperfect). Indeed, according to the rationalist duality of soul and body, or mind and matter—a polarity assumed in all debate—only reason was perfect, and the passions were just so many obstacles along the path which established its empire.

This doctrine might first appear to be politically neutral. In fact, however, an ideological position came to be attached to it. The defense of French against Latin was not only the defense of one language against another. This same struggle was at the heart of the "Querelle des Anciens et des Modernes." In 1669, Le Laboureur's *Avantages de la langue française sur la langue latine,* referring to the Cartesians, used the natural order to justify a general theory of language. Le Laboureur did not trouble himself to weigh evidence; he simply declared outright that, since all men share common principles of logic, the Latins, who commonly employed inversion, did not speak as they thought; while in French, conception and expression coincide. Of course, Vaugelas had questioned the authority of the rationalists as early as 1647, and supported popular usage over reason. But these objections were moderate and indirect, since Vaugelas (like many others) disliked inversion, preferring the "proper arrangement of words," in which he saw "one of the greatest secrets of style."[1] Meanwhile, Bouhours, in the *Entretiens d'Ariste et d'Eugène* (1671), defended the natural order against usage, respecting the latter in matters of choice and meaning of words, but not with respect to the arrangement of those words into sentences.[2]

The same ideological bias inspired subsequent contributions: in 1675, the *Défense de la poésie et de la langue française,* by Desmarets de Saint-Sorlin; then, in 1683, a massive work by Charpentier, one of the principle partisans of the "Modernes,"—*De l'excellence de la langue française.* Its author affirmed the superiority of French over Latin: the free word order found in the latter deviates from what he calls *construction directe,* (possibly translating Quintilian's *rectus ordo*), a term that would return to favor in the eighteenth century. "Direct," because the word order was presumed to be a direct reflection of the order of thought. And, at the end of the seventeenth century, the great dictionaries of Richelet (1680) and Furetière (1684), mention the natural order in the articles "arrangement," "construction," "inversion," and "transposition," identifying this order as an obvious logical requirement (and characteristic of French).

Thus the natural order debate, far from the purely scholastic pursuit of grammarians, constituted the cornerstone of defense for the French language, and even for the prestige of the French state. At the end of the seventeenth century, this doctrine became the foundation of what would be called general grammar. This, then, was hardly the simple affair of philologists or glossers. The general grammar of the classical period was nothing less than a philosophical discipline. It proposed to study language as the domain of a natural logic or spontaneous analytical method. Such a system would not be the pure reflection of immediate sensorial data, but, on the contrary, an embryo of scientific organization. If, however, the philosopher-grammarians generally agreed upon this vision of language as an elementary form of critical thought, their faith in natural word order as the reflection of the order of reason was soon to be badly shaken.

The debate on the imagination would provide one serious challenge. Having suffered the well-known criticism of Pascal and Malebranche, the imagination would be somewhat vindicated by the sensualist esthetic inspired (in the case of Du Bos,[3] for example) by Locke.[4] Here, imagination was treated as a faculty founded upon sensual perception, and serving as a criterion of taste entirely apart from—and in conflict with—reason. Furthermore, from the second half of the seventeenth century, the Cartesians de Cordemoy[5] and Lamy[6] had challenged the very implications of the rationalist duality, and granted a more important role to the psycho-physiological foundations of speech.

The repercussions for the natural order are not difficult to imagine. Lamy, for whom stylistic devices were the language of the passions, insisted (in his 1701 edition) that it was the ability of these devices to subvert natural word order that accounted for the powerful impression they make upon listeners. This may be observed in various figures of speech: exclamation, suspension, antithesis, and especially *hyperbat* (which, as its Greek name suggests, involves the fragmentation of a syntactically homogeneous phrase through insertion of one or several words). The most natural word order, then, would apparently be one that connects ideas in discourse according to relations similar to those that link them in the mind. This position already foreshadows Condillac, and would be reinforced by Fénelon's intuition[7] that the rigidity of French word order and the condemnation of inversion resulted in dry French prose—subjugated, obedient prose, devoid of eloquence, variety, or charm.

In the second quarter of the eighteenth century, the controversy over word order began to play a decisive role in philosophical debate. The defense of the supposed natural order of French continued to be used as evidence against Latin, a free word-order language. Under these circumstances, the Abbé Girard's 1747 work, *Les vrais principes de la langue française,* achieved instant celebrity, guaranteed by the adulation of its supporters as well as by the few criticisms it aroused. This work may even be considered—terse though it may be on this particular point— the principal word-order-based typology of languages produced in France in the eighteenth century. Girard was no doubt acutely aware of the stakes. This is attested by an episode of his biography:[8] Russian interpreter for Louis XV, Girard was on good terms with the poet and linguist V. K. Trediakovsky, then living in Paris. In fact, Trediakovsky was a member of the group of Russian nationalist grammarians and writers who, with Lomonosov, decried the literary monopoly of Slavonic.[9]

Girard, in a famous passage from the first pages of his book, proposes to divide the languages of the world into three types, and to use this division as the basis of a grammatical method. The first language type he calls "analogous" (i.e., to the sequence of ideas according to the tradition of the *ordo naturalis*). Their constructions "ordinarily follow the natural order and the gradation of ideas: the acting subject comes first, next the action accompanied by its modifiers, and afterward its object and goal." Obviously, French (as well as Italian and Spanish) are analogous languages. In contrast with these we find the second type, in which word order is determined by that "mistress of error and falsehood" (according to Pascal), and the central theme of the debate: the imagination. Constructions in these languages "follow no order beyond the flame of imagination, beginning sometimes with the object, sometimes with the action, and sometimes with the modification or circumstances of that action." Using the natural order as the standard, Girard calls these languages "transpositive;" the characteristic example, of course, is Latin. Finally, he calls "mixed, or, in more learned manner, amphilogical" the type of language that "resembles both the others," giving Greek as an illustration. Girard offers no real explanation for this apparent contradiction, except to say that Greek possesses both an article, characteristic of analogous languages, and declensional cases, a feature of transpositive languages.

Girard's rationalist fervor takes him beyond all reason. He assures us that the genius of Latin, a transpositive language, and that of French, an analogous language, are so different that the one could not have been the ancestor of the other; French simply borrowed a great deal of Latin vocabulary, preserving its own analogous roots inherited from populations previous to the Roman invasion. In this, Girard declares allegiance to an old and powerful politico-"scientific" tradition: since the Renaissance at least, defenders of Celtic (who were hostile to Latin) had argued that French had a basically Gallic foundation. But although this tradition might seem useful for Girard, his intention being to contribute to the nationalistic enterprise of the defense and illustration of French, his own point of view was anything but historical. In fact, it was anti-historical, if not purely achronological—similar, in this respect, to others in a century which was, however, far from indifferent to the real weight of time.[10] If we use contemporary criteria to evaluate

Girard's enterprise, we must be highly suspicious of such a procedure: to infer from typological difference an absence of any relation would, in modern terms, be a methodological error; for structural resemblance and historical filiation are now held to be two independent, if often parallel, discriminants.[11] Two languages with the same historical origin are often quite close (e.g., French and Italian, of the same Indo-European family and the same Romance branch), but this is not always the case (English and Hindi are very different, although of the same Indo-European family); inversely, two languages without a genetic relation may demonstrate strong typological resemblance, due for example to prolonged contact, as is the case with Armenian and Georgian. However, the article "Langue" of the *Encyclopédie*, written by Beauzée and Douchet (1765), echoes this confusion between two distinct principles of classification, and illustrates the intention of the philosohers: to substitute general grammar for philology, typology for etymology, and syntax for semantics. Indeed, the abbé Girard must be recognized for his eminent role in the history of French grammar, precisely because he so emphasized syntax and word-order-based typology.

Among the champions of natural order that Girard must have read, one of the most influential figures was Du Marsais. At the beginning of the eighteenth century, Du Marsais had become known through certain works[12] in which he advocated the teaching of Latin by "reestablishing" the logical order (that of French, naturally) in the Latin sentences that deviated from it due to the disordered predominance of imagination and passion! However, in the opposing camp, the main challenge to the natural order was to come from the sensualist philosophy of Condillac. According to this system, thought was nothing other than transformed sensation. The *Essai sur l'origine des connaissances humaines* (1746) argued that the respective order of words—for example, the adjective with respect to noun—depended upon the speaker's impression: one may say *grand arbre* ("tall tree") or *arbre grand* depending on how strongly one is struck by the sensation of tallness. Given this assumption, the two orders of Latin and of French are equally natural, and inversion is only seen as such if one accepts a priori the word order of French as the point of reference. The so-called inverted constructions are as natural as the French ones; meanwhile, the French language, if examined objectively, contains as many "inverted" constructions as "natural" ones. The following observation of Fléchier provides only one example of how French, by "violating" the so-called natural order, may adapt syntax to the faithful expression of the soul: *Déjà prenait l'essor, pour se sauver vers les montagnes, cet aigle dont le vol hardi avait d'abord effrayé nos provinces.* [13] ("Already took to the air, to escape toward the mountains, this eagle whose brave flight had first brought terror to our provinces.")

Batteux, in his *Lettres sur la phrase française comparée avec la phrase latine* (1748), pursued Condillac's line of argument and maintained that French, contrary to the assumptions of the partisans of direct order, is full of inversions. Batteux attempted to avoid the circularity of defining inversion in terms of the natural order itself: instead, the term "inversion" would designate divergence from the order of ideas, and not necessarily from the common word order accepted by the users of a particular language, and erected as a purely intuitive model. According to Batteux, it is the choice of what we wish to name first that determines the sequence of words, sometimes causing it to differ from the sequence of thoughts. Batteux's analysis lacks a theory of informational hierarchies, and a strict separation of perspectives (see chapter 9); but his arguments against the dogma of the natural order are convincing. The same is true for the *Lettre sur les sourds et muets* (1751), in which Diderot demonstrates that there is no real reason why the expression of substance must naturally precede that of circumstance or quality.

The debate was to become even more bitter when, in response to Batteux as well as to Condillac and Diderot, two contributors to the *Encyclopédie* came to the defense of the natural order. Du Marsais, official grammarian of the project until his death in 1756, addressed the issue in his article "Construction;" Beauzée followed with "Inversion," and also devoted a chapter of more than 100 pages of his *Grammaire générale* (1767) to the question. According to both Du Marsais and Beauzée, what *is* must logically be named before the action *(prius esse quam operari)* and the manner or modification *(prius esse quam sic esse)*. The Latin formulation itself, in a language that violates this very order by placing *sic* before *esse*, produces a strange impression! In any event, Beauzée took the offensive:

> Mr. Batteux confuses passion with truth, interest with clarity, rhetoric with grammar, and the accidental painting of the movements of the soul with the clear and precise exposition of the intuitive perceptions of the mind. . . . Once and for all, what is natural to Grammar is accidental or foreign to Rhetoric; what is natural to Rhetoric is accidental or foreign to Grammar. (*Grammaire générale*, II, p. 526s)

The two positions are clearly irreconcilable. For Beauzée, the only grammatical order is the natural order. Any violation of this sequence is necessarily inspired by the passions, and does not come under the heading of grammar but belongs instead to the domain of rhetoric, which is concerned with precisely those figures of speech in which the natural order is disturbed.

The polemics continued. Once again Batteux responded to the rationalists. In his *Nouvel examen du préjugé de l'inversion, pour servir de réponse à M. Beauzée* (1767), he reproached his adversaries as purists, mistaking rules of their own fabrication for reflections of reality: "Soon grammarians, who had merely based their rules on pre-existing language, succeeded in convincing themselves that their rules were the very Nature that had presided over the formation of Languages" (p. 29). We see here a denunciation of the innatist and anti-historical rationalism of the natural order camp, which rejected the concept of gradual evolution, and posited organizational principles a priori instead of conceiving them as the products of a dynamic process. Batteux also recalled an essential argument, long exploited by the adversaries of the *ordo naturalis*, and never denied even by its partisans. All participants in the debate, from Lamy to Beauzée (by way of Girard, Condillac, Diderot, and Du Marsais), had observed that the nominal inflections of Latin sufficed to indicate function, fulfilling the same role as word order in French, where the subject and the "object," instead of being indicated by nominative or accusative endings, are marked by position (before and after the transitive verb, respectively).

But it is well known that, in learned quarrels, the same facts may very well be used to support opposing theories. Some grammarians judged that Latin inflections compensated for the "violation" of the natural order in cases of inversion; for others, exalting the merits of the "natural" subject-verb-object sequence was simply making a virtue of necessity: since French is unable to indicate function through form, it must do so through position. French, therefore, has no synthetic formulas like the Latin *hominem fecit Deus*, which strikes the imagination with the anteposition of the complement: word-for-word, "man (accusative) made God (nominative)," i.e., "God made man." This argument, and this very example (later echoed by all the grammarians), were pointed out as early as 1676 by Lamy, a Cartesian well aware of the limits of rationalism. It is notable that no one in either camp was troubled by the almost anthropomorphic intentionality attributed to language in its "decision" to compensate for the absence of form by fixing word order. The subconscious activity of the speaker (see chapter 10) was given no consideration.

In the mid-eighteenth century, the controversy continued in these terms. The opening of the *Aeneid*, among other illustrations, provided fresh ammunition. *Arma virumque cano*, "Arms and hero I sing," i.e., "I sing the battles and the hero." According to Du Marsais, this exordium is possible precisely because the accusative inflection *-um* permits the restitution of the natural order in which Virgil began mentally to compose his verse; inflection thus attenuates the constant transgressions found in Latin word order. But Batteux inverted this argument: a preposed transitive verb with a complement in the order considered natural by Du Marsais presupposes this very complement; similarly, a complement preposed and declined in the accusative presupposes the verb that follows. Beauzée had been inspired by another example, cited by Condillac and often reiterated: *Darium vicit Alexander*, "Darius (accusative) defeated Alexander (nominative)," thus "Alexander defeated Darius." For Batteux, neither the original word order nor the permutation *Alexander vicit Darium* is natural. The operations of the mind are no better reflected by the one than by the other. Further, Batteux observed that the relative clause in the French fragment *Darius, que vainquit Alexandre . . .* ("Darius, whom Alexander defeated . . .") contains the (objective) relative pronoun *que* in preverbal position exactly as in the first of the two Latin versions. This "violation" cannot be explained merely by saying that the relative is in the oblique case, preserved in French pronouns but not in nouns.

Grammar and Politics, Ancien Régime and Revolution, or, The Clarity of French

It is within the context of this debate that we must consider an essay whose title, at least, is well known. Its fame is rather due to the talent of its author than to the depth, much less the novelty, of its content. In 1783, Rivarol won the prize of the Berlin Academy of Sciences and Letters for his *Discours sur l'universalité de la langue française* — but only after considerable argument among the members of the jury. The author, who knew the works of all the partisans in the controversy, simply summarized the theory of the natural or direct order. Indeed, this theory, paraphrased by many authors in the hundred and fifty years preceding Rivarol, had finally become nothing more than a series of clichés. The lasting influence of the *Discours*, which often overshadows the much more serious (and no doubt less amusing) works that made it possible, is largely attributable to its outrageous and frequently exaggerated tone, which does, however, include many brilliant turns of phrase. Thus in the most famous passage:

> French first designates the subject of the sentence, then the verb that is the action and finally the object of this action; this is the logic natural to all men. . . . Moreover this order so favorable, so necessary to rational thought, is almost always contrary to the senses, which first designate the object that strikes them first: this is why all peoples, abandoning the direct order, have resorted to more or less daring turns of phrase, depending upon their sensations or the harmony of the words required; and inversion has prevailed on earth. . . . French, by a unique privilege, has alone remained faithful to the direct order, an instrument of pure reason; . . . in vain the passions . . . entreat us to follow the order of sensation: French syntax is incorruptible. The result is that admirable clarity which is the lasting foundation of our language. What is not clear is not French.[14]

If Rivarol's essay brought no new substance to the debate, the criticisms it inspired were themselves a reiteration of the sensualist doctrine of Condillac. However, at the end of the eighteenth century, the debate took on obviously political overtones. Linguistic theories are rarely disinterested, much less in this case. In 1785, two reviewers attacked Rivarol's theory. The first article, by Domergue, was published in his *Journal de la langue française,* a well-known and valuable source of information on the French of the revolutionary period, "when style is endowed with the energy of liberty" (*Journal,* 1791). The other, by Garat, appeared in the *Mercure de France.* During the Revolution, Domergue was named "grammarian patriot." Garat was to become Robespierre's Minister of Justice. Later, under the Directoire, he taught Condillac's philosophy at the Ecole Normale where, as professor of "the analysis of understanding," he was the colleague of other illustrious Ideologues. The name of the first section of the second class of the Institute, where Cabanis and Volney taught—"analysis of sensations and ideas"—gives us some idea of the Ideologues' debt to Condillac. The convergence between their libertarian political ideals and the theory of free word order is not gratuitous. The arguments of Rivarol's critics illustrate the point. Here, observation is opposed to metaphysi-

125

cal speculation, as science is to religion: "The Philosophers made the grave mistake," wrote Garat in his commentary (p. 26),

> of trying to create systems of grammar, logic, and metaphysics which already existed in languages. Had they only observed languages, they would have found the systems: but they wished not to observe, but to create; and when one wishes to create without having observed, one finds only illusions and absurdities. It was by reflecting upon languages that Locke was first inspired to write his "Essay on human understanding," which has done so much to advance that very understanding while however circumscribing its author's career.

Rivarol's famous axiom on the clarity of French merely lends a peremptory (and nationalistic) air to a myth that, like the prejudices about imagination and inversion, had been central to the word-order debate for over a century. Even if this axiom were not totally contradicted by the simple facts, it would still be true that clarity can only be appreciated in relative terms. Despite popular belief, clarity is not even universally recognized as a source of merit. Paraphrasing Rivarol, T. Suzuki wrote: "What is clear is not Japanese."[15] This, by the way, was in reference not to Japanese word order (which Rivarol might have called "confused," since the complement precedes the verb), but to the abundance of absolute synonyms that result in Japanese from the many pairs of words corresponding to a single ideogram, one member from the native base, the other a Chinese borrowing. The Japanese lexicon is thus highly homosemic and lacking in univocity. But in the domain of the sign, as in that of word order, a presumed absence of clarity is apparently not perceived as a disadvantage. In France, however, the myth of clarity (linked, in Rivarol's view, to direct order) is today as tenacious as ever. The assumption is simply not submitted to objective examination; any argument in its favor is embraced. And yet, even as the *Discours* was being published, Garat was already arguing that the real factors of clarity were suitability of terms, and word order appropriate to thought—quite independently of the constraints of the so-called natural order. "The direct order is not the only source of clarity. Well-determined and well-ordered ideas, rendered either by the appropriate word or by the word that gives a true image, are clear in all languages" (p. 31).

Garat was not the only critic who opposed the sensualism of Condillac to Rivarol's tirade. For Domergue, clarity was not achieved through rigid sequence, but only when the emotions were freely expressed by individual choice, which would assume a variable word order.

> The author equates the clarity of our language, and hence its influence, with direct order. But first, what is direct order? Surely not the successive arrangement of subject of clause, verb and object; but the arrangement of ideas in the order in which they are perceived by the mind. When I see a snake . . . , the snake being the first thing my eyes convey to my spirit, I follow the direct order (whatever my language), if my sentence begins with *snake.* Whether I cry out in Latin, *serpentem fuge,* or in French, *un serpent! Fuyez!* ("A snake! Run!"), I am equally faithful to the direct order; and Heaven help the cold and absurd language that . . . would have me say, "Sir, beware, there is a snake approaching!" . . . Yet the author claims that the French speak thusly, calling it the direct order (p. 886).

If what we call "natural" word order conforms to reason but conflicts with the senses, we must conclude that the latter are not natural!

Here again, the debate was politically charged. The arrangement of words according to the succession of ideas amounted to a liberty of expression opposed by the guardians of order. The rationalist hypothesis paradoxically came to consider transgression the norm. If one wished to avoid this contradiction, it was no longer possible to describe as "normal" the highly variable reality of phrase structure in French (and in many other languages as well); for direct order was only one possible structure, and not even the most common one. This is pointed out by Domergue, by Court de Gébelin before him (1778), and by Laveaux, whose 1784 work[16] is apparently an answer to Rivarol. Laveaux was to become editor in chief of the *Journal de la Montagne* during the Revolution. It is not by chance, then, that we find these words at the end of a passage hostile to rationalist prescriptive word order: "The language of a nation enriches itself through the breadth of its ideas, and ideas can expand only with liberty. Religious despotism, maintained by political despotism, debilitates humanity more than harsh climate or poverty."

This ideological conflict underlies a related point as well. Partisans and adversaries of neology had been engaged in lively debate since at least the end of the seventeenth century. As we might expect, the latter were also supporters of rationalist grammar and direct order: among them, the abbé Desfontaines, author of a *Dictionnaire néologique à l'usage des beaux esprits du siècle* (1726). On the other hand, those who defended liberty of phrase structure were also in favor of the creation of new words, as well as the use of metaphors, "inversions" with respect to the supposed natural order, and all forms of expression for which Condillac's thought, countering Cartesian rationalism, had provided theoretical justification. The Académie was divided. In his reception speech, Desfontaines made a virulent attack on neology; but two decades later (at a time when, according to one historian, "the neological revolution was taking the academic Bastille,")[17] Moncrif would claim in 1742 that "a living language cannot, and should not, be fixed." Forty-three years later, Marmontel wrote in his discourse on *Autorité de l'usage* (1785): "Every day, it [language] is obliged to observe foreign customs . . . ; every day, the historian, poet or philosopher is transplanted to faraway lands . . . ; what will become of him if his language is not also cosmopolitan, if it does not have the analogies and equivalencies of the language of the countries and eras it frequents?"[18]

The controversy over cosmopolitanism in language is thus a very old one. But unlike the direct Anglo-American borrowings that inspire the current debate on the defense of French, the equivalents recommended by Marmontel were to be produced by an *internal* creative process. From the earliest days of the Revolution, such neologisms were both numerous and well-received by the new powers. In 1791, the Société des Amateurs de la langue franaise (which had replaced the Académie française) took on the task of "presenting the list of words we owe to the Revolution." Mercier, though not a disciple of Condillac, was quite carried away by the sensualist wave. Inspired by the colorful nature of revolutionary prose—in which classicism is, however, still apparent—he wrote the following: "Prose is ours; its flow is unchecked; we ourselves may endow it with more life. . . . May not words, and even syllables, be placed in such a way that their association produces the most surprising effect? Our constructions are not so rigid as has been claimed." This, from the introduction of an 1801 work appropriately entitled *Néologie ou vocabulaire des mots nouveaux*, in which Mercier announced his intention to produce a sequel in the form of a treaty on inversions.

The political nature of the debate is reflected in various events. The Count de Rivarol emigrated, along with most of the monarchist nobility, when the Convention called for his arrest on the grounds of his correspondence with the king. The son of a Piedmontese innkeeper (of Bagnols-sur-Cèze, near Uzès), Rivarol had been successively knighted, then made a count, under circumstances which remain obscure. What *is* clear, however, is that he took the side of the aristocracy of the Ancien Régime both in his writings and in his actions. The champions of word order were also the defenders of the social order. The great thinkers of the Restoration would further embody this convergence. Witness de Bonald:[19] "A language is more or less analogous [in Girard's sense—see above] depending upon whether the society obeys more or less natural laws. It has been observed that during the storms of the revolution, the French language itself lost some of its natural character, and that forced inversions and barbarian constuctions supplanted its noble and beautiful regularity." De Maistre, the other leader of monarchist catholicism after the Empire, wrote in a letter to de Bonald that Condillac was "the guiltiest of all modern conspirators."[20]

For both de Bonald and de Maistre, the theory of direct order was bound to political conservatism: a strict succession of words reflected the natural form of the State. Contrary to Condillac's sensation-based dynamism, this static view supports the immutability of the political order: any transgression of the rules established by dominant "reason" was inspired by the revolutionary resistance to the monarchy (i.e., the political order of reason). Neologisms, "inversions," and all the other features of the Convention's eloquence were to be exiled from memory, like the very events they reflected: "It seems that the surest way to banish the memory of these disastrous times would be to strike the savage idiom from our vocabularies."[21] Thus events are inextricably linked to the form of discourse that depicts them.

Word Order, Deaf-Mutes, and the Relativity of Naturalness

No linguistic theory may escape the problem of word order. The direct order debate illustrated the importance of the matter, and the ideological suppositions involved. There is much data to suggest that the notion of "natural" should be relativized; this was already implied by Rivarol's critics, disciples of Condillac who, lacking more extensive data and an adequate scientific apparatus, made no headway beyond the threshold of this domain while nevertheless perceiving its significance. If we assign the letters *S, V,* and *O* respectively to the subject, verb, and "objective" complement of a simple transitive sentence, we may assign the structure SVO to the French strings *l'enfant a cassé le bâton* ("the child broke the stick") or *un chat aperçoit une souris* ("a cat sees a mouse"). But this word order, typical of written rather than of oral style, is far from the only possibility: one may, for example, say *le bâton, l'enfant l'a cassé* or *il y a une souris, il y a un chat qui l'aperçoit.*

Furthermore, SVO structure seemed natural to the rationalists only insofar as they persisted in the belief, based on written French, that both ideas and words must proceed from the designation of the agent as source, to that of the action accomplished, and from there to the goal. But we need only study the order of gestures in most sign languages to find SOV (the most frequent in American Sign Language), or OVS (the inverse of SVO), or OSV, but not SVO. In these systems, a sentence like *le chien chasse le lièvre* ("the dog chases the hare") may correspond to the series of signs "dog" + "hare" + "chase," in which agent and patient are designated before the relation in which they are involved; or "hare" + "dog" + "chase," or "hare" + "chase" + "dog," as in a gestural narration of the scene (since the hare, in the lead and being pursued, appears first).

The natural virtues of these types of sequences were pointed out by Goguillot nearly a century ago:

> It could be argued that it is in fact our modern speech that is full of inversions, not the ancient languages such as Latin. . . . It is incorrect to consider the word order of Latin prose "inverted." Let us take Tacitus as an example. In the very first sentences of his *Annals,* we find that he adopts the syntax of the deaf-mute: *Urbem Romam a principio reges habuerunt.* We translate in French, *Des rois eurent (ou gouvernèrent) d'abord la ville de Rome* ("Kings held (or governed) first the city of Rome"). A deaf-mute renders it exactly as Tacitus does: *Ville Rome autrefois rois avaient* ("City Rome once kings held"). . . . The deaf-mute, like [still spontaneous] peoples, expresses himself using the order in which ideas are generated [from gesticulation].[22]

Diderot, in his *Lettre sur les sourds et muets,*[23] suggested studying the systems of signs used to teach mutes to speak, considering them invaluable to the analysis of language. He saw in them the possibility of a solution to a contradiction at the very heart of discourse: an experience is perceived globally, while its linguistic representation is necessarily sequential. If we knew the natural ordering of ideas, we might at least imagine how reality, first perceived as a totality, is then analyzed. Following Condillac,[24] Diderot felt that in order to learn this succession, it was necessary to adopt as criterion the order in which the corresponding gestures would have been arranged, had they been chosen as the means of expression.

Indeed, according to Condillac, actions were originally represented by gestures. Adopting the hypothesis of the chronological precedence of nouns (a circular argument: see chapter 6), Condillac believed that nouns were originally the only real linguistic elements. When gestures expressing actions were later replaced by verbs, the noun remained first because of this historical precedence. Consequently, word order was first "fruit" + "want," and when the subject came to be expressed, it was placed in final position. In modern terms, this results in OVS, exactly the inverse of the canonical SVO order assumed in the antihistorical view.

Thus, despite certain inadequacies of Condillac's method, it seems that, if we think about the world according to the order of space and time as represented by deaf-mutes, the sequences OVS, OSV, SOV are just as natural as SVO, the latter moreover being far from unique in observed languages. The conclusion is self-evident. There is more than one kind of "natural order," and much data has been obscured by this generalized notion. One of Rivarol's critics had already observed: "Almost all of those who have written on this subject have confused direct order with grammatical arrangement. Grammatical arrangement consists of placing first the subject of the clause and its dependents, then the attribute and its modifiers, and finally the complements. Direct order consists of placing each word according to a mental hierarchy of ideas."[25]

OVS is a natural order if, taking clarity as the criterion, we agree with Condillac that the clearest way to express the relation between participants in a process is to place the relation word *between them*. If, however, we assume with the deaf-mutes that *perception* in space begins with the patient, or the effect, or the goal, and is followed by the agent, or the cause, or the process, OSV will be "natural." If the agent is *conceived* as the motivation, and thus placed first, we will find SOV. In both OSV and SOV, the relation associating subject and object is mentioned *in fine*. Furthermore, even from a strictly grammatical point of view, both are natural according to the criterion of directional uniqueness. The verb being the central argument to which the nominal arguments are subordinated, the sequence in both cases is from the determinants toward the determined: O → S → V, S → O → V; it is thus a unidirectional sequence, as would be VSO, which however proceeds in the opposite direction from the determined toward its determinants.

Thus we can account for facts observed in the most diverse languages. We must take care to avoid the reductionist trap of the rationalists, convinced that SVO was the only possible sequence, and consider a given order characteristic (but not exclusive) only when it is statistically dominant in unmarked discourse. We will then find the study of word order in different languages quite instructive. We see, in fact, that the unidirectional VSO accounts for 15 percent of known languages (including Semitic and Celtic); and that 39 percent (among them Turkish, Japanese, Hindi, and many Amerindian and Oceanian languages) are SOV—also unidirectional, but in the opposite direction. As for OSV, it is observed only among the 10 percent that also includes OVS and VOS (the latter being attested in Malagasy, as well as in some Polynesian and Melanesian languages). This unequal distribution between SOV and OSV suggests that the conceptual order, by which the agent is visualized and named first, dominates the spatial order, by which the patient may be perceived before the agent, especially when the action involves movement (as in the visual field of the deaf-mute). The three minority sequences, OSV, OVS and VOS, all offer the sequence O + S, and not S + O.

The remaining 36 percent are SVO languages (Romance, Slavic, Mon-Khmer, among others). Such a percentage does seem to suggest some form of naturalness. But this cannot be due to unidirectionality, since S ← V → O, combining two opposite orders, is a syntactic hybrid. Nor can the criterion be spatial or conceptual, since the succession is neither OSV nor SOV. The choice of criterion is determined by the enunciative point of view:[26] a universal discourse strategy often places in initial position the *theme* (coinciding in many cases with the subject), followed by the *rheme* (coinciding in many cases with the verb). If the rheme implies no other participant, we have SV; if another participant is indeed present, a complement is added, whence SVO. This is the only reasonable justification for the famous "natural order" of French (and many other languages). The notion of naturalness depends upon perspective. For that matter, we have been considering only the sentence unit. Once we exceed its boundaries and take into account the succession of utterances in a text, the rigidity of this same SVO order can be a hindrance to logical transition.

Ascending and Descending Sequences

Genetic and Social Speculations. Leaving aside for the moment the framework of the complete sentence, let us consider the simple sequence of two nouns. In French, for example, fixed order and the linking word *de* (see chapter 3) are used to mark various relationships, including possession (*le cahier du maître*, "the teacher's notebook"); containment (*une tasse de thé*, "a cup of tea"); origin (*l'oncle de Russie*, "the uncle from Russia"); and material (*un immeuble de verre*, "a glass building"). Within this limited framework, it is easier to show the properties of languages, and to contribute to the debate over word order as a reflection of hierarchical relations of dependence. For the inversion of the two nouns reverses or destroys the meaning; while substitution, in a complete sentence, of the order SOV for SVO does not necessarily have the same effect.

The importance of order phenomena within noun sequences was perceived by such linguists as Schmidt, Bally, and Tesnière in the early part of this century.[27] Using different terminologies, they nevertheless described similar facts. Independently of the various markers that may be attached to the sequence in different languages (affixes, etc.), the actual order in which the two nouns occur is itself the fundamental syntactic marker; linked to the very linearity of discourse, it is universal. One noun, the determined element, constitutes the center; the other, the determinant, is in the periphery of the determined, and is related to it through a hierarchical dependency. The succession Determined noun + Determining noun, that of French, for example, in *le livre de l'écolier* ("the pupil's book"), is called "genitive postposition" by Schmidt, "progressive sequence" (progressing from the center toward the periphery) by Bally, and "centrifugal order" by Tesnière. The opposite order is labeled "genitive anteposition," "anticipatory sequence," and "centripetal order," respectively. The former sequence is also designated as "descending," and the latter as "ascending."

Here too, apparently innocuous theories of grammar are based upon —if not directly motivated by—political or social ideology. Schmidt began by establishing that gender and number markers, as well as class affixes (see chapter 3), tend to occupy a position identical to that of the determinant with respect to the determined noun; and that this position is also that of the noun complement with respect to the transitive verb. For Schmidt, this alignment proved the importance, in the grammar of any language, of the succession of two nouns in a relationship

133

of determination: this order would be the model for the others. The explanation for the difference between the sequences Determined noun + Determining noun ("genitive postposition") and Determining noun + determined noun ("genitive anteposition") was thus at the center of any theory of word order. The author claimed to have found the answer to this variance in social conditioning.

Schmidt defined three cultural domains: matriarchal societies, cultivating with axe and sickle; nomadic herders, ruled by patriarchal law; and hunters organized into totemic clans, also patriarchal. Schmidt, observing a correlation rather than developing an argument, claimed that genitive postposition could not have originated among the patriarchal societies. In fact, the sequence is not found in zones still ruled by primitive patriarchal law, such as central and northern Australia, Polynesia, and Sonora (northern Mexico). The exception that "confirms the rule," would be the so called boomerang cultures, all of whose languages display genitive postposition although the societies are patriarchal. However, in these cultures (Tsimshian country of North America, Tasmania), postposition is the result of borrowing. Thus, genitive anteposition would be of "organic-psychological" origin and characteristic of archaic, patriarchal societies; while postposition would be "analytical-rational," a property of more highly-evolved matriarchal communities.

How can we justify such a differentiation between two levels of rationality, or between affective spontaneity and reflective detachment? According to the author, the determining "genitive" noun carries new information, indicating the exact species of the determined noun, or *genus;* consequently, anteposition of the species before the genus would be naive, and contrary to the order of scientific description (which, in biological taxonomies, gives genus before species). Postposition of the genitive, reflecting a better mastery of reason, could only be a later development!

> In all of conceptual development, the genitive represents the *differentia specifica* by which the new species is constituted from the generality of the genus. Thus, for example, in the concept *Haus-Schlüssel* ("house-key"), the word *Schlüssel* is the global genus for all types of keys; the pre-posed genitive *Haus* is the *differentia specifica*. The genus is naturally the prior, already-known element. The *differentia specifica* is what has been unknown up to the present; and, as new information, this element attracts attention. This is why, in

naive, natural, spontaneous thought, the genitive is structurally preposed. In a cooler, constructive, "logical" mode of thought, the genitive, expressing the *differentia specifica* or later element, is postposed—just as it is in the zoological and botanical designation of genus and species.[28]

It is not true, however, that the natural specifier position is after the specified element. Diderot recalled this fact with respect to substance and quality.[29] In any case, at such a level of sheer speculation, we have not only abandoned scientific inquiry: we have crossed over into the domain of a rather poetic fantasy. If any further proof were needed of the fragility of such a theory, it could be found in the fact that the psychologist Wundt, working with the same data, reached a conclusion diametrically opposed to that of Schmidt, and equally undemonstrable: according to Wundt,[30] languages following the order Determined noun + Determining noun are primitive—for this is the order of gestural speech.

At the beginning of the twentieth century, etiologies based on psycho-socio-cultural reconstruction were still much in fashion. Even before Schmidt, we find an illustration in the work of another ecclesiastic, Van Ginneken.[31] Such reconstructions were common in the nineteenth century, and not excluded from the "rationalist" tradition. Weil, in 1844, distinguished two types of complements:

> French places many adjectives before the substantive that they determine, and permits adverbs and adverbial expressions to precede the verb; but object position is fixed. We may thus distinguish two types of relation between complement and completed element. Consider first the sentence *Tuer un homme, payer sa dette à la patrie* ("Kill a man, pay one's debt to one's fatherland"). Here the relation between action and object is a sensual and material one. Then consider *Un grand appartement* ("a large apartment"), *bien parler* ("well to speak", i.e. "to speak well"). In this case the relation of grammatical determination is not drawn from the sensual world, but is instead a more abstract process of restricting the meaning of one idea by attaching another to it. In the former (verb-complement) relation, the two terms may be more easily detached from each other; the imagination may conceive of a progressive movement from the antecedent to the consequent. In the latter (i.e., adjective-noun or adverb-verb), there is only a decomposition of reflective

analysis, in which the imagination no longer finds two different elements to which to assign roles of priority and posteriority.[32]

A Latin example is later used to illustrate the claim of greater clarity when complement follows verb:

> When I say . . . *Scipio Carthaginem,* it is impossible to stop there; an accusative is floating in the air, so to speak; it must be supported, please give us a verb to prop it up, add *expugnavit.* If I begin the sentence with *Scipio expugnavit,* you naturally wish to know what city was conquered by Scipio; but from the grammatical point of view, the words stand alone and need no other support.[33]

These arguments, which take French word order as reference and model, are without solid foundation. Although they may reflect valid intuitions (about the position of adjectives, for example), they do not justify the claim that a given word order is "preferable" to another. And even if Weil were right to judge ascending order more faithful to the unity of thought, and descending order better suited to illustrate its stages, this would not suffice to assign greater prestige to one or the other. Like every language, French has constructions using both orders. And there is no reason to prefer one of them, V + O, as did Madame de Staël (abandoning herself, like so many before her, to ethnocentric imagination): "German lends itself much less than French to rapid conversation. By the very nature of its grammatical construction, meaning is not usually understood until the end of the sentence."[34]

Cultural assumptions are apparent even among more prudent linguists. Bally claims that the progressive sequence "satisfies the demands of linearity."[35] It so happens that this order, in the group Determined noun + Determining noun, is that of French, his native language! The opposite sequence, which he calls "anticipatory" (already implying a value judgment), is "synthetic and antilinear;" for here, "a part of the utterance, whose interpretation depends upon another part, precedes this element instead of following it. . . . In reducing sentences to their constituent terms, the determinant must not be uttered until after the determined; compare *de mon père* ("of my father") and *la maison de mon père* ("the house of my father")."[36]

Even supposing, as the francophone linguist does, that speakers of languages with anticipatory sequences do indeed feel this incompleteness when confronted with a fragment of a noun phrase like *de mon père*, we do find such cases in French. The possessive, equivalent to a determining noun, is placed before, not after, the noun it qualifies: *mon chapeau* ("my hat"). Bally himself, rightly emphasizing the essential and often neglected relation between word order and stress, notes that *chapeau* is stressed, while *mon* is unstressed; thus the rhythmic constraints of modern French, a language that stresses the *final* word or group, subverts meaning when the sequence is not progressive. Indeed, one would expect the stress to fall on the elements bearing new information through specification, as is the case for *le* and for *de Jean* in *prends-le* ("take it") and *le chapeau de Jean* ("the hat of Jean"). But this is not true for *mon chapeau*, where the stress falls on *chapeau* instead of *mon* (unless the possessive is being emphasized).

Tesnière takes a more coherent position, claiming that "all structural syntax rests upon the relations between structural order and linear order."[37] The first is the hierarchical order organizing the sentence around a core (the verb, according to Tesnière), to which the other terms are subordinate. Speaking a language, then, requires that we translate this universal order into the specific linear order of that language; while comprehension involves carrying out the same operation in reverse. Tesnière then proposes a classification "according to linear arrangement,"[38] similar to the early-nineteenth-century classification through typological affinity rather than through genetic relation. (By the end of the century, classification by family was so dominant that Meillet would later declare this the only conceivable system.) Like Schmidt and Bally, Tesnière used the noun phrase, rather than the sentence, as criterion (although some of his examples are complete sentences). The world's languages would then be centrifugal or centripetal depending upon whether the determinant follows the "core" noun (as in Semitic, Bantu, and Polynesian languages) or precedes it (as in the Uralic-Altaic, Caucasian, and Dravidian languages). But Tesnière also defines intermediate cases. Thus, French is a "modified centrifugal" language, since we say *Alfred frappe Bernard* ("Alfred hits Bernard"), in which *Alfred frappe* is centripetal and *frappe Bernard* centrifugal. Latin, like Greek and Slavic, would be a modified centripetal language.

The division is a rather schematic one. Actually, languages like Latin permit a certain freedom of word order, with agreement assuring the identification of related elements. A famous apostrophe by Cicero begins with the most important word *(constrictam)*, which is clearly associated with *conjurationem* (the noun with which it agrees in gender and number) despite five intervening words: *Constrictam jam horum*

omnium conscientia teneri conjurationem tuam non vides? (Cat. I, 1).
("[It is] paralyzed, because everyone here knows about it, your conspiracy, don't you see?") Despite its theoretical interest, the distinction between centrifugal and centripetal orders is too rudimental to cover the complexity of the data—even allowing for intermediate degrees between the two systems. Finally, the criterion used to define the notion of the "core," or principal element in the hierarchy, is itself not clearly defined. This is however an essential point if we wish to characterize word order with respect to the order of thought or, for that matter, the order of the real world.[39]

Variation of Word Order. One problem with labels like SVO, SOV, etc., is that they suggest a fixed order for each language—an assumption belied by the facts, as we have seen. Varying word orders, responding to varying expressive needs, are basic to speech. The rigidity of a single, constant order would make discourse impossible. These variations reflect the conflict between two types of harmony: one ordering sequences according to historical patterns; the other ordering them according to contemporary language use. In fact, in the course of grammaticalization, which we may see as a vast *cyclic movement commanding the evolution of languages,* "tool-words" (morphemes) are distinguished from lexical items (lexemes) through specialization of meaning, and often through formal reduction.

Those morphemes that function as instruments of relation (e.g. prepositions in French), will for some time maintain the position they occupied as lexemes. This is why, to illustrate the point, relators that evolved from former present or past participles in French are still found (at least, in literary style) as postpositions. Such is the case of the words *excepté* and *durant* in examples like: *que tout le monde sorte, les fillettes excepté* ("everyone leave, the little girls excepted"). Here there is no written agreement in gender and number, since the status of *excepté* is no longer that of participle-adjective. The same is true of *il a peiné des années durant* ("He labored years during," i.e., "he labored for years"). These are examples of a historically-induced sequential harmony. Another type of sequential harmony, which is both structural and synchronic, tends to order relators according to the dominant sequence: in French, then, they are uniformly assigned the status and position of prepositions. This is why it is more common to find *excepté les fillettes* and *durant des années.* The few French postpositions tend to be found as prepositions as well. These stylistic variations mediate

138

the struggle between two types of sequential harmony: historical and structural.

Comparable examples are to be found in other languages. In Finnish and Hungarian (languages with postpositions, typical of Uralic syntax), the prepositional use of relators exists and seems even to be increasing. In other cases, evolution respects sequences, and the latter bear the trace of their origins. Thus Chinese has both prepositions and postpositions, but the two evolved from different sources. The prepositions are former verbs, and thus precede their nominal objects just as the verbs preceded their complements; the postpositions are former nouns and thus follow their objects just as those nouns, in the typical Chinese sequence, followed their determinants. Consequently we find the schema *sòng* ("send") + *gěi* ("give" = "to") + *xuésheng* ("student") meaning "send to the student," where *gěi* behaves as a preposition, coming *before* its nominal object. On the other hand, we have *zhuōzi* ("table") + *shang* ("top" = "on") meaning "on the table", in which *shang* behaves as a postposition, coming *after* its nominal object. Thus it is not surprising that Chinese, while preposing determinant nouns, also possesses prepositions. J. Greenberg, author of an important study on word order,[40] *does* find this situation startling, recalling that relators are postpositions in languages with the order Determining noun + Determined noun. But this is, in fact, the case in Chinese; and if the language also has prepositions, it is because their origin is not nominal but verbal. Here, then, sequential harmonies are perfect, and the system is both historically and structurally coherent.

There are other illustrations of variation of word order. Adjective position in French is one of the most famous examples. In Old French, adjectives were pre-posed more easily than in modern usage. As for the many cases in which both positions are still possible, it appears that the sequence Noun + adjective (i.e., determined + determinant) implies the analytical adjunction of a qualifier, while the opposite order (or ascending sequence) implies greater solidarity of the two elements of a synthetically-expressed unit. Examples include *lois iniques / iniques lois* ("iniquitous laws"), *plaisir réel / réel plaisir* ("real pleasure"), *idée bizarre / bizarre idée* ("bizarre idea"), and *obligeance extrême / extrême obligeance* ("extreme kindness").

This greater cohesion of the construction with pre-posed adjective is demonstrated by certain facts. The sequence is more common in idiomatic expressions, and resists analysis: *passé simple* ("simple past") and *procès-verbal* ("police report") may be interpreted as constituent sets; *blanc-seing* ("blank document"), *sage-femme* ("midwife"), and *sauf-conduit* ("safe-conduct") are not so easily broken down. Other phenomena reinforce the hypothesis. For one thing, it seems that *glorieux souvenir* ("glorious memory") and *second tome* ("second volume") are pronounced more rapidly that *souvenir glorieux* or *tome second:* only the latter have a pause at the word boundary. Further, since French has group-final stress, *souvenir glorieux* appears to emphasize the notion of glory. Finally, a liaison is ordinarily made within *profond abîme* ("deep abyss") or *excellent homme* ("excellent man"), but not within *un froid extrême* ("extreme cold") or *un remplaçant aimable* ("kind substitute").

The same formal distinction explains differences in meaning such as that observed between *un savant [t] aveugle* ("learned blind man," where *savant* is an adjective) and *un savant aveugle,* without liaison, ("blind scholar," where *savant* is a noun). Of course, this distinction is not universal in French; and in any case, liaison, like the pre-posing of the adjective *savant,* are not observed among all French speakers. Besides, it is true that beyond this one case, in which each of the two associated words may be a noun or an adjective depending upon its position, the examples given above do not involve a major semantic difference between the two orderings. The contrast is largely between a more intrinsic qualification (ascending sequence) and a more extrinsic one (descending sequence).

In other cases, however, language displays a tendency to polarize meaning according to position. The sequence *heureux poète* describes someone "happy" or "fortunate" as a poet, i.e., he writes with skill; but he is not necessarily *un poète heureux* ("happy poet"). Similarly, the slightly archaic *furieux menteur* is one who lies "furiously," or very frequently; but not necessarily a *menteur furieux* ("furious liar"). Postposed adjectives apparently tend to have a purely relational meaning: in *autorité paternelle, paternelle* = "of the father." Meanwhile, the ascending sequence, which is not a dominant feature in contemporary French, is for that reason an available source of non-relational qualification. Relational adjectives themselves are sometimes placed before the noun; and, no longer subject to the constraints of the descending sequence, they may then be modified. One cannot say *l'autorité très paternelle* ("very paternal authority"), or *ces élections assez présidentielles* ("these rather presidential elections"); but one can say *la très paternelle autorité du maître* ("the master's very paternal authority"), or *cette fort présidentielle assurance* ("this quite presidential assurance"). The relational adjective has become a qualifier.

Above all, as is well known, French has profited from this tendency toward polarization and has constituted around sixty sequential pairs, each based upon a single adjective. The semantic nuances here do not reflect regularities, and are not predictable, except on the basis of the very general opposition already mentioned, between more or less inherent. This phenomenon is one of the most exotic features of French. The following sentences demonstrate certain of the best-known pairs:

1. Ce benêt, ce *pauvre enfant,* n'appartient pas au milieu des *enfants pauvres.*
That simpleton, that *pathetic child,* doesn't belong among the *poor (destitute) children.*

2. *Brave homme* dans le civil, serait-il un *homme brave* à la guerre?
A *fine man* in civilian life, would he be a *brave man* in war?

3. Une *certaine compétence* ne signifie pas une *compétence certaine.*
A *certain competence* does not imply an *indubitable competence.*

4. Napoléon apporte la preuve qu'il n'est pas besoin d'être un *homme grand* pour devenir un *grand homme.*
Napoleon proved that it is not necessary to be a *tall man* to be a *great man.*

5. Le *sale type* était bien trop soigné pour paraître un *type sale.*
The *shady character* was too well-groomed to seem like a *dirty fellow.*

6. Ce sont ses *propres termes,* et ce n'étaient pas les *termes propres.*
Those are his *own terms,* and they weren't the *proper terms.*

7. Dans la chambre, un *simple tapis,* aux volutes assez compliquées.
In the bedroom was a *mere rug,* with a rather complicated pattern (i.e., not "simple").

8. Voilà une *vraie phrase,* mais ce n'est hélas pas une *phrase vraie.*
This is a *real sentence,* but it is unfortunately not a *true sentence.*

We know as well that a *chaud lapin* ("philanderer") is not a *lapin chaud* ("warm rabbit"), a *foutu cochon* ("damn swine") is not a *cochon foutu* ("defeated pig"), and a *fière canaille* ("real bastard") is quite different from a *canaille fière* ("proud bastard").

The Heavy Close Law (HCL)

The various criteria commanding word order may compete with each other, and the resolution of such conflicts can shed light upon the profound nature of languages. Most known languages possess expressions consisting of two terms of the same category and function, coordinated or simply juxtaposed, and irreversible in idiomatic usage. The order of succession of these two terms follows a tendency which we propose to call the Heavy Close Law. *Law*, because of the rarity of known exceptions, and because a strict formulation facilitates invalidation should a greater number of counterexamples be found. *Heavy* is defined as having more syllables, or longer (or more) posterior consonants or vowels, or consonants in the lower frequencies of the acoustic spectrum. By virtue of the HCL, languages tend to place the heavier term in the second position of such binomial constructions.

The consciousness of the human speaker is usually the point of reference with respect to which spatial or temporal distances are judged, and values are defined: more generally, the *ego* is the center around which any *deixis* or designation of the universe is arranged. This deixis normally makes us perceive spatial and temporal proximity, and the notion of "more," as positive terms in the sphere of the *ego*, while lesser quantities and distant referents are negatively-marked terms. These determinations are then recorded in the hierarchy of values and the relative order of mention. Interestingly, the HCL normally prevails over this generalized point of reference. We find in French, without violation of deixis, *ici et là* ("here and there"), *tôt ou tard* ("soon or late"), *plus ou moins* ("more or less"), in which the latter term follows the HCL.

In other languages, obedience to HCL sometimes results in binomials that violate the deixis. Thus we find the Russian *tam i sjam* ("there and here"), Spanish *tarde o temprano* ("late or soon"), and Urdu (under the influence of Persian) *kəm o béš* ("less and more"). In all these cases, the second element is heavier, but the negative term precedes the positive term—otherwise the first element would be the heavy one.[41] In all other cases, the rule applies without conflict, for there is no hierarchical relation between the two terms of the binomial: French *bric-à-brac* ("odds and ends"), *prendre ses cliques et ses claques* ("to pack up bag and baggage"), *de bric et de broc* ("some way or other"), *méli-mélo* ("hodgepodge"); English *flip-flop, by guess and by gosh,* etc. This is an *iambic affinity* of speech, imposing the succession Weak element + Strong element.

The HCL has never before been explicitly formulated; but its effects have long been observed. Pâṇini, an Indian grammarian of the fifth century B.C.,[42] noted that Sanscrit binomials tended to place the longer word in second position. Grammont[43] observed that, "no matter when we begin to listen to the sound of the clock, we always hear *tick-tock, tick-tock,* never *tock-tick.* . . . The change of vowel in doubling onomatopoeias . . . demands that their accented vowels be . . . / i /, / a /, / u /, going from the brightest to the darkest, and this order may not be inverted." More generally, Ibn Khaldoun[44] claimed that the poet works with words; and that ideas, in comparison to words, are minor. The HCL illustrates in a striking fashion this priority of spoken forms. Languages produce meaning, but they do so through sound. The phonological constraints to which the message is subjugated prevail over the logic of meaning. This is why any linguistic theory of exclusively logico-semantic inspiration will find the system aberrant or paradoxical.

Division and Stratification of the World through Speech

Unlike a symphonic score, which displays notes played simultaneously by many instruments, linguistic discourse is a series of signs without counterpoint. Sound signifiers may only be articulated successively; new signifieds result from linear relations, these relations being potential sources that are sometimes cyclically exploited (as in the case of French adjectives—see above). The arrangement of circumstantial complements provides another illustration. This ordering is variable, and linked to stylistic effects, but it may also have a more general interpretation. Thus, in French, certain temporal complements are often closer to the predicate than spatial ones (most languages reflect the opposite tendency). Permutation modifies the degrees of information: the structure *il est arrivé hier à Paris* ("He arrived yesterday in Paris") bears information concerning *il;* while in *il est arrivé à Paris hier,* most French speakers identify the main piece of information as *hier.* The rest of the sentence is interpreted, if not as a pure presupposition, as less informative in any case.

Some regularities seem to emerge, however. In many languages, adjectives of color, dimension, and quality succeed each other in that order either from the noun-center toward the anterior periphery (the ascending sequence of German, English, Hungarian, etc.), or from the noun-center toward the posterior periphery (the descending sequence of Persian, Basque, etc.). In German, for example, we have *ein schöner kleiner roter Ball*, and in English *a beautiful small red ball*. We might hypothesize that the order of qualification follows that of degrees of inherence. Color, a relatively objective feature, is expressed in immediate proximity to the noun, and quality, a subjective feature, over distance; while dimension, an intermediate feature,[45] occupies the interval between them. Languages with mixed sequences, like French, seem to confirm this hierarchy: *une jolie petite balle rouge*, and not *une rouge petite balle jolie* or *une jolie balle petite rouge*. But such hypotheses are conditioned by linearity constraints, which they attempt to justify *a posteriori*. Unified thought and global representations are inevitably dislocated when put into words. Further, however we may try to explain the order of adjectives, this order already corresponds to an *interpretation* of the universe, and not to real relations between objects and properties.

Language abolishes the simultaneity of the world and the unity of thought. Its physiological constraints are those of successivity and phonological balance, as illustrated by the HCL. Speech may produce only an articulated version of the world and of human thought. It creates its own analytical time frame, within which signs succeed each other and real time is dissolved. Word order, varying between languages, linked to linear constraints, is an order unto itself. It cannot be the order of the world. In the world, phenomena are perceived in a uniform way: causes precede effects, even if they are known only afterwards, and movements are directed toward goals. Word order has little to do with these circumstances. Nor is it the order of thought, which also varies among cultures. Reflecting neither the universe nor our ideas, word order has its own orientation: the order of speech.

But this latter depends a great deal on the discourse relation. The organization of words, reflecting the dialogue process in which the speakers are engaged (transmission of information, interrogation, intimation, expressive emphasis, etc.), is not a neutral strategy. By analyzing this relation, linguistics makes a double contribution to anthropology. First, it links word order to the needs of verbal situations peculiar to human society. Second, as we have seen in this chapter, the linguistic study of the word-order controversy reveals the relation between language facts and the history of ideas. This contribution of linguistics to history is no doubt a fundamental indication of its importance as a social science.

8

Wordmasters

The Dream of Language Perfection

The dream of a universal language is linked to the ancient notion of an original God-given tongue. In the Western tradition, this obsession is reflected by the myth of Babel. If indeed there is a harmonic relation between world and speech, it must be a unique one; the notion of such a relation would correspond to the image of the universal language. Thus there is nothing new about the passion for *pasilalies*, artificial languages whose transparence and perfection render them ideal for all mankind. Dr. Zamenhof's Esperanto, which first appeared in 1887, is merely the best-known and the most enduring of the international languages invented at the end of the nineteenth century, all of which were attempts to realize this dream of perfection. The tendency may be traced from the prophet Zefania (seventh century B.C.) to the German cleric Schleyer, who invented Volapuk in 1879; it includes Saint Hildegarde (twelfth century) and the speech philosophers or scientists Leibniz, Ampère, and Poincaré. Zamenhof and his disciples, including Jespersen (who invented Novial in 1928), hoped to construct a unique code that would spare men the trouble of learning each other's languages. During this period of internationalist idealism, it was even believed that the multiplicity of languages was itself the "cause" of dissensions among peoples.

These attempts were conceived as real language systems; others remained theoretical illustrations of the virtues of simplicity, univocity, regularity, and logic. Meanwhile, inventions like J. F. Sudre's musical language (1866) associated precise sound combinations with individual senses. All these creations share an ambition that extends beyond the perfection of clarity: the inventor seeks to rise above the social convention imposed by the language system, i.e., a tyrannical mandate, imposed from earliest childhood, to integrate with the majority. One way or another, and to varying degrees, the inventors of languages are all rebelling against this tyranny. One example may suffice, however, to demonstrate the flaw in such a utopic vision: the Sevarambes imagined by Vairasse[1] speak a language with declensions, like Latin or German. Since functions are marked by declensions, word order should theoretically become freer; but this economy with respect to sequential constraints is offset by the additional memory burden of learning inflected noun forms. A simplification of one aspect of speech is counterbalanced by an encumbrance of the grammatical system. This is the opposite of what occurs in pidgins, as we have seen (see chapter 2). Yet artificial languages claim to be simple languages. The goal of transparency is deeply rooted in the subconscious: we find it even in sleepwalking or subliminal states of language invention. All of us wish to break the bonds of the language socialization in which our dreams are imprisoned.

The revolt is a futile one. For although the dialogic species has some influence over language, it is an illusion to believe that we can escape its confines. We may invent "universal" tongues, or try to rediscover a *uglossia* (original language); we may continue to project our fantasies into utopic kingdoms, and, in paramnesic states, we may produce incomprehensible idioms. But none of that will do. Our only hope of mastery lies in a concerted intervention in the very real material of living languages, of whose development we have been, throughout our own history, both active spectators and blind participants.

Word Demiurges

Human action upon language may be carried out in either the public or private domain, although the separation between the two is not absolute. The support (or at least the benevolent indifference) of state authorities may advance private endeavors. It even happens that these authorities take over such enterprises altogether. From Italy (the Cruscan Academy, 1582) to Israel (the Academy of the Hebrew Language, 1953), the history of languages is marked by the founding of organizations for their reform or preservation. During periods in which the national consciousness most strongly identifies with its culture and language, there is a strong temptation to intervene in its "natural" course of development. In societies with a written culture, the best journalists and authors play a considerable role in such actions. Models of the educated public, their actions balance the unconscious construction of the history of the language by the anonymous speaking masses. In France, from Vaugelas to Grevisse, these cultured few are the *guarantors* invoked by the *language arbiters.* Scholars and technicians play their own role: within their fields of specialization (chemistry, law, the petroleum industry, etc.), they create technical lexicons which we propose to call *technolects.*

But instances of true "language builders" are more rare. Collective memory and official history associate certain great names with decisive stages in the destiny of a language. The "first grammarians" are often creators of orthographies, like Saint Mesrob in the case of Armenian (fifth century), and Saints Cyril and Method for the so-called Glagolitic notation of Slavonic (ninth century). This is an essential task, certainly less trivial than has frequently been suggested by linguists (see chapter 4). More usually, these language builders are founders of an authorized form of their language at some turning point in history. Examples from the sixteenth and seventeenth centuries include Luther for German, Agricola for Finnish, and Sylvester for Hungarian; from the eighteenth century to the present we have Lomonosov for Russian, Koraís for Greek, Karadžić for unified Serbo-Croatian, Aasen for modern Norwegian, Ben Yehuda for Israeli Hebrew, Kemâl Ataturk for Turkish, Aavik for Estonian, and Prince Wan for Thai.[2]

Can such voluntary actions suffice to (re)construct an entire language? Or is this goal largely illusory? We have seen considerable accomplishments. Luther, Agricola, and all the translators of the great religious texts established a lexicon and phrase structure system by making judicious selections from available material. Ben Yehuda, supported by a highly motivated public and assisted by educators, gathered from Biblical and Talmudic literature a considerable number of elements that were to constitute the basic vocabulary of Israeli Hebrew. Ataturk, a nationalist scholar as well as head of state, carefully selected experts to revitalize Osmanli by borrowing words from other Turkish languages (a more "authentic" source, which replaced Arabic). Aavik, Prince Wan, and other champions of individual cultures created technolects, specialized words, and entire modern vocabularies. This was accomplished by borrowing from prestigious ancient languages, which constitute a virtually limitless source of material even when the models are not genetically related to the target language (as is the case of Pali in relation to Thai).

In some cases, the ascendency of a state is accompanied by the publication of major lexicographical or grammatical works, codifying the usage considered most representative. In 1492, the power of the Catholic kings in Spain was reinforced by a threefold action: the Reconquest was completed, the American expedition began, and the Jews were expelled. That same year saw the publication of Nebrija's *Grammar*, a work glorified by many and read by few, as is so often the case. And at the dawning of a new nation that did not establish a new language—since the colonists could not bring themselves to abandon English for any of the native Indian languages, which they deemed inferior—Noah Webster's *Dictionary* (1828) fixed the spelling of American English.

All of these works belong to the history of the languages concerned. They are not passing incidents, but major events. It is true, however, that they remain on the periphery of any real restructuring. They simply reorganize and modernize. Language "treasuries," while they obviously have a political and cultural influence, are monuments to the established order; they are a powerful reinforcement of the status quo, not a creative enterprise. They do not deviate from accepted usage, but consolidate the past and trace the contours of a norm. Comprehensive dictionaries, especially when they are panchronic (describing the language at all known stages of its history), reflect the speech of dead societies as well as that of the living. This past haunts the present and seems to trace a destiny. Thus the dictionary, far from an innovative effort, appears as a socio-political tool for representing history according to an accredited point of view.

Of course, the more daring of the word demiurges inserted their own creations into the list of "accepted" entries. In certain dictionaries, we find words that are the product of pure invention. Their success is explained by two properties, and may be measured by two criteria. First, they satisfy a need when the designated notion or object is present in the environment but does not yet have a name, and they do not violate familiar structures. Secondly, they are accepted by the public as well as by the all-powerful masters of audiovisual information; ideally, their artificial origin is forgotten or ignored. Ben Yehuda declared that he would be satisfied if only one-fourth of his lexical innovations became standard in Israeli Hebrew and were no longer recognized as his creations. In fact, two-thirds of these words were accepted. The same is true of certain lexical items contributed to Estonian by Aavik, and of the creations of the most devoted participants in the *nyelvújítás* (language renovation) in Hungary at the end of the eighteenth and beginning of the nineteenth centuries. But these are isolated cases; the failures are much more numerous.[3]

The fact remains that these linguistic founding fathers deftly exploited traditional means of vocabulary enrichment: learned borrowings, whether internal (from the native language) or external (from an ancient or foreign language); native fabrication, either by composition or by derivation (especially affixation and truncation of an initial or final segment); and finally extension, which is the adjunction of a new meaning to one or several meanings already associated with an existing form. Using these procedures, groups of specialists have created, and continue to create, technolects capable of responding to the vast need for words arising from the considerable increase in human knowledge and power. Both private initiatives and acts of state bear witness to a single tendency: the nationalist transparency of motivated formations (descriptive compounds, various types of derivations) is preferred to the internationalist opacity of borrowings. Borrowing from American English—which, particularly since the end of World War II, has become a kind of technolectal Esperanto—results in universal forms; however, these do not speak to the consciousness of national cultures. The case of motivated formations is exactly the inverse. They dominate in many enterprises of lexical modernization: the reformers of Vietnamese, Tamul, Somali, and Georgian preferred indigenous creations.[4]

Even in languages that do resort to extensive borrowing, native habits play a role. One of the most vigorous strategies is the creation of acronyms, a particuar type of composition in which only the first syllable, or the name of the first letter of each word, is retained. An example is the French *cégétiste* for a member of the C.G.T., or "Conféd-ération Général du Travail" (here the procedure is combined with the derivational suffix -*iste*). Russian and Indonesian offer numerous examples; so does modern Hebrew, in which the national army is called *tsahal*, from *tsava* ("army") + *haganah* ("defense") + *leisrael* ("of Israel"). Similarly, radar (which itself derives from "radio detecting and ranging") is called *makkam*, from *megalle*, ("discoverer") + *kiwwun* ("direction") + *maqom* ("position"). Meanwhile, there are middle tendencies between borrowing and creation. One of these is the half-playful, half-chauvinistic procedure of "pun-borrowing," the exploitation of an accidental and felicitous resemblance of form and meaning between the foreign word and the native one. The resulting terms sometimes gain wide acceptance. Hungarian has *elem*, "element," from the root *elö*, "what is in front;" in Turkish we find *okul*, "school," based on *oku*, "read;" and in Israeli Hebrew *ilit*, "elite," based on *ili*, "superior." Another process, found in learned neologisms as well as in spontaneous creation, is the naturalization of borrowings. Swahili takes the Arabic noun for "book," *kitabu*, but gives it the plural form *vitabu*, exploiting the coincidence by which this word fits into the system of Swahili noun classes, where plural *vi*- corresponds to singular *ki*-.

Vocabulary enrichment, controlled neologisms, the establishment of lists of recommended or rejected words, the elaboration of dictionaries, the introduction or reform of orthography—in many countries, these tasks are assigned to assemblies of experts. Often, legislative bodies (like the French Parlement or the Norwegian Storting) vote on these decisions. Another area under their authority is *normalization*, i.e., the adoption of a single linguistic means of expression to be promoted to the rank of national or official language (or both). This may be a supra-dialectal norm, as was the case in nineteenth-century Italy, and in China as of 1955. The absence of a norm, or of a unified authority to impose one, has in some societies coincided with extreme political instability. Usage is then determined by the interactions of daily life: such is the case, in Europe, of Carelian (USSR), or Sardi; and in New Guinea, of the languages of the Emenyo tribes of the Upper Plateaux. Breton, Basque (despite unification efforts), Rhaeto-Romance in Switzerland, and Circassian in the Caucusus also remain dialectal groups rather than languages in the process of unification: there is no indentifiable norm that could be imposed by political or literary authority. To compensate for the splintering of nationalities, governments may try to officialize one of the national languages, like Amharic in Ethiopia and Tagalog in the Philippines. Or a foreign language may be chosen: in India and in much of Africa, English and French may well have been the languages of the imperialist oppressors; but they are less politically

151

explosive than any of the rival ethnic tongues, any of which would be an affront to speakers of the others.

Lexical reform, unlike normalization, does not take place at the periphery of the language itself. Still, even when it succeeds, it touches only the least-structured elements. Of course, morphosyntax has not escaped modification. But interventions in this area are more often designed to conserve than to reform: most known cases involve restorations. To take the case of modern Norwegian: when the feminine was on the verge of disappearing from nominal morphology, it was reintroduced from the most conservative dialects of the language, where it had remained. In Dutch, initiatives by "purist" grammarians (motivated by a desire to mold the written language to a Latin ideal) had artificially preserved the feminine until the middle of this century; but official interventions, in Belgium as well as in the Netherlands, have weakened its position with respect to the masculine. In addition, certain vanishing forms have been revived, like the Hungarian -*ik* conjugation, or the verbal patterns *puʿal* and *šafʿel* in Israeli Hebrew.

Similarly, in Finnish, the nominal and verbal declensions that had been eliminated from the spoken language by the fall of short atonal vowels in final position—producing *metsä-s* ("forest-in," i.e., "in the forest") or *tule-m*, ("come-we," i.e., "we come")—have been restored, yielding *metsä-ssä* and *tule-mme*. Finally, there are cases of local word-order modifications. Thus, in modern Norwegian, the sequence "ten + one" was substituted by decree for the sequence "one + and + ten;" i.e., *tjue-to* replaced *to-og-tjue*. Overall, as we have seen, these actions support tradition over innovation; their scope is limited, their results modest.

Pronunciation, as we might expect, is also largely unaffected by attempts at modification—or actually resists such attempts. In Israel, there was an effort to impose the pronunciation of the eastern Jews, rich in guttural sounds like those of Arabic, as a phonetic norm more faithful to classical Hebrew. But this pronunciation clashed with the articulatory habits of the western Jews who had founded the state, and who until quite recently maintained exclusive control. The political dominance of this group thwarted the linguistic initiative.

Language: Source or Resource?

Computers and Linguistics. Would-be word demiurges are not discouraged by this resistance. Their perseverance is really quite remarkable.

Although only the lexicon is accessible to real intervention, they do not confine themselves to that domain. On their daring quest for the Holy Grail of better expression, they question the implicit assumption of every grammar book: that language is "a driving force," and that it is madness to try to control it. Of course, if language is considered a "natural" phenomenon, then it is conceivable that humans may affect it. Since the dawn of mankind, the control and the rational use of nature have distinguished human communities from those of other living beings.[5] *Homo sapiens* is, in truth, a singular species. We do not passively accept our natural environment, or the properties written into our genetic code; we try to transform them. According to Pico dela Mirandola, God said to Adam, "I have established laws within which Nature encloses other species; but thou, who knowest no confines, I have placed thee under the authority of thine own judgment, that thou mayest define thyself."[6] For the reformer, then, languages are not inaccessible to modification.

Certain assumptions should, however, be recognized. If language is considered a natural resource, it then belongs to a nation just as do petroleum or iron ore. In that case, language must be accessible to efforts of regulation and development. But such an instrumental conception implies that communication—which is only one of the functions of speech—is the most important, if not the only, determining element. According to this perspective, language planning is no longer a secondary effort, a simple footnote to linguistics; it becomes instead a major aspiration. Jespersen said[7] that theoretical linguistics was the means, and language planning the goal. And in a recent work we find the following: "A syntactic theory providing a conception of syntax that contributes to the characterization of human speech as an instrument, or as goal-oriented behavior, is preferable to a theory that cannot do so."[8]

If this point of view is carried to its logical extreme, linguistics becomes a science directly determined by its application, just as anatomy, physiology, and pathology are frequently associated with medicine. Further, certain scholars[9] predict that the superiority of machines (presently computers) will one day be such that they will replace speech as the auxiliary of thought. Therefore, humanity would naturally be forced to adopt the language best adapted to harmonious collaboration with these machines. Linguists, then, should direct their efforts to fashioning such a language. This goal would assign to linguistics a role in the history of civilization which can scarcely be imagined today. The linguist's primary task would become the evaluation of degrees of economy, motivation, analyticity and simplicity (whose theoretical importance is clearly demonstrated by pidgins—see chapter 2). The typology of morphological indices, using an improved version of the trilogy of inflectional, agglutinating and isolating languages (see chapter 3), would no longer be an arcane field for technicians; instead, it would be the basis for a pure value judgment, i.e., the choice of the best language in terms of flexibility and "easiness."

If we set aside its rather mythical aspect, this futuristic view is not to be shrugged off. At least one of its implications should be examined: language does not change by its own blind rules, as has been taught. We modify our languages, as we consciously or unconsciously modify everything else, from the technologies that determine our relations with nature to the very defining properties of the dialogic species. However, the procedures of language reformers are instructive. Why is it that in the lexical domain, most accessible to intervention, they generally prefer native formations to borrowings (as seen above)? If languages were pure natural resources to be modeled at will, would we not predict the triumph of artificial idioms like Esperanto? Natural languages have been forged by the contingencies of history; they are collective, unsupervised creations whose vocabularies, morphosyntax, and even spelling systems contain obsolete elements and various unanalyzed residue. From the purely utilitarian point of view, they are highly imperfect. Yet, not only have artificial languages failed to replace them, but reform attempts tend to preserve original purity as much as possible. Individuals and groups identify themselves with these "imperfect" systems. The desire to direct the evolution of vocabulary and grammar, far from being iconoclastic, implies a symbolic appropriation of one's own language. And for the reformers themselves, mastery over language guarantees their own continuity.

We might then imagine that in a few hundred (or perhaps a few thousand) years, the fate of the most widely-spoken human languages —and of those dominated by them—will fluctuate between the instrumentalism of adaptation to machines, and the symbolism of diverse cultural representation. Unless it happens that one day the two goals should coincide, on a national or perhaps even a world-wide scale. In the latter case, a unified human race would face the challenges of nature and of human invention. We can always dream, of course . . . and meditate upon the implications of the present and continuing adventure of speech for mankind and his destiny. In any case, this is a far cry from the tirades of those who decry the multiplicity of languages, and who are impatient to see their numbers diminished. On the contrary, if nations were bound by a real sense of human solidarity, the first step in forming a unified front against the common dangers presented by the future would be the respect of differences—including differences of language.

The Language Conservationist: Public Enemy? Of course, human history offers few illustrations of such mutual respect. Linguistic unification has almost always been effected through violence, or through the forced expulsion of natural variants. The advancement of French, for example, was first facilitated by the monarchy: under Saint Louis (and later under Philippe le Bel), the choice of language was a choice of power. The dissemination of the vernacular throughout the royal kingdom was a corollary to the strengthening of a centralized authority. When, with the edict of Villers-Cotterêts (1539), François I made French the exclusive language of justice, he was simply confirming the de facto situation, established in the provincial parliaments and administrations by agents who brought with them the language of the king.

To consolidate this position, the Revolution made the national language an instrument of political struggle—not only against the dialects of the anti-revolutionary western provinces, but against all languages and minority dialects, whether or not they were being used to express resistance to the Republic. Dialects or *patois*, in any case, were not perceived simply as reflections of ancient feudal divisions. They were major obstacles to civism. A good citizen must understand the government's decrees. How can men be equal before the law when they are not equal before language?

Consequently, in Barère's Report (in the month of Pluviôse, year II of the Revolutionary calendar), we read that "federalism and superstition speak low-Breton." Grégoire, in that same year, wrote of "the necessity and the means to exterminate patois and to universalize the use of the French language." Under this absolute regime, local dialects could only become museum pieces. The policies of centralization continued during the Restoration and under Louis-Philippe, arousing furious reactions from language conservationists. Thus, in 1834, Nodier wrote:

> It is in the name of civilization that the complete annihilation of patois is being carried out today. . . . Destroy low-Breton, you say? . . . And how would we go about it? Do we

even know what a language is? Or how deeply its roots may penetrate the spirit of a people? Or what emotional chords is strikes for them? . . . Those who embrace such theories ought to have the terrible courage of their convictions: they will have to burn down the villages and bludgeon the inhabitants to death.[10]

The status of minority languages is equally precarious in the great empires in which a dominant state language is a matter of practicality. Almost all of the national languages of the Soviet Union, including Cheremis in the Volga basin, Koriak in the Siberian north, Abkhaz in the Caucasus, and Kirghiz in the central Asian mountains, contain a large number of Russian borrowings. Only languages like Georgian or the Baltic dialects, spoken on the scale of a Soviet Socialist Republic and rooted in a tradition of cultural and political nationalism, have resisted the tendency. For all the others, the publication of dictionaries and grammars following massive literacy campaigns among national groups only underlines the fragility of these languages in comparison with Russian which, as the language of power, can only benefit from generalized bilingualism. Russian is also served by "liberal" measures masquerading as freedom: a 1958 law allows parents to choose the language in which their child will be educated![11]

Those political states that impose a dominant language in the course of normalization support the linguistic traditions of the dominant socio-cultural community in its attempts at reform and modernization. French is a perfect example. The language owes its political and cultural preeminence to measures of the state; however, and contrary to the common perception, it owes little of its lexical and morphosyntactic structures to government intervention. More precisely, political action has only succeeded when it coincided with certain ideological models, whose decisive influence has triumphed over all the individual governmental reforms implemented since the dawn of the state in the fourteenth century. These are the models of the dominant social groups, the guardians of the French language, who consider it their legacy. Of course, their consciously conservative efforts have always controlled or inspired official interventions; but this could hardly restrain[12] the "spontaneous" evolution of the language as it was imperceptibly shaped and transformed, in the anonymity of everyday usage, by the great multitude of ordinary speakers who have no political influence. Yet the fact that the guardians' conservative action, however limited, was at all possible, suffices to demonstrate the power relation that language can institute among speakers of unequal social status.

Language, the Anonymous Power. Why is it that political authority tends to support and extend the efforts of scholars to preserve and perfect language? Why should the normalization of language and the reform of vocabulary be political activities, and not simply innocent games among speech enthusiasts? Why do languages so often become grounds for violent confrontations, as they have in Greece, India, and Belgium even in this century? The language professions are not without their dangers: the Iranian historian and philologist Kasravi, who proposed the de-Arabization of part of the Persian vocabulary, was assassinated in 1946 as an enemy of Islam; and in 1936, Stalin sent the linguist Polivanov to Siberian camps because he was in favor of the Turkish languages and hostile to the prevailing doctrine of Marrism. Ironically, it was Stalin himself who ended Marr's reign in 1950 (see chapter 11), writing the following in a purported response to the questions of a "group of young comrades": "As I am not a linguist, I am naturally unable to answer our comrades fully. But as for Marxism in linguistics, as in the other social sciences, this is a matter that concerns me personally."

Stalin's affirmation of a *personal* interest in linguistics is rather surprising. How can it be explained? No doubt as a particular interest in the phenomenon of language itself. The Soviet regime, which has been called a "logocracy,"[13] is a striking example of this. It might be useful, in fact, to analyze in linguistic terms the French expression "langue de bois," defined as a style that assures total control by masking reality with words. The aim of Orwell's Newspeak was to drive out all unorthodox thought by banishing the very words that sustained it. Words became their own referents. Official Soviet texts reveal a scanty use of verbs compared to that of nouns derived from verbs, this type of nominalization being extremely productive in Russian.[14] The great number of nominalizations makes it possible through discourse to circumvent reality, which normally involves also the use of verbs. Thus, one can present certain assumptions or hypotheses as evident and accomplished "facts." To take an example, when we change *mes thèses sont justes* ("my arguments are valid") or *les peuples luttent contre l'impérialisme* ("the people are struggling against imperialism") to *la justesse de mes thèses* ("the validity of my arguments") or *la lutte des peuples contre l'impérialisme* ("the people's struggle against impe-

157

rialism"), we pass from assertion to implication. The speaker thus eludes responsibility as well as objection; for the hearer, who can interrupt at the end of the sentence "my arguments are valid," has less of an opportunity to do so after the portion of an unfinished sentence such as "the validity of my arguments."

Naturally, dictatorships do not appreciate being identified as such. How then could they remain indifferent to language? This potential for secret power is precisely a property of language. Is it not a seductive tool? Its exercise represents a kind of implicit supremacy. Certain words express this more clearly than others.

> The man we call "emperor" in Mexico bore the title *tla-toani*, "he who speaks," from the verb *tlatoa*, "to speak." The same root is found in words relative to language, for example *tlatolli*, "speech," and in those concerning power and command, for example *tlatocayotl*, "state." Both senses meet in the word *tlatocan*, designating the supreme council, i.e., the place of speaking and of political authority. It is not by chance that the sovereign is called *tlatoani*: underlying his power is the art of speaking, the debate within the council, the elegance and dignity of the pompous and colorful speech that the Aztecs so appreciated.[15]

Even when linguistic forms do not express this equation as clearly as they do in Nahuatl (the language of the Aztecs), those who possess speech are invested with authority—a greater authority than those with a hesitant command of the language. If the statesman can succeed, as did Ataturk in Turkey, in controlling the languge at a decisive stage of its evolution, he adds another dimension to his power. This is why linguistic interventionism, and the notion of language as natural resource, are far from innocuous. Intervention may be well-intentioned, especially if anti-purist and opposed to the sanctification of the usage of a conservative minority. But language is political property. Linguistic politics always plays into the hands of authority by providing it with a very powerful kind of support. The norm established by intervention is not the simple recording of the form of expression common to the greatest number of speakers. It is an idealized norm. The interests of the state are served when a fictitious stability of language erases the oscillating progress of speech. For the unity of language is of interest to those in power. Variation is inconvenient: variation in speech, already an obstacle to economic exchange,[16] suggests variation in

thought. Whether they like it or not, linguists who endorse the dominant usage risk becoming the patrons of the established order.

This is why human intervention in language, if it is to be something
other than a power play, must be developed outside of all political
authority. The linguist's role in the legitimate work of planning and
reform is one of the domains of application (including language teaching, translation, and the computer challenge) through which our work
can truly influence the course of human events. If we do not intervene,
we leave matters to those who will not hesitate to carry out their own
linguistic agendas in the press, the audio-visual domain, education and
law. If we abandon the field to engineers, scholars, and jurists who
invent—and often succeed in imposing—their technolects, we give
credence to the notion that language affairs are too serious to be left to
linguists. What is at stake here is not simply a technique of linguistic
expression. If languages make a major contribution to the shaping of
intellectual processes, influence upon the former translates as influence upon the latter, and consequently upon the civilization itself.

Of course, languages do not belong to linguists. But linguists do have
the right, and even the duty, to express an opinion on linguistic destiny.
They may even at times play a legitimate role in that destiny. If scientific inquiry based upon the need to know is distinguished from practical application, this is only a prerequisite to research—not a vow of
purity opposed to the presumably impure procedure of working with
raw matter. By taking their rightful place in the enterprise of linguistic
reform, linguists can help to guide the destiny of languages—and, to
some degree, that of their speakers—onto a safer course.

PART THREE

Theoretical Goals

OR

Our Dialogical Nature

9

The Three Viewpoints Theory

Linguists of many backgrounds are more or less in agreement about the existence of four traditional domains of language study: phonology, semantics, syntax, and morphology (see chapter 3). But although these areas are considered in the context of concrete speech production, the data and methods are actually ordered in a different manner. We cannot limit ourselves to the association of meaning with sound at the word level. What we find in reality are sentences, and groups of sentences forming texts. This is the actual language material produced and perceived by all speakers. Within this framework, it is more realistic to say that linguists begin by analyzing whole sentences, and eventually reach the level of identifying individual words. Thus the study of sound goes beyond word boundaries; and intonation, which operates over entire phrases or sentences, has its place beside the study of phonemes, the units that distinguish between words.

We propose here to study the actual manifestations of languages in discourse using the three viewpoints theory.[1] The sentence is accordingly defined by two criteria. First, it is the word or series of words that the native speaker accepts as complete, that is to say, sufficient unto itself and requiring no additions in order to be grammatically correct and semantically interpretable. The second criterion is a formal one: a certain intonationl contour defines sentence boundaries, although the material form of this contour may vary between languages and even within a single language.

Defined in this way, the sentence may be considered according to three complementary viewpoints. The first viewpoint examines the sentence in relation to the entire language system. Thus, we may study the relationships between terms and the material forms that serve to express these relationships. This is the *morphosyntactic* viewpoint. The second viewpoint links sentences to the external world of referents. In this case, we focus not on forms, but on the meaning they transmit, hence the name *semantico-referential* which we propose for this second viewpoint. Finally, the sentence may be considered in relation to the speaker, who is in turn linked to a hearer. The speaker chooses a certain strategy or mode of presentation, introducing a hierarchy between utterance and referent. We therefore propose the name *information-hierarchic* for this third viewpoint.

Notice that these are *viewpoints* (or *perspectives*), and not *levels* (as is clearly indicated in figure 1, where the three are arranged horizontally rather than vertically). The concept of levels, and the corresponding representation, would imply a hierarchical relation, or a transformational mechanism by which one level could be derived from another. But such a mechanism would have no phenomenological reality; nor would it even be of operational use. Besides, each of the three viewpoints provides uniquely essential insights; none of them dominates the others. All three contribute equally to the characterization of language acts as prototypical human behavior.

Research undertaken from any one of these perspectives, isolated from the other two, is an artifice that denies the reality of the indissoluble links between the three. From the morphosyntactic point of view, languages are natural objects, and their study involves several disciplines. First, phonology for describing the sound systems that constitute the physical aspect of words; then, morphology for studying the structure and alternation of words, and their arrangement into classes in different languages; finally, syntax for ascertaining the relations between words or groups of words, and the markers for these relations.

If we restrict ourselves to the first viewpoint, we ignore meaning, and the relations between constituents. If we work only from the semantico-referential point of view, we arrive at a formalization (fre-

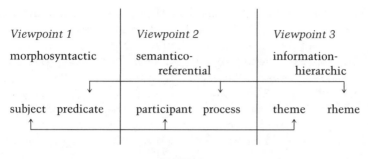

FIGURE 1

quently developed through mathematical logic) of the phenomenon of meaning and the operations that assure its production and interpretation; at the same time, we lose sight of the morphosyntactic constraints that characterize languages, and of discourse rules as well. Finally, if we regard all data according to the third viewpoint, we can obtain a characterization of discourse and of the interactional relations involved in it; but the essential components of speech escape us.

Since language behavior occurs in three dimensions simultaneously, it is clear that the three viewpoints must correspond to three zones in a single field of vision. Although it may be uncomfortable or dangerous to sit on the summit of a pyramid, the linguist who wants to do justice to the complexity of his subject has no choice; and his point of view, within the metaphorical area of his investigation, will necessarily shift from one to another of the three faces of language study defined by the three angles of this pyramid: natural sciences, mathematical logic, and sociopsychology.

To facilitate this task, let us consider one of the simplest and most instructive types of minimal utterances found in most languages, those consisting of two terms. From the morphosyntactic viewpoint, a French sentence such as *Pierre chante* ("Pierre sings") institutes a relation between a predicate *chante* (to be distinguished from *predication*, the name of the phenomenon itself), and a subject that determines this predicate, *Pierre*. From the semantico-referential point of view, *Pierre* represents the participant who takes part in an event, and *chante* is the process or event itself. Finally, from the information-hierarchic perspective, *Pierre* is the theme, the element about which the utterance says something, and *chante* is the rheme, or thing said about Pierre.

The three viewpoints theory does more than point out these three types of relations between terms. There is also a binding link between

165

the perspectives. Often (but not always), the word functioning as subject according to perspective 1 also represents the participant for perspective 2, and the theme for perspective 3. The same correspondence
will therefore exist, symmetrically, between the predicate, the process,
and the rheme. Thus, in *Pierre chante*, in *il court* ("he runs"), *l'enfant
bavarde* ("the child talks"), or *les invités sont arrivés* ("the guests have
arrived"), the words or groups of words *Pierre, il, l'enfant,* and *les
invités* figure as subjects in morphosyntactic terms, participants in
semantico-referential terms, and themes in information-hierarchic
terms. Similarly, *chante, court, bavarde,* and *sont arrivés* are analyzed
as predicates in terms of the first, expressions of a process in terms of
the second, and information provided about a theme (i.e., rheme) in
terms of the third perspective. This correspondence may be sketched in
the fashion shown in figure 1.

However, it sometimes happens that it is the predicate that corresponds to the theme, which is conceived as the less informative element constituting the background, while the rheme, providing new
information, coincides with the subject. Thus, in *il reste trois poires*
("there remain three pears"), or, in the relation of events, *survient un
homme armé* ("(there) appears an armed man"), the second part of the
sentence bears more information than the first.[2] This can be seen in
cases where the speaker expresses the principal information ellipti-
cally. The existence of utterances such as *trois poires!* and *un homme
armé!* does not mean that the other constituent is useless, but simply
that it is obviated by the situation. Thus it is not the initial words, *il
reste* and *survient,* that bear the principal information, although they
do function as predicates. However, even without coincidence between
predicate and rheme, or subject and theme, there is always a relation of
correspondence between the three types of sentence structurings.

Before returning to each of these types, we must again emphasize an
essential point. The very numerical ordering of the viewpoints adopted
here seems to imply a hierarchy, or at least a preferential ordering.
However, this is not the case. We must take into account two different
directions of analysis. If a Francophone listener receives the message
J'ai acheté "L'éducation sentimentale" hier ("I bought *L'éducation
sentimentale* yesterday"), he will decode it using the available forms
and the rules of French, eventually arriving at the content which was
the point of departure for the speaker. If, on the other hand, the Francophone is the speaker, and wishes to give some information about his
purchase of a particular book, he will encode the equivalent content,
again according to the rules of French, eventually producing the form

of the same message. In other words, if one is operating according to a *listener's strategy*, one follows a *semasiological procedure* from form toward meaning, that is, a decoding process from message as data toward an interpretation into content. If one chooses instead a *speaker's strategy*, one starts from an intention to signify and a hierarchization of the information to be transmitted, and encodes a message in terms of the language system, following an *onomasiological course* from meaning toward the forms that express it. In the latter case, the order of the viewpoints would be the opposite of that adopted here: the information-hierarchic point of view would come first, the morphosyntactic third. Yet if we substitute this order for the preceding one, we persist in a conception in terms of hierachically ordered levels, when, as we have said, the notion of viewpoint implies no hierarchy. If any significance is attributed to the numbering, we must remember that the processes of encoding and decoding meaning are in fact complementary, given the interchangeability of speakers.

In any case, the order adopted here may be considered a dynamic reflection of the situation of the child language learner, who necessarily begins as a listener. Yet this does not mean that we wish to foster a listener-centered linguistics, in answer to the speaker-centered linguistics characteristic of various modern currents. In classical generative grammar, for example, neither of these two directions is explicitly chosen; but the proposed rules progress from underlying schemata to realized structures, and no symmetric algorithm is provided allowing a reverse derivation. In such a framework, it is impossible to study realized messages as results to be decoded; one considers only the encoding process, the construction of messages.[3] This implies a hierarchy that, like its inversion, must be rejected.

The Morphosyntactic Viewpoint

The autonomy of syntax is a fantasy nourished by certain facts. It is possible, to some degree (as in certain literary works like Joyce's *Finnegans Wake*), to shatter the lexicon, explode individual words, and create an appearance of incoherence without, however, failing to transmit meaning. On the other hand, despite this latitude of distortion, we cannot violate syntactic rules at will. Certain types of languages absolutely require agreement between subject and predicate, or between predicate and complement; others insist upon obedience to word order constraints, especially when they are essential to meaning. As for morphology itself, it is generally impossible to modify the forms of function words, declensions, or temporal, aspectual, gender, and number markers. In cases of so-called semantic aphasia, the patient retains the syntactic structures of determination, coordination, subordination, and predication, but the strings almost never make sense. It is as if only syntax were preserved, and meaning lost. Further, in phenomena involving borrowing or interference from other languages, syntactic structures are more resistant than vocabulary. A primary property of languages—a rather odd property in terms of "common sense"—is that they subjugate spontaneous expression to the yoke of syntax. Meaning must pass through the sieve of rules, even though many badly-formed sentences are interpretable. Various experiments reveal that very early in life, man acquires an awareness of linguistic constraints. Corrections of errors committed by foreigners are oriented toward syntax rather than meaning; and corrective behavior by child-grammarians may be observed as early as age four-and-a-half, especially if the child is bilingual.[4] The ability to express a single meaning through two syntactic systems—that is, two different languages—seems to encourage attention to syntax rather than to content.

Despite these considerations, syntax is not an end in itself. Since syntax is in part the result of a fixing of semantics over a period of time, it may sometimes appear to be a closed system characterizing the very identity of each language. But we do not speak in order to apply or illustrate rules of grammar, except in language classes or textbooks—and even here, the grammarian communicates (sometimes consciously) through the examples he chooses. We speak to transmit meaning. This is why languages are radically different from logical systems, whose syntax is also believed to be autonomous. In the tripartite model adopted here, we do not find this illusion of syntactic autonomy endorsed today by theories like generative grammar. The rules of construction for utterances are not independent from the meaning they express, or from the choices organizing the information. In a language, syntax errors committed by the child, the foreigner, or the unschooled adult are tolerable as long as they do not compromise meaning; while in formal systems of logic, any syntax error, any order violation, any propositional inversion, destroys the entire edifice.

The Semantico-Referential Viewpoint: The Production and Reception of Meaning

Is it possible to set up a typology of minimal two-word utterances? The study of a large number of languages allows us to arrive at the model in figure 2 (representing the most common cases), which we will consider an empirical hypothesis to be verified over an even larger number of cases (see chapter 3):

As we have seen, the minimal two-word utterance brings into relation a process and a participant. The latter may be conceived in various ways, as illustrated in figure 2. The participant may be defined or definable, as in the equative utterance *Jean [est un] menteur,* ("Jean [is a] liar") (French and English, which must express the article and the verb "to be," involve more than two words). The participant may instead be attributive, as in *Jean [est] généreux,* "Jean is generous." It may be localized, in the literal sense ("in," "on,") or figuratively ("with," "for"), as in *Jean [est] ici,* "Jean is here." We find an existential participant in the spoken French *ya* (= *il y a,* "there is / are"), for example *ya un problème* ("there is a problem"). Notice, by the way, that in many languages without a verb "to have" (including Arabic, classical Hebrew, and Russian), possession is expressed through a situative utterance of the structure "Y is with X," or through an existential utterance of the structure "Y exists" with adjunction of a possessor "with X." A participant may be the scene of the event, as in the descriptive utterance *Jean dort* ("Jean sleeps"). Finally, the active utterance *Jean travaille* ("Jean works") illustrates a participant having a certain degree of control over the process, assuming a state of consciousness or will, as opposed to the other five types, in which the participant is conceived as nonactive.

Semantic types		*Participant*
non-active	1 equative	defined by the process
	2 attributive	qualified by the process
	3 situative	identified by its situation
	4 existential	posited as existent
	5 descriptive	conceived as scene of process
active	6	having a certain control over the process

FIGURE 2

169

We have seen that from the morphosyntactic perspective, the two-word utterance is a convenient structure, allowing easy identification of recurrences, types of relations, sequences, correspondences between word classes, and the determining relations characteristic of each language. This structure also provides a practical framework for isolating the simplest semantic relations, distinguishing them from the discourse situation which participates in the elaboration of meaning. But the two-word utterance is not the fundamental operating unit. Meaning is not produced in the smallest isolated utterance, but in the text as a set of sentences (when speaking of a string within a coherent whole, the term "sentence" is more appropriate than "utterance"). The text expresses a homogeneous message, sometimes divided into parts (paragraphs in written notation) through which this message is articulated. Naturally, the text may be either oral or written. All languages possess coordinating words, grammatical structures, or intonational curves that signal the addition or progression of ideas, and the choices made within the argumentative or narrative hierarchy. Cohesion and accumulation are observed not only within sentences, but also within the framework of the homogeneous whole constituted by oral or written paragraphs. Cohesive markers exist between the sentences of a text: anaphors recall earlier sections; cataphors anticipate later portions, etc. In certain languages of South America and New Guinea, it is even common, within a narrative, to connect sentences with summary-propositions that repeat textually or in substance an entire segment of the earlier context. In other languages (in Colombia, for example), special morphemes indicate that the directional thread changes from one sentence to another and that, for example, the speaker is proceeding from the exposition of events to the description of circumstances.

Assuming, then, that we must operate on the level of the text, and not on that of the single utterance, what elements constitute meaning? A daring question to ask! We refer here not only to the signified of each sign, a contribution called "signification" to distinguish it from "meaning" in general, but to the much wider phenomenon surrounding it: the meaning of a given sentence of text, or of any exchange of sentences in a dialogue, or of an entire oral or written text. It is clear from all evidence that meaning, while not limited to the mechanisms of linguistics, lies largely within its domain. To point out only one striking ontogenetic phenomenon, we observe that from earliest childhood, neurological awareness of sound sequences and meaning progress in parallel fashion.

In the table shown in figure 3, the components of meaning are divided into three zones, while its modalities are represented as two fields.

The fundamental characteristic of zone A is the *encoding* of the components of meaning. These components will thus correspond to the established formal means of the language. The label "reconstructed referent" (see chapter 6) recalls that language is not a simple reflection of the world, but rather a reorganization of it. The second component, the signified of signs, is the contribution made to the senses by the addition and combination of the signifieds of each sign—in other words, signification. The actual signifieds can be analyzed into minimal semantic units, or *semes*. The semic organization of any language reflects the praxis of the society and the specific way in which it culturalizes referents, so that words may be considered as *praxemes*, or linguistic expressions of this praxis. The object of praxematics, a discipline anchored in the real nature of language vocabularies, is characterized by the fact that, unlike traditionally static lexical studies, this object changes with the praxis and its representation, which, in modern societies, evolve quickly. On the other hand, the signified does enjoy relative autonomy. It is an entity defined by knowledge of the language as

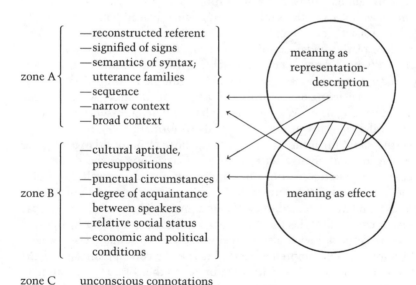

FIGURE 3

well as by contextual use of it: the signified may appear in very unusual contexts, and may even be in conflict with its surroundings, and yet still be recognized.

The semantics of syntax refers to a word's membership in a category of the language (noun, verb, adverb, etc.), and its function in the text (subject, predicate, etc.) Thus, verbs and complement markers (prepositions, postpositions, etc.) express relation, as opposed to nouns (see chapter 6 and references to Russell). Another aspect of the semantics of syntax is the meaning that arises from relations between utterances belonging to the same family. These include conversions, as in *il est venu et j'en ai été heureux* ("he came and I was happy about it") and *j'ai été heureux de sa venue* ("I was happy at his coming"); paraphrase, as in *Jean a menti* ("Jean lied"), *Jean n'a pas dit la vérité* ("Jean didn't tell the truth"); and antonymy, as in *tu leur as prêté de l'argent* ("you lent them money"), *il t'ont prêté de l'argent* ("they lent you money").

We have already noted (chapter 7) the contribution of sequence (word order) to meaning in the case of adjectives in French; many other examples could be found to illustrate the point. The contribution of context is well known, although, as we have just seen, the signified of signs is an independent entity. The narrow context involves immediately contiguous words, or those within a single sentence (for example, *grand* does not have the same meaning when placed before *garçon* ("a big boy") as it does before *connaisseur* ("a great connoisseur"). The influence of the wider context is seen in the question *qui as-tu rencontré?* ("who did you meet?"), which provides the elements necessary to interpret the response *Pierre,* which would be incomprehensible in isolation. We *learn* our "natural" language in infancy; we *construct* formalized languages. We should emphasize here an essential property of natural languages: unlike the words of formalized systems, which have the same meaning in any context, those of natural languages are sensitive to, and change with, context. This is one of the conditions necessary to poetic creation. In continuous speech as well as in dialogue, the volume of information brought to bear upon different parts of a text, and not repeated in each new sentence (except in pathological cases, or narrative styles like those of some languages of South America and New Guinea, mentioned above), constitutes a semantic stock necessary for mutual comprehension. This may be conceptualized as *activated common knowledge.* Its assignment to the zone A of meaning is based upon the fact that previous parts of the text are formal phenomena, falling within the domain of ordinary linguistic analysis.

In contrast to zone A, zone B is a domain of contingency. This aspect of meaning is not encoded, since all of its components are linked to ever-changing and unpredictable circumstances. Under the heading of *cultural aptitude,* we include knowledge shared by speakers about the physical, social and cultural environment, knowledge specific to each language and to each discourse situation. While membership in a single perceptual world may be necessary to mutual comprehension, it is not sufficient; meanwhile, the asymmetry between transmission and reception, given the accidental and transient state of each participant, may constitute an obstacle. In any case, the members of a language community possess a similar cultural aptitude. The foreigner who does not speak the language is thus excluded. Even if translated texts are available, cultural ignorance can make it impossible to distinguish between certain homologous forms. Thus, in Shawnee, an Algonquin language of North America, the two sentences corresponding to "I bend the branch by pulling on it" and "I have an extra toe" are almost identical: the first is *ni-l'θawa-ko-n-a,* that is "I-forked-branch-manually-action of an agent on a patient," and the second *ni-l'θawa-ko-θite,* that is "I-forked-branch-toe."[5] This language, of course, possesses no clear opposition between noun and verb; what would be a noun in English or French occurs in Shawnee as a classifying suffix (here *-ko,* an element applicable to any object in the form of a branch). Yet it is not only their morphosyntactic structure that makes these two sentences so striking to us. It is also the fact that in our culture, the relation between branch and toe is metaphoric at best, while in Shawnee this is considered self-evident.

Even so, it is true that shared knowledge of the cultural environment is not entirely separate from knowledge of the linguistic code. Experiments have shown that in certain languages that allow elliptical speech, such as Japanese, speakers reduce the number of ellipses according to their familiarity with their interlocutor; this reduction is greatest when speaking to a foreigner, even one who speaks fluent Japanese.[6] Cultural and linguistic aptitudes are closely related. Structural linguistics, by overemphasizing the common code of speakers, has neglected to recognize that this code is not sufficient. Speakers must also agree upon the meaning of saying, or not saying, the same thing; they must therefore be members of a single culture, or of two closely related ones. Misunderstandings still occur, however (see chapter 10).

Presuppositions are a part of cultural aptitude; but, for those with a universal value, they are also a part of the world experience of the entire species. The sentence *Il commence à dire "maman"* ("He's starting to say 'mama' "), for example, presupposes the proposition "He is a child" — except, of course, in the very unusual case of an adolescent raised in the wild. Punctual circumstances of the verbal exchange also participate in the construction-interpretation of meaning. Thus, *il nous quittera bientôt* ("he will leave us soon"), applied to a dying patient, cannot mean that the person is getting ready to take a trip. The interpretation of many messages in everyday conversation involves components of non-verbal communication: body language, especially movements of the head and arms, other physical constituents, attitudes and actions. Moreover, meaning is also linked to the degree of acquaintance between speakers, to everything they know about each other: acts, ideology, moods, lifestyle, *habitus*[7] in various domains. If we are unaware of the political orientation of our interlocutor, especially at the beginning of a conversation, we cannot have a clear idea of what the words *left, right, democracy, communism,* or *feminist* represent for that person. Given the diversity of situations, the mutual acquaintance of speakers is as variable as cultural aptitude and punctual circumstances.

The same is true of the last two components of zone B: relative social status, and economic and political conditions. We see, then, that the five components of this zone, unlike those of zone A, are not systematically encoded (unless they arise directly from morphosyntax, like the personal forms of politeness and hierarchical relation found in many languages of eastern Asia and elsewhere). The constituents of zone B are variables: thus, despite their importance as factors in the construction and decoding of meaning, they do not lend themselves to interpretive rules expressing systematically recurrent and predictable facts — i.e., rules for the production and reception of meaning. As for those factors conceivable within a semantic ethnography of daily life, which are mentioned by contemporary interactionist theory, the only ones that may be codified in linguistic terms are Goffman's so-called "verbal utterances":[8] "The ultimate behavioral materials are the glances, gestures, positionings and verbal statements that people continuously feed into the situation, whether intended or not."

Zone C is also virtually impossible to codify. We speak here of *connotations* (Fr. *signifiances*), since what is involved is neither *signification,* a phenomenon proper to the sign, nor *meaning* (Fr. *sens*), a phenomenon proper to the text as a combination of signs in a given speech situation. Connotations, embedded in the unconscious, are by this very fact unavailable to an encoding characterized by explicit consensus. This consensus is in fact largely theoretical, even for those components that may be encoded (zone A), and especially for those that may not (zone B). Ambiguity is a constituent of linguistic communication, as we shall see (chapter 10).

As for the two modalities of meaning, the first, meaning as representation-description, has long been recognized; while the second, meaning as effect, has only been systematically studied (in the twentieth century, at least) through considerations of concrete discourse events. Meaning as representation-description does not apply exclusively to zone A, nor is meaning as effect limited to zone B. As is indicated by the hash marks and directional arrows of figure 3, the two modalities of meaning overlap, each applying to the two zones, A and B. The reconstruction of meaning as representation-description may call upon noncoded components, cultural aptitude for example. In a relative clause, the status of the antecedent is theoretically determined by the syntax; yet this coded component is not always recoverable through the application of syntactic rules. In the French sentence *il s'agit d'un écrivain ami de Flaubert, qui est l'auteur des "Convulsions de Paris"* (it's about a writer friend of Flaubert, who is the author of the "Convulsions of Paris"), the antecedent cannot be identified unless one knows that this book was written by Maxime Du Camp, and not by Flaubert.

To take another example: the imperative, which is clearly encoded in the morphology of most languages, does not simply transmit information: it instructs the hearer to do something. It is remarkable that, in many languages which inflect verbs in other modes, the linguistic encoding of commands corresponds to the bare verb form. Since the function of the address is clear from the situation, those languages that do not designate the interlocutor are a negative reflection of the participation of discourse circumstances in the construction of meaning. Interrogation is also encoded in language: through intonation, with or without special words (such as *est-ce que* in French), or a particular word order (such as the inverted form *viens-tu?* in formal French). Symbolically, at least, the question takes possession of the interlocutor, since an answer, usually verbal, is expected: "The question, ostensibly a request for information, is also a seizure of another speaker whom it designates as respondant—even if this response is limited to a refusal to answer. It constitutes a symbolic hold over the body, time, and speech of the interlocutor, by virtue of the simple fact that it breaks the silence and opens a verbal space."[9]

The Information-Hierarchic Viewpoint

Pragmatics. By focusing upon problems of theme and rheme, that is, upon the speaker's choice, and the listener's understanding, of an informational hierarchy, we broaden the field of linguistics without however immersing it in that of *pragmatics.* This term applies to a current of research that has been greatly developed in Europe and North America over the last several decades. The concept was presumably originated by C. S. Peirce; but it was his student, the semiotician C. W. Morris, who integrated pragmatics into a theoretical framework in which the term denotes the relation between signs and their users. This model, in fact, considered speech only as a system of signs, and only within the domain of scientific discourse.[10] However, subsequent developments in research on the relations between speech and speakers have so extended the frontiers of pragmatics that its boundaries are no longer clear.[11]

Theme and Rheme. In contrast to this rapid burgeoning of the field of pragmatics, the information-hierarchic perspective considered here is limited to the polarity of theme and rheme as we have defined the terms. Thus the three viewpoints may be anchored in a single reality, with enunciative strategies explicitly linked to syntax and semantics. To take yet another simple example, the French utterance *l'enfant s'est endormi* ("the child fell asleep") may be analyzed in three complementary manners: the first part, *l'enfant,* is subject (perspective 1), actor (perspective 2), and theme (perspective 3); the second part, *s'est endormi,* is respectively predicate, process, and rheme. Theme and rheme are determined with respect to one another, not as absolute values. The result is that the theme does not necessarily bear old or established information, nor is the rheme always a vector of new or unknown material. In a given utterance, the rheme is simply *more informative* than the theme, although the latter may still, on occasion, carry new information. In general, a speaker posits a theme when he is not satisfied with the situational data or the previous context that he is addressing, but wishes to reinforce it through linguistic expression. Thus, it is useful to distinguish at least two aspects of this opposition. On the one hand, the theme can be considered an element defining the discourse universe or identifying the subject, i.e., as supporting material, in contrast with the rheme as focus. On the other hand, we can see the theme as old information, or a reprise of what is known, in contrast with the rheme as new information, or exposition of what is less well known. "Known" implies here a degree of knowledge or consciousness possessed by the speaker, and which he has reason to believe are shared by the hearer.

The statistical correspondence between theme and subject may be verified for each of these two interpretations of the notion "theme." If the subject coincides most often with the theme defined as supporting element within the utterance, we may predict that elements functioning as subjects will occur less frequently than other elements as centers of determination corresponding to various information. If the subject coincides most often with the theme defined as old information, we may predict that the kinds of words referring to the known, especially pronouns, will occur more frequently as subjects than in other functions.

A recent study has in fact verified these two predictions for French.[12] Still, certain languages use two distinct markers for subject and theme; but, in this case, the preferred use of the theme marker reflects a specific intention. This was noted in a study of Japanese news broadcasts (Fr. *informations*, an appropriate term, since they identify a new element, or theme, in order to say something even newer about it, i.e., a rheme). Over a given period, the first element in approximately half the sentences carried the theme marker *wa*; in fact, in languages which distinguish between the definite and indefinite article, *wa* is often translated as a definite article (since what is presumably known is considered identifiable).[13] Yet this first element ought to bear the subject marker *ga* (often translated in French by the indefinite article *un*), which would signify it as unknown. We may conclude that the procedure reflects an intention, that of reducing the mental distance between announcer and listeners.[14]

Intonation and preposing are universal markers distinguishing theme from rheme. But certain languages also have special morphemes, like *wa* in Japanese; other strategies exist as well. French distinguishes between two types of themes in conversation: the theme as old information or reprise of known materials tends to be postposed, while the theme as supporting material is generally preposed. Thus we find, on the one hand, sentences like *ça s'élève tout seul, les enfants* ("it raises itself, children," i.e., "children raise themselves"), or *il n'est pas là, papa* ("he isn't here, papa," i.e., "papa isn't here") in which *les enfants* and *papa* are contrastive postposed themes representing information already given. On the other hand, we have *les chiens mordent quand on les provoque* ("dogs bite when provoked") in formal style, with weak thematization of *chiens*; or *les chiens, ça mord quand on les provoque* in spoken style, with strong thematization of *chiens*, recapitulated as subject through the resumptive pronoun *ça*). The first strategy, postposing of the contrastive theme, may take the form of a different word, with anaphoric reiteration applying to the same referent; this is one of the characteristics that contribute to the familiar tone and dramatic rhythm of Céline's prose:

> Je venais de découvrir la guerre tout entière. . . . Faut être à peu près seul devant elle comme je l'étais à ce moment-là pour bien la voir, la vache, en face et en profil.[15]

> (I had just discovered war in her entirety. . . . [One] has to be pretty much alone before her as I was at that moment to get a good look at her, the bitch, full face and profile.

The sequential presentation of the opposition between the two strategies of thematization is not systematic, but it does reveal the importance of the distinction between types of themes.[16] Languages do seem to be the only known codes in which supporting material (the theme as a given) is explicitly stated.

Languages, in addition to their role as instruments of analysis or logical interpretation, are also mechanisms permitting their users to construct hierarchies of information. Even in the most austere scientific (especially mathematical) style, information is organized into a hierarchy based on a contrast between supporting facts and new material. This is all the more true in dialogue, where the interaction between speakers is much more obvious, and largely conscious. Such interaction calls for more complex strategies. In particular, a pure and simple linear progression of information[17] is not the only possible discourse strategy. The speaker may change perspectives, alternately placing one argument or another in the forefront, then relegating it to the background. This, of course, applies not only within the sentence but at the paragraph level as well. In fact, when we consider any text longer than a simple isolated utterance, we discover that a given word order, preferred within the framework of a single utterance, may actually compromise the clarity and coherence of a text comprising a series of utterances.

Within this textual framework, it is easier to organize information if the language has some freedom of word order. In this respect, French literary prose (unlike the spoken language, or even ordinary French prose) is characterized by a certain rigidity which favors the once-heralded "natural" word order (see chapter 7) consisting of subject + verbal predicate + complement; yet this order may in fact mask logical transitions. Complements, which were new information in the preceding utterance, should appear at the beginning of the following utterance since, as themes, they represent information that is no longer so new.

Thus, in literary French, the sequence of ideas is sacrificed to a purely grammatical order. The following passage by Voltaire (*Le Siècle de Louis XIV*, chapter 30) provides an illustration:

> Ce n'est point en effet l'argent et l'or qui procurent une vie commode; c'est le génie. Un peuple qui n'aurait que ces métaux serait très misérable; un peuple qui, sans ces métaux, mettrait heureusement en oeuvre toutes les productions de la terre, serait véritablement le peuple riche. La France a cet avantage avec beaucoup plus d'espèces qu'il n'en faut pour la circulation.[18]

> (It is not in fact silver and gold that procure a comfortable life; it is genius. A nation possessing only these metals would be quite destitute; a nation bereft of these metals, but which knew how to administer all of the earth's bounty, would be the truly rich one. France has this advantage, with more than enough currency to go around.)

The informational hierarchy would be clearer if the sequential constraints were broken. This could be accomplished simply by preposing the element in each sentence that represents old information (i.e., the theme, which may be deduced from the preceding sentence); in other words, transitions could be made *through themes*, resulting in a text more faithful to the informational hierarchy; but, by that same token, the text would be less acceptable in literary French:

> Ce n'est point en effet l'argent et l'or qui procurent une vie commode; c'est le génie. Ces métaux, un peuple qui n'aurait qu'eux serait très misérable; (ces métaux), un peuple qui, sans eux, mettrait heureusement en oeuvre toutes les productions de la terre serait véritablement le peuple riche. Cet avantage, la France l'a avec beaucoup plus d'espèces qu'il n'en faut pour la circulation.

This word order, often avoided even today in written French, is nonetheless that of the spoken language. As long as the various elements have been introduced into the dialogue, or belong to the discourse universe, they may be embedded to the limits of comprehension: *moi, mon copain, son père, il est pilote* ("me, my buddy, his father, he's a pilot"). In this case, *moi* is the theme with respect to the rest of the sentence; but within the following rheme another theme, *mon copain*, has been embedded, and, at still another level, *son père*.

This order of progression, reflecting the distinction between foreground and background, is often found in Greek and Latin texts. Homer's transitions are quite natural, while the French translation generally muddles them. Take, for example, *tòn d'apameibómenos proséphê pódas ôkùs Achilléus*, [19] word-for-word "him then answering declared feet light Achilles." The only available French translation is *Achille aux pieds légers lui répondit*, ("Fleet-footed Achilles answered him"). But Achilles is not mentioned in the preceding line; the sudden appearance of this new element breaks the continuity. Instead, the Greek text first mentions the previous speaker (the demonstrative pronoun *tòn*), who has been identified, and to whom Achilles is responding.

Thus, viewpoint 3 deals with an essential aspect of the study of languages, which is not addressed by the morphosyntactic description of viewpoint 1. To what degree, then, might this study of the relation between language and its users be independent of the study of *meaning* as the primary goal and permanent mystery of linguistics? Can the information-hierarchic domain of viewpoint 3 be considered autonomous with respect to the semantico-referential domain of viewpoint 2? In order to answer this question, we must first take a position on a dichotomy that recurs, in various forms, in almost all modern theories: language as *system*, and speech as *activity*.

This distinction has played an essential role in twentieth-century linguistics—although, given the excesses it has inspired, it has largely been considered a negative model. Saussure, whose formulation has been the most criticized, claimed that the "linguistics of language *(langue)*" and the "linguistics of speech *(parole)*" are "two routes that cannot be taken at the same time." [20] He himself was interested only in "linguistics in the strict sense, i.e., the study of *langue*." Pursuing this line of thought, Saussure later observed that the sentence "belongs to the realm of speech, not language." This is sufficient to eliminate it from consideration, since, a few pages earlier, we read that "if [the sentence] falls within the domain of speech, it cannot be considered a linguistic unit."

This proscription, and this collaboration of strategies—one separating linguistics from speech, the other eliminating the sentence—have proved cumbersome to Saussure's disciples. The history of linguistics since Saussure has, in large part, been a restoration of syntax, whose principal concern is in fact the sentence. There has also been a greater appreciation of the speaker's construction of sentences in the act of speech. An entire tradition represented in the classical period by Port-Royal, then by philosophical grammar through the first decades of the twentieth century, and illustrated by the word order controversy (see chapter 7), placed strong emphasis on syntax. Generative grammar completed the revival in the second half of this century,[21] or rather renewed its prestige.[22] But in its over-emphasis on syntax, generative grammar neglects the fact that this domain does not constitute an end in itself, and that languages transmit meaning.

The development of generative grammar has been followed by a series of trends catalogued under the (often vague) headings of pragmatics (taken over from Morris) and enunciation. Despite the obvious differences between them, enunciative theories, pragmatics, and our information-hierarchic viewpoint 3 share a basic focus upon the activity of the subject in the exercise of speech, a realm that has been neglected by purely systemic models of language. Yet this focus, within the three viewpoints theory, is closely linked to semantics and enunciation (see figure 1). Thus, within the theoretical framework adopted here, *there cannot be two distinct linguistics* as proposed by Saussure and Benveniste.[23] It is no doubt useful, from a methodological point of view, to distinguish language as system from speech as activity; but language, while indeed the foundation of speech, may only be perceived through this very behavior. Using various terminology and pretexts, most modern speech theories misunderstand this essential unity.

According to the earliest formulation of generative grammar—which has been frequently revised—all deviations and individual variations are labeled *performance* phenomena, which are to be distinguished from *competence*, a notion defining the user's knowledge of the language system (see also chapter 1). Competence would also exclude all phenomena involving memory limitation, restrictions on embedding, and constraints on recursiveness. Thus, there would be no theoretical prohibition against the accumulation of nominal determinants, as in "the school's director's brother's friends," or against embedded relative clauses of the type "this is the cat that caught the rat that ate the cheese that." Only performance limitations could explain the standard limits of these accumulations. Such a hypothesis fails to recognize that the organizing principle of these structures is a factor of competence. The language as system must itself contain the mechanisms that adapt rules, or permit their violation, in the exercise of speech: for as long as these violations do not interfere with the construction and perception of meaning, no one can deny that the interlocutors are speaking the same language. Speech and language cannot constitute two independent domains.

Therefore, and despite all protestations to the contrary,[24] Chomsky's paradox is simply a restatement of Saussure's. Both firmly reject any sociological perspective. The price of creating such a homogeneous scientific domain is much too high: after eliminating individual variation, there remains only the code shared by all the members of a speech community. But the variations themselves are the reality, and any reductionist theory that ignores them will result in a linguistics void of social content. A theory creates its own goals. Saussure, for whom "the single and true object of linguistics is language considered in itself and for itself" (the final, oft-quoted and perhaps apocryphal sentence of his *Cours de linguistique générale*), excludes the individual speaker and, by the same token, ignores interaction between speakers. In this conception of language, it is as if no one ever spoke to anyone else. Living language users, and the relation created between them by the exchange of words, are dismissed as the linguistics of speech, to be dealt with at some (unspecified) later date.

Meanwhile, progress in the study of discourse acts under the inspiration of Austin[25] and Searle[26] represents the swing of the pendulum so often observed in the history of science. This reaction has resulted in a tendency, especially among pragmatists, to ignore the fact that speech is inconceivable outside of the system of language upon which it is based. Texts are results, and may not be separated from the code. Inversely, the activity of the dialogic species is the manifestation of this code; through history, usage even defines the system, by inspiring periodic changes.

Countless facts attest to the essential unity of the domain defined by the polarity of language *(langue)* and speech *(parole)*. In the lexicon, most words (aside from grammatical tools like articles and conjunctions) may, when used in discourse, take on values linked to this usage. The evolution of vocabulary is effected by, among other things, the annexation of connotation, (or meaning in relation to a specific situation) to denotation (or primary meaning given by the dictionary). The situation creates its own relation to a certain signified; when the frequency of a given situation is high enough, the language integrates the new signifieds. Among countless examples, we may cite the classic French farmyard series *pondre* ("lay," i.e., an egg), *couver* ("set / hatch"), *muer* ("moult") and *traire* ("milk," i.e., a cow).

In circumstances linked to rural life, established in France since ancient times, these words have taken on their contemporary technical meaning; while in Old French, they were more often used like their Latin ancestors *ponere* ("place"), *cubare* ("recline"), *mutare* ("change"), and *trahere* ("pull"). The unified view proposed here allows us to interpret a phenomenon which has long been a subject of theoretical controversy along the frontier between syntax and semantics, i.e., *ellipsis*. Ellipsis may be considered the voiding of one position in the speech chain, a process subject to constitutive properties of the code and not to personal or stylistic choice, but which is, at the same time, carried out by the speaker in discourse. Ellipsis is thus coded, and yet at the same time open to the speaking subject's activity, as are other linguistic phenomena involving a dialectic of constraints and freedom (see chapter 10). In this, ellipsis resembles another puzzling phenomenon, that of *ambiguity*. Both may be seen as epistemological guides toward a unified course, which will be seen in chapter 10 as a discourse model of the subject.

The unity of language and speech is illuminated by another essential phenomenon: intonation, which is often ignored in the study of written language isolated from the real conditions in which texts occur. Specialists are becoming increasingly proficient at analyzing intonational curves, and at recognizing variations of voice register, from the ultra-low to the ultra-high, including all intermediate levels, whether the contour is flat, ascending, descending, or bidirectional.

However, it remains difficult to identify intonational encoding. In fact, the ever-changing and unpredictable meaning of intonation is situation-dependent—except for very specific cases such as the opposition of theme and rheme,[27] or interrogation (and even these domains are subject to random variation). Speakers do not always agree on the content of intonation, as we have seen. But in those cases—and, fortunately, they are many—in which there is consensus, the observation of intonational behavior is obviously quite instructive.

Intonation, which is a contrastive phenomenon of the speech chain, may nevertheless be integrated into the coded language system. This is demonstrated by an example as simple as the French question: *vous avez l'heure?* ("You have the time?") Pragmatists would claim that a contradiction exists between the syntax, which appears to be questioning the possession or nonpossession of the time, and the semantics, which asks the listener to respond with the correct time, or to say "no" —but not, presumably, to answer "yes." In our framework, the contradiction would be resolved by taking into account the pragmatic dimension according to which this question is asked only when one wishes to know the time. In fact, the decisive factor is intonation, which has habitually been ignored when linguists study artificially isolated utterances, flattened onto a blackboard or a piece of paper. If the question is asked with ascending intonation, this intonational contour is coded in the language system, as established by the listener's invariable response of giving the time if he knows it. If on the other hand the second syllable of *avez* is pronounced on a high note progressing into a rapid descending curve, and *heure* is spoken on a low tone, then, for any French speaker, the interrogation is in fact on the possession of the correct time (i.e., a dependable watch). In this (admittedly rare) case, the expected response could be "yes," as well as "no." It would be "yes," for example, if the questioner has no watch and wishes to be sure that the listener, who does have one, will be able to give the time later if needed (say, if some person or event is expected at a certain time).

But sometimes intonation is not sufficient, and the implications of a given utterance depend upon the situation and the connections between speakers. This brings us back to the issue of the inclusion of these factors in the general study of meaning. The response of the pragmatists (or of many among them) is that semantics should instead be subsumed under pragmatics. Thus, the utterance *il fait froid ici* ("it's cold in here"), spoken in a room with the windows wide open in the dead of winter, is interpreted within the situation as an invitation to close them. Assuming that the listener who does not comply has not understood, the underlying theory of this position is that the reconstructon of meaning is linked primarily to circumstances. But this aspect corresponds to zone B, which, as we have suggested (see also figure 3), is the domain of the non-codifiable; and meaning is also involved in the components of zone A, which *are* coded. Thus semantics—and, correspondingly, the enunciative-hierarchical aspect of speech— enjoy a certain autonomy. If viewpoint 3 were enlarged into an immense field of pragmatics, it would annex zone B; within the three viewpoints theory, however, the information-hierarchic aspect is limited to the clearly coded opposition between theme and rheme. We do not have decisive criteria to evaluate situation-dependent meaning; nor do we possess a dependable procedure for defining a consensus over a variety of suppositions.

Moreover, we do not always say what we mean or mean what we say. Lewis Carroll's formula reminds us that even so-called indirect speech acts, the favorite terrain of the pragmatists, may be ambiguous or inadequately understood. The above example illustrates the case of observations interpretable as commands. These are not always understood, nor are other speech acts like questions constituting attenuated or direct commands, requests for forgiveness disguised as explanations, etc. It is true that certain indirect formulations seem clear: such is the case for personal pronoun substitutions as in *maintenant nous allons nous laver les mains* ("now we are going to wash our hands"), uttered by a teacher to young pupils designated as "we;" or in *on en vient à la conclusion qu'il y a là une erreur* ("one comes to the conclusion that there is an error here"), where *on* ("one") really means "I," and *il y a* ("there is") means "you have made"—both terms politely disguised.

Further, it is generally true that in making what Austin has called performative utterances, we accomplish through the discourse situation the very thing that we claim to do: *j'ordonne qu'il s'en aille* ("I order that he leave"), or *nous te permettons de revenir* ("we permit you to return"), or *la séance est ouverte* ("court is now in session"). But in considering the use of tropes and figures of speech as indirect means of transmitting meaning, of convincing a listener, or of acting upon that listener,[28] we start from linguistic facts, and from the encoding of meaning in the material of discourse. This is equally true in the field of indirect communication studied in rhetoric—the ancestor of modern pragmatics.

We enter upon an uncertain path when we posit conceptual categories without bothering to establish traces of these categories in the stream of discourse. When we attempt to consider all factors, coded or not, which contribute to meaning, we suffer under the twin delusions of boundless knowledge and unlimited prophecy, as suggested by Bloomfield and echoed, thirty-five years later, by Eco.[29] Science requires a closed domain, and the linguistic terrain cannot be drowned in an ocean of calculations and predictions unsupported by formal data. Speakers themselves, producers and decoders of meaning in the social environment which constitutes their natural milieu, constitute the only bridge between semantics and pragmatics (in the broader sense) which concerns linguistics. Let us then consider the speaker in those terms.

10

Socio-Operative Linguistics:
Toward a Theory of Communication

The Discourse Relation

Classical structuralists study only language *(langue)*; pragmatists worship speech *(parole)*. By isolating the two domains, these schools fail to recognize either the constraints imposed by the former, or the discourse relation established by the latter. This relation is more or less ignored in the structuralist tradition, which is preoccupied with language in itself—as if no one ever affirmed, denied, questioned, invited, or exclaimed. And if no one perceives speech, then no one answers, executes or reacts. In fact, however, when we put language into use through the activity of speech, we adapt the language system to the discourse relation. Such behavior is not purely operational or logical, but regulative. The properties linked to discourse must be integrated into the definition of language. Dialogue is natural to humanity.

We use the word *dialogue* here in the broad sense, that is not only as question / answer pairs (although this is an important component), but as discourse in general: all face-to-face linguistic interaction, an essential defining property of the human species. Moreover, despite the fact that an erroneous etymology of the word generally results in a limited notion of *dialogue* as activity between only two partners, we include here exchanges by more than two speakers ("plurilogues"). In any case, the activity of the partners is characterized by the joint construction of meaning. Questions, injunctions, and negations play an important role.

The question establishes a narrow relation to the extent that it naturally calls for an answer (see chapter 9). But the question, used itself as an answer, may be an avoidance strategy or a bid for control of discourse. An old Jewish precept from the rabbinical wisdom of the oral tradition teaches this very tactic. Injunction often uses verbal means to solicit a nonverbal response. Negation refutes an assertion, perhaps attributed to the partner, or answers a question. It is crucial that the actual negation be understood, thus clearly perceived by the ear, in order to avoid misinterpretation. By virtue of this discourse weight, negation often has a certain phonic weight. This occurs either as a recapitulation after the negated element (such discontinuous negation is found in 17 percent of languages, including French, Mooré (Burkina-Faso), Afrikaans, Guarani (Paraguay), and Burmese[1]), or through adjunction of reinforcing elements. Since, generally speaking, more features are needed to say that something is not than to say that it is, negation involves more marked morphosyntax, and is at the same time more charged with presuppositions and more psychologically complex. Negation thus provides a perfect illustration of the influence of discourse situations upon the very structure of the language.

But dialogue involves other strategies as well. Strong affirmation often takes the form of a so-called rhetorical question, which in French calls for an answer of *oui* ("yes"), *non* ("no"), or *si* ("yes" in contradiction of a negative). Thus: *N'est-ce pas en France qu'on trouve les meilleurs fromages?—Si!* ("Isn't it in France that the best cheeses are found?—Yes, it is!")

The progression is assured through the cooperation of the participants. Not in the moralizing sense of Grice's maxims,[2] which exhort the speaker to give all and only the information required by the situation, to be honest, to be pertinent, to be clear; for the mythical obligation of harmony implied by these maxims is continually belied by the bravado, humor, trickery, and personal interest of interlocutors. Instead, speakers cooperate in the construction of a meaning[3] which is the foundation and justification of their relation; this is true even

187

when, to maintain linguistic contact, they fill voids with meaningless sequences. Examples of such *suspensive words* include, in French, *ben, eh bien, alors, c'est-à-dire;* and in English, *well, y'know, I mean.* A syntax of dialogue is evident in the many cases where this cooperation consists of echoes or even linking of sentence fragments: A: *Ce type-là . . . — B: . . . c'est un voleur . . . — A: . . . peut-être pas un méchant homme . . . — B: . . . mais dangereux tout de même.* (A: That guy . . . — B: . . . he's a thief . . . — A: . . . maybe not a bad fellow . . . — B: . . . but dangerous in any case.) Subtle interpretation may lead a speaker to head off questions with anticipatory responses; or to give an answer which, despite appearances, correctly grasps the implications of the question. Inversely, questions may be dodged when the hearer wishes to elude interrogation; and answers may be evasive, which does not however impede the progression of meaning, but rather determines its direction according to the quality of information that each speaker agrees to give and the type of relation desired with the interlocutor.

All of these cases illustrate a *discursive interaction* that calls upon various linguistic strategies barely hinted at in academic grammars. These latter often list some of the most remarkable linguistic devices under the condescending label of "particles," revealing an ancient and persistent distrust of certain vital words of oral registers, little-used in written style. Indeed, it is in languages with a mainly oral tradition that we find great numbers of these short regulating words; languages like French and English can furnish only a few clumsy equivalents *(quant à moi, vois-tu, en quelque sorte, si on veut, tout bonnement, c'est à peu près sûr, c'est bien connu;* "as for me," "you see," "in some way," "if you like," "quite simply," "almost definitely," "as everyone knows"). Meanwhile, in Lapp, Finnish, Swedish,[4] and Czech, for example, we find nimble monosyllables. These *utterance modifiers*— whose function is distinct from that of the suspensive words mentioned above—implicate the hearer as an active participant in the dialogue.

The Psychosocial Speaker

How can we conceptualize the dialogic species in such a way that the science of linguistics may make some real contribution to the humanities? The study of speech, as has become increasingly clear in this last quarter of the twentieth century, is the study of mankind defined by our use of speech. Enunciative and pragmatic theories, while they do consider speech activity, have not until now given sufficient consideration to its social, cultural and historical dimension. Will recent innovations beyond structuralism, such as that of the study of speech acts, lead to a theory of personality? While it is true that linguistics must remain attentive to psychology (in addition to its ongoing and fundamental interest in sociological research), it cannot endlessly expand a domain which is already vast enough, if we intend of explore it fully, without its being subject to continual enlargement. The human subject must indeed remain the center of attention, but as a speaking subject, not as a pure subjectivity who happens to speak. We propose then to try to conceptualize a *psychosocial speaker.*

The notion of psychosocial used here has nothing to do with the assumptions of the old *Völkerpsychologie,* which was concerned with the mentality of peoples as reflected in their languages. We wish only to emphasize that, in discourse situations, interlocutors build a relation in which all the components of their psychology and their social nature are engaged, the situation itself permitting the expression of these components. "Speaker" is to be understood here in the sense of speaker + hearer, and not that of "speaker-hearer," as if these were two interchangeable entities. It is time we gave up the comforting myth of the latter formula. In psycholinguistics, the nonconvertible relation between mental processes of encoding and decoding is now being recognized; and sociolinguistics is revealing the differences in status between speaker and hearer at various points in the dialogue, differences which transcend or redefine social distinctions.

These advances should now be taken into account. The psychosocial speaker is neither an ideal nor a mythical permutation between a speaker and a hearer with equal abilities and virtues. We must resist the temptation to short-sightedness which makes us forget that the child acquiring language begins necessarily as a listener. Moreover, this role also remains essential for the adult. All hearers know more speech registers than they use, and, "bilingual" at least, they understand, in addition to their familial or local speech, the norm spoken by the dominant classes, whether taught in school (in written cultures), or learned by ethnic minorities when the (national or official) language is foreign to them. Saussure's *langue* is perhaps nothing other than this norm. In any case, the concept of the psychosocial speaker recognizes the asymmetry of speaker and hearer, without however suggesting that the linguistics of one should dominate that of the other.

It is important to emphasize that the notion of the psychosocial speaker does not result in a weakening of linguistics with respect to psychology or sociology. On the contrary, it is because neither of these disciplines is capable of furnishing specifically linguistic propositions, or of providing linguistics with the operational modes needed within its specific domain, that the recognition of the psychosocial nature of the speaker retains its primary focus upon this *speaker*. The same may be said of the biological encoding of speech aptitude as part of the genetic code. Biology, although directly implicated here, is no more able than the humanities to provide a foundation for purely linguistic assertions about speech. Thus the autonomy of linguistics, like that of any science, is the subject of a curious epistemological debate: while the object of study is almost never entirely accessible to the linguist, the other sciences legitimately implicated in a thorough investigation of this object are not able to provide a foundation appropriate to what linguistics itself may have to say.

The psychosocial speaker is involved in all sorts of situational language use. This is why logico-semantic distinctions are not always useful for defining the speaker in a discursive and textual perspective. What we find, depending on the circumstances, is both the articulating speaker and the acting interlocutor; when we are not speaking, we are both the interlocutor to whom words are addressed and the patient of speech acts,[5] or, to continue the categorizations, the audience addressed by a narrator. On the other hand, the plurilinguism of speech in acts, to use Bakhtine's terms,[6] is essential: the counterpoint of uttered words and reported speech, the interlacing of direct and indirect discourse. In many languages that encode this plurality, a special marker is used to indicate reported speech for which *ego* does not assume the responsibility. The so-called free indirect style merits a detailed study in terms of its relations with both direct and indirect style; the same is true for specific cases like the German subjunctive of assignation and its French equivalent, the conditional of distance: *Un type révolutionnaire d'ordinateur serait bientôt lancé sur le marché* ("A revolutionary type of computer would (= will *reportedly*) soon be launched on the market").

Once we have established the concept of the psychosocial speaker, the socio-operative model of linguistics proposed here may be characterized as the reflection of the *dialectic of constraint and freedom* linking language and speaker. The table below presents the main components of this model:

190

Toward a Theory of Communication

I. Domains of constraint

1. Language system
   - phonology
   - morphology   ⎫ operations for
   - syntax   ⎬ producing and
   - organization of the lexicon ⎭ interpreting meaning
2. Circumstances of dialogue

3. Biological factors
   (token: biolectal
   indices (see Chapter 11)

4. Status and linguistic imagery
   (token: symbo-, socio-,
   polito-lectal indices (see
   Chapter 11)

II. Domains of initiative

1. Construction of the language system
   a) by a collectivity of speakers, unconscious agent of long-term change
   b) by groups of speakers forming identifiable societies: genesis of creoles, creation of special languages
   c) by individual speakers through conscious acts: creation of neologisms, poetic activity, planned intervention in languages
2. Involvement in shaping situations
   a) variation (see Chapter 11)
   b) use of speech as an instrument of power (see Chapter 8)

The concept of socio-operativity implies that we cannot limit our focus either to the speaker's operations in discourse, or to the social aspect represented both by the inherited language system and by the ever-changing circumstances of dialogue. These are inseparable givens. It is the speaker who constitutes the measure of the relation between them, and of the degrees of constraint and initiative. Of course, these two domains (distinguished here for facility of presentation) constantly interact in the reality of discourse. We never have pure liberty or pure constraint, but rather a reciprocal balancing.

Domains of Constraint. Grammar may be defined as what is obligatory. If there is choice within paradigms, as there is with cases (accusative, genitive, etc.) in inflectional languages, this choice is selected from a set of possible options according to the speaker's intention. Thus

191

each choice is surrounded by impossibilities. In those languages which require that a designated object be assigned to a class (see chapter 3), the speaker does not have the option of not matching noun and classifier; nor can he decide that verb and noun need not agree in those languages in which this agreement is the rule. Such rules are often quite complex to the outside observer. Thus, in Hungarian, conjugations vary according to whether the verb agrees with the number and person of the subject (subjective conjugation, without a definite complement), or with these two parameters *and* with a definite complement (objective conjugation). Further, there is a special form when the subject is in the first person singular and the complement in the second person; finally, if the subject is not in the first person, a complement in the second person is not marked (the verb form is again in the subjective conjugation). Speaking Magyar, for a nonnative, is like navigating between icebergs—assuming that the speaker has indeed learned how to avoid them.

Thus the speaker faces a set of requirements, defining features of the grammar. Of course, grammatical constraints like agreement often consist of redundancies which, while they force the speaker to give more information than would be "logically" necessary, are not entirely inoperative (besides, in others cases the speaker is forced to give less information than may be needed). Redundancy is a kind of breathing condition in discourse, if not an agent of cohesive reinforcement. But the effort of acquisition is arguably linked to the degree of complexity of the grammar, vague as this notion may be.[7] Even the lexicon is a zone of constraint, not to mention the phonological structure which, beyond considerable individual and collective variation (see chapter 11), forces all speakers to analyze the sounds of words into phonemes, whose number and possible relations constitute an obligatory minimum.

Of course, individuals are "free" to formulate their ideas as they please. Still, through a *conventional violence* specific to languages, a speaker may not assign other meanings, or another phonological structure, to an existing word. Images, analogies among designated objects, and formal confusions and contaminations result in the construction of innumerable fields within the lexicon. Speakers confronted with this material can only, through a lifetime of usage, become themselves the unconscious agents of the changes that affect them. Some tendencies are linked to degree of usage. Certain words are more frequent than others, and the number of their contextual meanings is therefore higher.

The speaker is also constrained by a type of fossilization that characteristically results from extensive use: idiomaticity. We must learn and remember more or less demotivated forms. Spontaneous analysis is inapplicable to a French expression like *casser sa pipe* ("break one's pipe," i.e., "die," equivalent to English *kick the bucket*), the meaning of which is not the sum of the meanings of its parts; or to a Yoruba formation like *kpā-rí* ("cut-head," i.e., "finish"). Of course, not all idiomatic expressions are equally opaque. In French, *passer l'éponge* ("to pass the sponge," i.e., "to erase or forget"), *jeter de la poudre aux yeux* ("to throw dust in the eyes") are interpretable to those who are not familiar with the formations. But the form is not modifiable; the speaker cannot alter it to an individual case. The same is true of the figurative phenomenon that explains why *va voir à côté si j'y suis!* ("go next door and see if I'm there!"), for example, is not an order to be executed to the letter, but a way to get rid of someone by giving that person an absurd task. In Japanese we find the parallel *ototoi koi*, word-for-word "come day-before-yesterday!", which places this absurdity in the dimension of time instead of space. The idiomatic property of these expressions is confirmed by the questionable result when various syntactic operations are applied: French speakers are quite divided on the acceptability of utterances such as *on coupera, s'il le faut, la poire en deux* ("we'll cut, if necessary, the pear in half," cf. *couper la poire en deux*, "reach a compromise"). While this insertion is accepted by many, passivization is questionable in *la hache de guerre sera difficilement enterrée* ("the hatchet will be buried with difficulty"); even worse, it seems (except in a contrastive or ironic context), is the focus construction *c'est dans le plat qu'il a mis les pieds* ("it's in the plate that he put his feet," cf. *mettre les pieds dans le plat*, "to make a gaffe"); similarly, at least in the north of France, topicalization is unacceptable in *des vessies, il ne faut pas les prendre pour des lanternes* ("bladders, they must not be taken for lanterns," cf. *prendre des vessies pour des lanternes*, "believe something better than it is"). When experience and perception are integrated into linguistic categories, arbitrariness and distortion are the result. For languages, which produce meaning through forms, allow the latter to evolve more rapidly than the former.

Thus speakers have no recourse against the externality of the language system. We must simply learn it. The domain I.1 of table 10.1, the only "strictly linguistic" domain according to a minimalist structuralist conception, is beyond the user's control, at least in a synchronic sense. The "socio" component of socio-operativity is found in the principle as well as in the goal: the language system, a defining convention of every human society, preexists any speaker who may use it; further, it is in the social environment of dialogal activity that this system is put into use, and this use, in the dialectic history of the language, modifies it. Thus operativity is manifested, but with certain conditions: rules for combining phonemes, arranged in paradigms that the speaker has learned in infancy; compounding, derivation, and, in some languages, rules of formal word variation, or irregularities of alternation (cf. the French verb *aller* ("to go") has four stems: *v-*, *all-*, *aill-*, and *ir-*); rules for constructing utterances; and relations between utterances linked through conversion procedures.

Domains of Initiative. Despite all these constraints, the speaker has considerable freedom of initiative. This may be seen in the many areas of apparent rigidity in which speakers can play with the very restrictions imposed by existing forms. Thus, one may or may not accept the credit or the responsibility for what one is saying. In many languages (Turkish, Bulgarian, Quechua of Peru-Bolivia, Kwakiutl of British Columbia, Oksapmin of New Guinea), we find an alternation of affixes or verbal forms, depending upon whether the speaker wishes to take responsibility for the information or the narration being delivered, or whether the source is a direct participant or a simple witness. Even a category as integral to verbal inflection as is aspect in the Slavic languages remains a flexible instrument with a range of usage so wide (depending upon the choice of expression in oral or written discourse), that it cannot always be predicted, or strictly coded. Examination of texts and attention to dialogues reveal the flexible use of functional markers themselves. We would normally expect these integral components of morphosyntax to be automatic; but the occurrence of *ko* in Burmese, and especially of *râ* in Persian (both indices of an "object complement" corresponding to the role of a definite patient), depends in large part on the choice of the speaker. The same is true for *a* in Spanish, the marker of what is called (in a strange and contradictory formulation) a "prepositional direct object." The grammar explanations of language handbooks would be less torturous, and the confusion of students could perhaps be reduced, if it were simply stated that the speaker may choose between the maximum (presence of *a*) and the minimum (absence of *a*) of singularization of patient and efficiency of verb.[8] The decision may or may not crucially affect meaning: for example, in the same newspaper article, we find *defender la sociedad* and *defender a la sociedad* ("defend society").

But furthermore, if we wish to relativize the overly rigid formulation of Saussure's opposition between historical evolution of languages and synchronically observable states, the trace of the human speaker is everywhere clearly evident. Not of course as the conscious inventor of a freely-chosen system; but at least as the transitory and more or less willing agent in the successive stages of evolution carried out through speech activity. Over time, these innovations are woven into the morphological fabric.

Four examples will suffice to illustrate the point. The first is that of quantifiers, both universal (ex. *all*) and existential (ex. *someone*). In 76 percent of languages, quantifiers are derived from interrogatives,[9] i.e., from question markers used in discourse. The second example is that of *anthropological case-marking (anthropologie casuelle):* we propose this label for the more or less universal (but variable) designation of spatial and temporal relations using names of parts of the human body —the ever-present body of the psychosocial speaker talking about the world around us, a world of which we ourselves constitute the measure (see chapter 3). The *axiological scale of beings in language* constitutes the third example: this is the term used for the underlying representation of articles such as the series of eight found in Kawi, an ancient language of Java. These eight articles were used to determine nouns divided into eight classes. The summit of the hierarchy, as we might expect, is occupied by beings revered by the human speaker: gods, saints, heroes, kings; and the lower degrees by the nonhuman, notably by the names of inanimate objects.

The last example is that of coding operations through which speakers record their speech activity in the structure of the language itself. Certain languages of New Guinea[10] and California, in addition to English, use an auxiliary "do" to emphasize the reality (affirmation) or the irreality (negation) of an assertion, which is presented as dependant upon doing or nondoing. The revelation of such coding operations allows us to understand other troubling phenomena. Thus, in Nahuatl (Mexico), the word *tla* is used to mark both hypothesis and its apparent contradiction, i.e., strong assertion. In fact, it appears that in both cases the speaker adopts the point of view of the listener—in whom the speaker senses a potential objection—and either recognizes this resistance (hypothesis) or tries to reduce it (strong assertion).[11]

Many languages (Russian, Georgian, Nahuatl, Chamorro of Guam, Ainou of Japan, Chukchee of the USSR, Mojave of Baja California, etc.) possess structures which are homologous between two or more of the following contents: passive, reflexive, reciprocal, plural, potential, and honorific address. If we consider the concrete enunciative operations involved, this correspondence is not so surprising: using passive to avoid mentioning an exterior agent as direct cause of an event is an operation comparable to the polite suppression (use of honorific address) of that agent's singularity (use of plural). Similarly, the absence of an explicit agent suggests spontaneity, and thus propensity of occurrence (potential) of the action that the patient exercises either reflexively, or in reciprocal exchange.[12]

Finally, we may refer to the *egophoric system*, the vast construction characteristic of languages by virtue of which adverbs of place and time, demonstratives, articles (if present), and terms of reference to another part of the text[13] are all organized around a center of designation constituted by the dialogue partners, indissolubly united in reciprocal relation by virtue of which each calls himself "I" and the other "you." A science of *ecolinguistics* might eventually study the manner in which culturalized versions of "natural" frames of reference are integrated into languages. These frames could include, for example, compass points, geographical particularities, human habitations, and cosmic elements.

The operations of the human subject are even more clearly recorded in the syntax. A very instructive example is that of semi-accusative / semi-ergative idioms, which use two of the principal types of transitive structures attested in languages. In the so-called accusative system, an utterance with two participants marks only the complement, i.e., the patient. In the so-called ergative system, on the other hand, the agent is marked. These markers (prepositions, postpositions, case markings, or a combination of these) have an informational foundation: basically, *the least expected element is marked* in order to draw attention to it; thus the most expected information is left unmarked. Meanwhile, if we accept that the *ego,* the source of all discourse,[14] spontaneously places itself at the summit of the hierarchy of expression (and power), it is quite natural that the probability of being an *agent* (definite) and not a *patient* is very strong for "I" (*ego*), less so for "you;" and that this probability decreases regularly through various third-person arguments and nonhuman animates to inanimate objects.

Consequently, in a language with mixed syntax, we might expect that *ego* be treated accusatively, that is not marked when agent and marked when patient. After *ego,* we find an *oscillation of the personality axis:* "you" may be placed before or after the axis, i.e., treated accusatively or not; so may even human third-person arguments, or those with stronger affinities with *ego.* In any case, inanimate objects and most animals are, in general, treated ergatively, i.e., marked when agent and not marked when patient. The transhistorical speaker, whose continuous presence determines syntax, has "decided" that it is normal for the latter group to be patients rather than initiators of actions, this latter being a human prerogative. Such is the case in many languages of North America and Australia.

In other languages we observe, if not priority of *ego,* an affinity at least of the person category with that of agent, whose status is perceived as a human privilege. In French compound verb forms, the auxiliary (inflected according to person) normally agrees with the agent, while the participle agrees with the patient, as if it were an ergative verb. Thus we find *je l'ai prise* ("I took her") or *je t'ai prise* ("I took you") with crossed agreement between *je* and *ai* and between *l'* or *t'* and feminine agreement in *prise.* The strings *tu as été prise par moi* ("you were taken by me") or *elle a été prise par moi* ("she was taken by me"), in which both auxiliary and participle agree with the subject, are conceivable only as utterances focused upon the patient taken as theme. Other Indo-European languages, such as Marvari (India), display similar phenomena.

In all these cases, it is clear the the speaker's choices have, in fact, resulted in the creation of constraints; it may then seem paradoxical to assign these constraints to the domain of initiative. But languages are in a continual state of transformation; consequently, motivated choices become fossilized forms until they are remotivated. Of course, the treatment of agents in semi-ergative languages is a syntactic phenomenon, and therefore a constraint. But this treatment bears the mark of discourse activity through which the dialogic species, marking its own presence, claims preeminence in the universe. It is this aspect which defines the phenomenon as an initiative. The same may be said concerning word order phenomena which establish priority relations among human participants. In many Australian and American languages (Algonquin, Navaho, etc.), word order is the same as in the French utterance *je le bats* (I-him-beat, i.e., "I beat him"). However, the same order may not be followed in the equivalent of *il me bat* (he-me-beats, i.e., "He beats me"), because then *ego,* who occupies the summit of the speech hierarchy, is not at the head of the sentence. Thus the word order of the former utterance must be preserved, with the addition of a passive or inversive marker indicating that "I" is now patient. Here, the parallelism of the three perspectives (see chapter 9) becomes quite clear: the highest actor in the hierarchy, necessarily chosen as theme (perspective 3), corresponds to the subject (perspective 1), whether this theme is agent or patient (perspective 2).

Finally, the speaker's initiative appears as a motivation for language evolution. This may take place over long periods, as with idioms in which morphology has been transformed by a rapid rate of speech: a striking case is that of Palauan (Micronesia), in which displacement of accents linked to speech rate have brought about a veritable typological mutation.[15]

Evolution may also take place over shorter periods (through a catastrophic change, in Thom's sense[16]). This is the case in Israeli Hebrew, which has created a verb of possession by taking a construction based on "be" and, selecting a human possessor, making it a structure based on "have." Thus, from the classical (Biblical) Hebrew *lo haya l-i ha-kesef ha-darūš,* word-for-word "negation was to-me the-money the-needed," we progress to *lo haya li 'et ha-kesef ha-darūš.*[17] This odd structure contains the complement marker *'et,* normally used after a transitive verb and before the noun referring to the patient. We must then assume that *lo-haya-li* is treated as a true transitive verb "have", although, since form evolves more slowly than meaning, the structure is still that of the verb "be" (*haya* = "was") with a benefactive personal complement (*li* = "to me"). But the use of *'et* clearly shows that reanalysis has taken place, as confirmed by a further possibility: preposing of *ani* ("me") before this utterance, which makes it a structure with the verb "have," just like the English equivalent *I didn't have the necessary money.* The possessive "have" construction (as opposed to the one based on "be") takes as its point of reference not the possessed object, but the possessor, which is most often human.

Wherever documentation is available or facts can be reconstructed with reasonable certainty, the study of the historical evolution of languages reveals a *morphosemantactic cycle:* a gradual progression from semantics to syntax, then from syntax to morphology and phonology; at the end of this path begins a slow movement in the opposite direction, closing the cycle as it begins anew. The evolution of pidgins into creoles (see chapter 2) provides a remarkable example of a segment of each branch of this cycle.

Here again, the facts bear witness to the speaker's "humanization" of structures. On the other hand, the speaker cannot be assumed to have absolute power. Since Freudian psychoanalysis has discovered in subconscious drives a means to remove the "I" from the center of analysis, and sociogenetic research has dissolved the integrality of "I" in the dynamics of the society, the traditional egocentric analysis based on a transcendental subject has become largely obsolete. The psychosocial speaker is "dialogal" by nature, even when the discourse situation is not interlocutory.

Speech Stratagems: Interruption, Double-Entendre, Paraphrastic Connivance, Connotative Violations. If we look beyond the most structured parts of language, the psychosocial speaker's initiative appears even greater. We are free to vary registers, adopting different styles and vocabularies for making a public speech, declaring our undying love, or asking our dinner partner to pass the salt. Moreover, the speaker's presence is continually manifested through "violations" of the linear continuity of discourse, in the form of elements that contradict the canonical structures of the examples found in grammar books: let us call them *word sequence shatterers*. These may intervene between preposition and object, as in the French examples *sur, mettons, tel ou tel plan,* ("on, let's say, some level or other") and *sans, bien sûr, intervenir,* ("without, of course, intervening"). They may also separate verb and complement, as in *il avait peut-être soif,* ("he was perhaps thirsty"); or emphasize, through extraction and repetition, a preceding element, as in *il a peur, entends-tu, peur!* ("he was afraid, do you hear, afraid!") or *ils ont disparu, je dis bien, disparu* ("they've disappeared, I say, disappeared").

Shatterers play an essential role; for they attenuate the effects of one of the principal obstacles to discourse activity, namely the *unavoidable simultaneity of speech transmission and discourse planning* in sentences and groups of sentences. Shatterers facilitate this planning as part of a strategy to circumvent both the contiguity of words in discourse, and the pressure of time, which continuously aligns them. A sentence or text has not always been completely formulated at the moment the speaker prepares to utter it. Through the mistakes, false starts, or suggestions of parallelism in what has just been said, speech is constructed, the representation is refined, the plan is clarified as the discourse progresses. "As we speak, the ideas come," wrote von Kleist,[18] and the formula is applicable to many (although not all) instances. The same author continues, "I notice, to my great surprise, that at the end of the sentence concepts appear in perfect clarity. . . . I punctuate my discourse with inarticulate sounds, I extend conjunctions, I sometimes insert redundant appositions, and I use many other artifices to gain the time necessary to the formulation of my idea."

Thus, shatterers are one of the rare means, not of abolishing time (which would be impossible), but of shaping it into manageable intervals. They do not merely permit the utterance to reflect the subjectivity of the speaker, who establishes distance with respect to what is being said. Interruptors also allow us a brief respite from time, a respite that allows us to listen to ourselves. For we must listen to ourselves as we speak, to insure that what we are going to say corresponds to what we want to say. Prince Henri's remark in W. Gombrowicz's *Marriages* is not so absurd as it may seem: "I don't know what to say, but when I've said it, I'll know." Moreover, shatterers provide the time necessary to apply morphosyntactic rules, an area in which hesitations may persist even in the adult speaker. But obviously, shatterers are not sufficient to deter all mistakes; in spite of their assistance, speakers build new grammars and contribute to the evolution of languages by producing incorrect but comprehensible sentences.

Ambiguity, a phenomenon inherent to languages, is yet another aspect of the speaker's initiative. There are lexical ambiguities linked to the disproportion between the lexical inventory of languages and the unlimited mass of objects in the world. In syntax, we may find not only structural homonymy, but actual referential ambiguities. In *la maison de Socrate* ("the house of Socrates"), Socrates may be the possessor, but also the builder, or someone who mentions the house in his discourse, or even someone whose name is associated with it. In *la crainte de l'ennemi* ("the fear of the enemy"), the enemy may fear or be feared. In *le marchand de drap anglais* ("the English cloth merchant"), either the merchant or the cloth may be English. Ambiguity is everywhere, and speakers, whatever their knowledge of the language or their ability to distance themselves, play with these possibilities: metalinguistic jokes exist in all languages and all styles of speech.

By studying only the "linguistics of *langue*," and ignoring that of *parole*, Saussure *separated* two perspectives that need only to be *distinguished*; further, his recognition of only those values found within the language system provided lasting support for the thesis of univocity, used by the structuralists as a pretext for expelling ambiguity from the field of knowledge and for distrusting *meaning* as it is constructed within speech activity. If it is this reality that we wish to study, the structures of ambiguous sentences and words can no longer be considered homonymic accidents, but must be seen as manifestations of a fundamental polysemy (homonymy being reserved for cases of historical evolutions which have resulted in the confusion of once-distinct signifiers, or for cases of divergence between signifieds whose common semes may only be discovered through etymological research).

Accidental homonymy on the one hand; analyzable structuring of polysemy on the other—the two hypotheses are irreconcilable. Before Saussure, the grammar inherited from the classical age did not separate the effects of discourse interpretation from the language code itself. This is attested by the integration of the catalogue of tropes,[19] and by the very name *rhetoric* being used for the study of language (and, at one time, for the highest class of the *lycée*). Socio-operative linguistics, like certain contemporary tendencies, aims at rediscovering the unity of language and speech, and sees in the psychosocial speaker the necessary link between the two. This goal places it at a point of intersection with a quite different critical aim: "Literature and speech are rediscovering each other . . . at least at the level of the writer, whose action may more and more be defined as a critique of speech." This comment by Barthes follows a passage in which he notes that rhetoric, after a reign of nearly two hundred years, had been overthrown by the end of the nineteenth century.[20]

The psychosocial speaker can encode ambiguity, whether intentional or not; meanwhile, as hearers, we try to understand—like the translator, who must make choices. The task is far from easy. Is "successful communication" (defined as the exchange of words stripped of all ambiguity) the norm, or rather a glimpse of light against a background of continuous misunderstanding? For that matter, misunderstanding exists in what is not said as much as in what, having been said, may have more than one meaning. It is time we gave up the notion (inherited from narrow versions of structuralism, and still strongly held in some circles) that a message must say all, or be dismissed as incomplete. Messages may be transferred between contexts, and these peregrinations affect their meaning; they refer to and clarify each other, often in unexpected ways and despite distance in time, space and culture. In various contexts, identical messages may have variable or even contradictory meanings. In discourse, as well as in literature, intertextuality reveals hidden meanings, relating sentences to each other, providing at a given point what is needed to account for the ambiguities of an ellipse situated well before or after that point. These shadowy texts are encoded and deciphered by the psychosocial speaker: a painstaking cryptographer, and a manipulator of intentional ambiguity quite apart from that imposed by languages or dictated by the subconscious.

However, if we focus our attention on ambiguity, we may forget the role of the situation in the establishment of univocal meaning. "The ability to understand simultaneously the different meanings of a given word . . . and, a fortiori, the ability to manipulate them . . . is a good measure of the usually learned ability to rise above a situation."[21] We may also too often forget that different intonational contours correspond quite frequently to the distinct syntactic structures of an "identical" utterance, which becomes ambiguous only in written form. Thus, the sentence *c'est le français qu'il parle* ("It's (the) French that he speaks") may, depending upon intonation, have two quite different meanings: either "that's the type (or style) of French that he speaks," or "what he speaks is French, and not English, Russian, etc." Finally, and above all, the hearer's principal job (although complicated by the ambiguities of speech and its use) is to deconstruct the constructed meaning that is received. If we are generally successful, it is because ambiguity, while an obligatory component of speech, does not rule alone.

Languages also have the power to confer the same meaning upon formally different utterances: for a given meaning, one may formulate several utterances which are paraphrases of each other and which thus constitute a single family. The existence of different ways of saying the same thing results from a dual phenomenon: the abundance of lexical synonyms (not excluding homonyms, for languages are historical and thus largely aleatory organisms), and that of different but semantically homologous syntactic structures. In fact, the variety of classes of words and functions allows different linguistic treatment for similar situations.

To know a language is, among other things, to be able to construct and identify formally diverse sentences to which we can attribute the same, or a very similar, meaning. The paraphrastic activity of the speaker is thus inherent to any theory of speech. The possibility of paraphrases as a fundamental feature of linguistic activity may be observed in the most common types of dialogue, for example in the form of question / response: *Est-ce qu'il est bien 9 h 50?* / *Oui, il est dix heures moins dix* ("Is it really 9:50? / Yes, it's ten to ten"); or *Est-il célibataire?* / *Oui, il n'est pas marié* ("Is he single? / Yes, he's not married"). The speaker's voluntary exploitation of paraphrase strategies opens a domain of relative freedom. This is in fact one of the issues for computer research in the near and distant future.

Ambiguity is one of those phenomena whose linguistic encoding allows for some choice on the speaker's part. Another phenomenon possessing this property is reference, through an anaphoric pronoun, to an element from the previous context, whether referring to the formal element itself or the extra-linguistic reality to which it corresponds (the linguistic problem of coreference criteria). A third phenomenon of this type is ellipsis. The success of computers as talking machines will depend in large part upon their capacity to integrate these phenomena, as well as that of paraphrase, i.e., to treat these nuclear properties of languages in a natural way. For the moment, considering recent disappointing results with translating machines, it seems that technology faces a quadruple challenge.

Connotation and *plural readings* are related to ambiguity and misunderstanding. While denoting meaning through words and their arrangement in sentences of text, speakers may unknowingly connote, i.e., transmit a parallel series of meanings about themselves, their history, their fantasies, and their social position. Only careful analysis can isolate the inherent ideology from everyday words; even so "simple" an expression as *mère de famille* ("housewife / mother") has aroused the ire of more than one feminist. But speakers may also deliberately decide to use connotation and to enrich the counterpoint of their speech. A sentence like *c'est un socialiste* ("he's a socialist") has different connotations depending upon one's political tendencies. The speaker's initiative may even, through extension, reach the lexicon: connotations, arising from the contingency of situations, may be integrated into the base meaning, and become solidified in denotations. This is one way in which the lexicon may evolve. Thus the French word *bureau* ("desk"), while still designating the same object, has also come to be applied to various things evoked by this object, such as the room in which it is found, or the people grouped around it for administrative work. The expression *tel qu'en lui-même* ("just as in himself") was taken from Mallarmé's famous verse about Poe finally being transformed into himself through the eternity of death; in very literary French, this expression is applied to a person whose personality appears to be immutable.

The choice of individuals or of anonymous groups is also apparent in *euphemistic reduction*, by virtue of which various resources of the language serve to repress meanings and the images associated with them by clothing them in the propitious magic of vague labels. In contemporary French we often hear *longue et pénible maladie* ("long and painful illness") instead of *cancer; demandeur d'emploi* ("seeker of work") instead of *chômeur* ("unemployed"); *troisième âge* ("third age") for *vieillesse* ("old age"); *pays en voie de développement* ("developing country") for *pays sous-développé* ("underdeveloped country"); and *nonvoyant* ("nonseeing") for *aveugle* ("blind").[22]

Similarly, in military parlance, *repli* ("withdrawal") or *redéploiement* ("redeployment") have long replaced *fuite* ("retreat") or *déroute* ("rout"). The word *mort* ("death") has always been supplanted by shadowy evocations like *départ* ("departure") and *disparition* ("disappearance"). The weasel, an animal feared in rural areas of France, was long ago assigned the name *belette,* a diminutive of *belle* ("beautiful"); the other Romance languages have similar names for this creature. In other cultures, harmful powers are similarly exorcised by replacing the taboo words with decorative substitutes through which we see the speaker's penchant for conciliatory opposites: classical Arabic contains a long list of such words, including *salīm* ("healthy") *'aqūq* ("pregnant mare") and *hāfil,* ("camel with swollen teats") to designate, respectively, a man bitten by a snake, a mare that has become sterile, and a camel whose teats are empty.[23]

We find many examples of an existing word which, on the initiative of speakers, begins to be used to designate a foreign object introduced through contact with another culture, while a new term, or the adjunction of a qualification to the existing one, is chosen to replace the name of the indigenous object. Thus the speaker gives a new meaning to an unmarked term (that is, frequent by virtue of the cultural frequency of the object designated). First, the term becomes marked; but later, the frequency of the new designated object assigns it unmarked status (as opposed to the one chosen to apply to the object relegated to the background). We find numerous illustrations of this *inversion of markers.* In Huastec, a Mayan language of northern Mexico,[24] the unmarked term *bičim* ("stag") began to be used to designate the horse, an animal unknown in the region until its introduction by the Spanish. Today, a marked term is used to designate the stag: *ic'a:mal,* literally "having horns." Comparable phenomena are attested in Navaho (Arizona), Kiowa (Oklahoma), Eskimo, and, at earlier periods, in many European languages.

Individual Invention, Poetic Language

Glossolalia, the invention of language in a state of delirium, may be situated on the level of the individual, beyond any possibility of consensus (see chapter 5). This phenomenon (commonly called the "gift of tongues") is presumably distinct from *xenoglossia,* the "miraculous" reinvention of existing languages. But the Miracle of Pentecost has given rise to at least two other interpretations:[25] Aramaic, the language of the Apostles, was understood by all the faithful, despite the diversity of the nations they represented; or else, the Apostles spoke a sort of universal language, which was transparent to all. Yet in these cases of xenoglossia, the inspiration is similar to the motives behind glossolalia.

Both reflect the dream of the original language of Adam, and the nostalgia for a lost Eden.

Thus, although glossolalia are individual and momentarily pathological phenomena, they are clear reminders of one of the oldest of human dreams: the destruction of the walls of language and the attainment of a longed-for domain of transcendence. This dream is a mere extension of the *expressive drive* which seeks diverse outlets. The soliloquies of the schizophrenic, the most uncontrolllable speculations, the most lyrical effusions, belong to the realm of expression alongside the most rational discourse or the most easily analyzable texts. The psychosocial speaker may not only hesitate, insert shatterers, start again, break off, and pause; the speaker *may also violate syntax, at least on certain points, as long as this violation does not interfere with meaning.*

Another path lies open to the desire of the speaker seeking to escape the prison of linearity of sign and utterance. The creations of this desire, literary inventions of gifted individuals, are no more sanctioned by the linguistic community than are glossolalia. We refer here to what Lewis Carroll called "portmanteau words"[26] (Fr. *mots-valises* or *mots sauvages*).[27] These are mainly the inventions of writers playfully subverting the continuity of sounds by overlapping or condensing two words with one or more syllables in common: some of the French examples below are attributed to Morand (1–12), Laforgue (13–14), Audiberti (15), Montherlant (16), Rimbaud (17), and Rostand (18).

1. *bourreaucratie*   (*bourreau,* "torturer / executioner" + *bureaucratie,* "bureaucracy")

2. *canaillarchie*   (*canaille,* "rabble" + *anarchie,* "anarchy")

3. *coiteration*   (*coit,* "coitus" + *iteration,* "repetition")

4. *délivicieuse*   (*delicieuse,* "delicious," fem. + *vicieuse,* "depraved." fem.)

5. *étudiamante*   (*étudiante,* "student," fem. + *amante,* "lover," fem.)

6. *hérésistance*   (*hérésie,* "heresy," + *résistance,* "resistance")

7. *mécontemporain* (*mécontent,* "unhappy," + *contemporain,* "contemporary")

8. *mélancomique* (*mélancolique*, "melancholy," + *co-mique*, "comical")

9. *mélomaniaque* (*mélomane*, "music lover," + *man-iaque*, "fanatical")

10. *prévoiricateur* (*prévoir*, "foresee," + *prévaricateur*, "prevaricator")

11. *romansonge* (*roman*, "novel," + *mensonge*, "lie")

12. *cosmopolisson* (*cosmopolite*, "cosmopolitan," + *polis-son*, "naughty")

13. *éléphantaisiste* (*éléphant*, "elephant," + *fantaisiste*, "whimsical")

14. *ennuiversel* (*ennui*, "boredom," + *universel*, "universal")

15. *nauséabondance* (*nauséabond*, "nauseating," + *abond-ance*, "abundance")

16. *nostalgérie* (*nostalgie*, "nostalgia/homesickness," + *Algérie*, "Algeria")

17. *patrouillotisme* (*patriotisme*, "patriotism," + *trouille*, "funk")

18. *ridicoculiser* (*ridiculiser*, "ridicule," + *cocu*, "cuck-old")

In German we find the example of *Hakenkreuzotter*, from *Haken-kreuz*, "swastika," + *Kreuzotter*, "viper." All these examples illustrate the richness of personal and ideological connotations invested in these whimsical words, saturating them with information and making them equivalent to complete utterances. Sometimes the wordplay depends on written forms with variously subversive content: the French *consti-passion*, pronounced exactly like *constipation*, contains *passion*. In similar fashion, we find

1. *ensaignement* (like *enseignement*, "teaching;" with *saigner*, "bleed")

2. *sangsuel* (like *sensuel*, "sensual;" with *sangsue*, "leech")

3. *effervessence* (like *effervescence*, "effervescence;" with *essence*, "gasoline")

4. *fainéhantise*   (like *fainéantise,* "laziness;" with *han-tise,* "obsessive fear")

5. *Alb'atroce*   (like *albatros,* "albatross;" with *Albion,* "Britain," and *atroce,* "horrible")

6. *seinphonie*   (like *symphonie,* "symphony;" with *sein,* "breast")

But even the most bizarre portmanteau-words cannot violate the system indiscriminately: the violations follow a coded pattern. At least one of the constituents must obey the law of continuity, and all portmanteau-words necessarily belong to one of the word classes recognized by the language.

In all cultures, we find games involving inversion of syllables (or of tones or accents), insertion of artificial segments, repetitions, recurrences, and many other playful manipulations of the language. Speakers in Turkey, Sardinia and Greenland engage in oral contests, with the prize going to the most virtuosic player. All kinds of verbal whimsy, puns, neological initiatives for sheer amusement (and, no doubt, for the honor of being considered a wit), attest to the immensity of the field of invention claimed by individual speakers in the apparently fixed territory of linguistic convention.

Poetry is another fundamental activity of the dialogic species, and one which cannot be characterized by the banal intuition of divergence from linguistic constraints. It is true that poetic activity arises from the desire to dominate speech by subverting its laws. But it is also much more. One technique is the establishment of correspondences between sounds through rhyme, assonance, meter, etc., whereby meaning is diffused, rather than concentrated upon words. These parallelisms and couplings suggest a relation of meanings under that of the sounds. But parallelism, contrary to popular opinion, does not define poetry; and diverse cultures and languages possess other techniques. All share the construction of the poem's meaning through analogy of forms, beyond the mechanics of the associations imposed by the language between meaning and sound. In extreme cases, sound becomes an end in itself, and the most daring poetry follows the path outlined by Artaud: "All true speech is incomprehensible."

But this brings us to the threshold of alienation. Even if the speaker wishes to shatter the unity of the sign by deserting communicability in order to enter the tempting realm of pure soundplay, the tyranny of semantics may not be entirely eluded. Poetry is not music, despite the affinity between the two. In the compositions of Beriot, Penderecki, and Crumb, syllables or entire words of certain languages are inserted into the scores. These elements are chosen only for their properties as pure sound material, and associated as such with classical instruments and various novelties: rubbing bows over crystal glasses, percussion, gongs, etc. But music is not an abstract schema of communication. The psychosocial speaker is characterized by his resigned or active acceptance of the social authority, manifested first and most inexorably by semiotic convention.

It is troubling, however, to note that Saussure, one of the greatest theoreticians of this century, carried out research in the two opposite directions of social arbitrariness and its violation. The linguist, whose work established the theoretical solidarity of the *signifiant* and *signifié*, spent the last years of his life in the stubborn search for sound correspondences in Greek and Latin poetry. This strange research, known today as Anagrams (and including a study of paragrams), was begun well before his famous course in general linguistics. Saussure considered both works incomplete, since he was not satisfied that he had found what constituted a complete demonstration. Yet the Anagrams clearly establish the role of sound as an autonomous component of poetry, noting the required correspondences between vowels and consonants in Saturnian verse, which is characterized by binary repetitions and by buried anagrams of the names of nations. An entire paratext arises, completely independent of the constraints of linearity—the very constraints which Saussure would establish, for generations to come, as inescapable!

The Speaker and the "Functions" of Speech

For those who are content to characterize speech as a human faculty, the study of functions may seem to reduce this faculty to the status of a simple tool. But an analysis of the uses of speech, and of its advantages for the species, need not imply a purely instrumental conception. Questions of function are not without interest, as long as we consider these functions within a hierarchy and demonstrate the links between them.

It is easy enough to observe that speech serves communication: the signs of a given language are *common* to all users. Since the 1930s, the application of structuralism to diachronic evolution and synchronic instability in language has shown the heuristic and methodological advantage of the conception of speech (and of spoken languages) as instruments of communication.[28] But we must avoid overly reductionist views. Discourse interaction does not mean a simple transfer of information. Discourse, through which languages are realized, institutes an exchange commanding a hierarchy of information based on its importance, and goes far beyond the pure transmission of messages. Further, if messages do communicate, it is because they have something to communicate which is not the product of a simple extraction from the world or the event. Languages are models fashioned by social life and the articulation of thought, through which reflection may order the world. Experience is perceived as a whole, but arranged in a linear hierarchy in the discourse stream. This operation is, dialectically, both the trace of thought and a source of nourishment for it. As analytical methods, languages are also essential factors in the formation of the personality, for the individual from the moment of birth as well as for the species throughout its history.

Analytical thought has been developed through the need to divide an event into words which have meaning, and which can be articulated by the human speech organs and perceived by the ear; in other words, thought reflects the indissoluble link between sound and meaning in discourse behavior. The human species has used organs that segment material (and were originally oriented toward different vital functions, such as breathing and eating) for linguistic ends, continually refining them through a long period of evolution. Consequently, the linguistic representation of the universe, while perceived as a synthesis rather than a series of fragments, has been analyzed into isolated units, i.e., words. But the refinement of the speech organs, like that of all organs situated in the region of the cortex, is dialectically linked to the increasing adaptation of the species to the surrounding environment and thus to the formation of human persons: within a group context, speech is both a method and a product of thought in the broadest sense. While it was perhaps created for practical ends and for collective uses, speech perfected the species and was perfected by it. The capacity of speech to translate and even construct extraordinary edifices of thought (if not always of the emotions) is nonetheless quite amazing.

As a means of articulation, then, speech is the center of cognition, despite its obvious logical inadequacy and the fact that it integrates contradictory states of knowledge in rather chaotic fashion. Any object that cannot be named or integrated into a defining proposition of language cannot be grasped by rational knowledge and remains purely intuitive. Speech does not possess the mystical power attributed to it by the ancient belief in the word as demiurge—languages permit us to speak of nonexistent entities without causing them to exist; they also allow us to lie.

On the other hand, speech does have the power to reinvent the world by ordering it into linguistic categories. Above all, through discourse activity, speech confers the power of interaction. The psychosocial speaker, even when not implicating an interlocutor through interrogation or intimation, acts or is acted upon: for discourse consists of arguing, refuting, and trying to convince. In the service of those who wish to influence behavior, speech is quite simply an instrument of power. We often learn the language of others in order to do business with them; but our goal is just as frequently to acquire some political or religious power over them. Still, such use for domination is only an isolated case, and a kind of deviation from a quasi-ritualized interactional function,[29] a source of solidarity linking speakers in discourse despite accidental or induced misunderstanding. In this respect, dialogue is the condition necessary to social relations, both in its formal substance and in all the informal components surrounding it, including silence.

Because speech is the foundation of the social relation, speakers invest something of themselves in their use of language. Speech is thus a privileged means of expression. For languages reflect both cognitive processes and subconscious drives. Self-expression may in fact be therapeutic, which is why it is employed in psychoanalysis. Other means, from a simple glance to the fine arts, cannot suffice and are not interpreted with the same degree of consensus. It is nonetheless true that speech has frequently been criticized in literature (especially poetry) as inadequate, and infinitely incapable of expressing the most subtle of emotional states. Languages remain unable to give a faithful rendering of what are sometimes called "moods."

However, we may distinguish various levels of inadequacy. It is true that this level is high with respect to emotional expression; but the language of the sciences (in particular those known as exact sciences) is by necessity entirely adequate to its subject, which is always very precisely defined. Scientific discourse tends to eliminate connotations, or at least to minimize them (for they are never entirely absent[30]); it is adapted to measurable and experimental expression. The inadequacies of speech are thus not always so devastating. They increase in direct proportion to emotional content. But there is always some portion that may be expressed, and the importance of the rest cannot suffice to make us doubt tbe expressive function of speech.

In a related function, speech is a mirror of psychic and social imagination. At every level, it reflects the inclinations of speaking-desiring subjects. Lastly, speech fulfills another need which defines the human species: the need for play. Linguistic invention and poetic activity are the most highly developed manifestations of this characteristic. Of course, poetry is much more than an idle amusement. It responds to a profound spiritual craving. But for certain forms of poetic activity at least, the link between poetry and play remains an essential one. An entire chapter of Huizinga's *Homo ludens* (1938) illustrates this in the most varied of cultures, from Scandinavia to Oceania, from the nations of Islam to Japan. Human beings are animals who not only play, but practice play as an art.

In fact, we play by vocation and need, and play constitutes a purpose parallel to, and yet independent of, all other purposes. Alongside the reproductive instinct, the drive to eat, and the need for shelter, we find eroticism, the culinary arts, and the esthetics of architecture—not necessary to survival, but vital in their own way. Alongside the need for expression we find, from earliest infancy, the irrepressible desire to play with words. How could humanity fail to use this aptitude, which defines us in opposition to all other living beings? Reprimanding someone for "talking to say nothing" (*parler pour ne rien dire*) ignores the very real desire to speak for purposes other than saying something. Speech without content may be an end in itself, like a toy in the hands of a child. Not all writers have lamented this passion for words. On the contrary, from Rabelais to Georges Perec, that explorer of the universe of expression, many authors have relished its perils, and their zest continues to define new and unexpected itineraries.

All of these inclinations are linked by a single thread. These "functions," apparently so different, may be summarized by the fact that speech produces meaning. It is a model generating interpretable texts. Still, we must guard against the illusions of an eternal and universal logic of meaning. When such a system of logic is developed based on Western languages, it succeeds only in "discovering" the logical constructions of Western thought. If the search for meaning is to be fruitful for the humanities, it must combine a search for constants (the necessary foundation for a theory of speech) with a three-sided anthropological model: linguistic representations, which always vary with cultures; social practices expressed in language; and the real discourse which reflects the imaginary dicourse unique to every human society. The determination of meaning seeks to evaluate this interaction of constants and diversity.

211

The Determination of Meaning

Meaning is the avowed or concealed obsession of all linguistics, the perpetual challenge to those who profess to analyze language. While the most elementary experience so clearly reveals its banal reality, meaning remains the scourge of learned research. Linguistics cannot yet bridge the gap between ordinary intuition and rational knowledge. Various artifices have been implemented to elude meaning by adhering only to form—this was particularly true of American structuralism in the 1950s.[31] It was a futile ploy. "What have we not tried in order to avoid, ignore, or banish meaning? But whatever we do, this Medusa is always there at the center of language, fascinating all those who behold it."[32] It is not our intention to avert our eyes from this intense gaze. We must instead study the operations underlying one of the most troubling mysteries of speech: despite the fact that the language and its organizational laws are imposed upon us from our birth, we as psychosocial speakers may nevertheless say virtually everything we wish to say.

In order to produce and interpret meaning, the speaker carries out operations which are complex and very poorly understood. And while languages display considerable typological diversity (see chapter 3), the process of production-reception of meaning is universal. Of course, some of the operations through which meaning unfolds are linked to the subconscious and thus inaccessible to direct analysis. Moreover, the neurological traces of these operations are still unknown. But by adopting the hearer's point of view, we may propose a mechanism for the determination of meaning. Understanding the sentences of a text involves applying a succession of cyclic operations to an ordered series of components as shown in the table of zones and modalities of meaning (see chapter 9, figure 3).

These operations must be cyclical, since once the meaning provided by one of the components is established, the operation begins anew on the next component, addressing what the preceding operation left uninterpreted, and so on to the last component in the order given in the table. Thus, the operations applied to zone A of the meaning of a text treat successively the reconstructed referent, the signified of signs, the semantics of syntax, sequence, the narrow context, and finally the broad context. We recall that these operational cycles concern the zone of meaning corresponding to identifiable formal traces, the only type which certain structuralist schools accept as linguistic. What remains after the application of the last operation treating zone A must, in turn, be dealt with. For it is rare that the comprehension process depends solely on the components of zone A. Those of zone B are thus the next object of ordered interpretive operations. These operations, as shown in the table of zones of meaning, address in cyclical fashion cultural aptitude and presuppositions, punctual circumstances, degree of acquaintance between speakers, relative social status, and finally economical and political conditions.

It seems possible to provide indirect proof of the phenomenological reality of these operations, which are more than a hypothetical simulation of natural comprehension processes. The daily observation of verbal exchanges reveals an order of priority in errors of interpretation, ambiguities, and transmission problems. What is first perceived is the letter of the messages, i.e., the part of their meaning involving the components of zone A (at least, in those cases where these components are sufficient for the reconstruction of some meaning). It is well known that long-distance communication, for example by telephone, obliterates certain factors external to the discourse stream that are integrated in the components of zone B, but not those of zone A. Moreover, we may formulate a hypothesis which, while not experimentally falsifiable given the present state of research, may be so one day: neurological traces may correspond not only to cyclical procedures of interpretation, but also to the order of their application; although their succession cannot, given the immediacy of comprehension in most cases, take place over measurable time, it must follow a sequence common to various nerve activities, which we propose to call *operative chrono-sequence.*

We may not be able to fully establish the framework of such a progression. Yet it is clear that it is governed by cerebral mechanisms, and that the operations applying to the zones of meaning occur in a determined order. If these mechanisms remain impossible to identify, we must temporarily assume that the speaker has greater liberty than we have imagined. Of course, the physical and mental state of interlocutors, as well as the diversity of situations, are beyond experimental control. But each of us has an individual way of perceiving a text. The figures of classical rhetoric clearly show the margin of uncertainty and the balancing act which dominate all verbal exchange. One may also choose to say less in order to suggest more (litotes), interrogate while appearing to state, intimate while pretending to invite. And the decoder may wish to perceive only the letter of these formulations and not their intent, even if the hearer is equally dependent upon nuances of meaning, various slips, misunderstandings, and ambiguities which are as basic to dialogue as is "clear" articulation.

Thus, by considering individuals within a discourse situation, we are able to unite the study of language and the study of speech, so often separated in linguistic theories. We may then avoid certain pitfalls of the speech sciences. We evade the distributionalist exaggerations of a structuralism blindly attached to the language system, as well as the extremes of an extensional logic which studies only the function of designation. We also escape the obsession with the contingency of words, which ignores the language foundation from which they spring. This is one of the fundamental challenges for contemporary linguistics.

11

Speech Fluctuation

Linguistic Time, Social Time

In the preceding chapter, the speaker was seen as both creator and implement of the language system activated by speech. This activation is an impetus for change. Change is inherent to the definition of all that is linguistic or social. Yet Meillet's ambition, to explore systematically the correspondences between linguistic structures and social structures, and between structural changes in both domains, is a vain one. The ancient and fruitful study of the relations between language and society must seek other territory: the constituents have virtually nothing in common, and, further, they evolve at entirely different rates. This can be illustrated by a single example.

As has long been observed, especially in English- and French-speaking countries, language clearly reflects masculine supremacy. The feminists often refer to texts like the following, written more than eighty years ago and yet entirely modern: "The feminization of the words of our language is more essential to feminism than orthographical reform.

215

At present, there are no words to express qualities that by right belong to women. We do not know whether we should say *une témoin* (*témoin*, "witness"), *une électeure* or *une électrice* (*électeur*, "voter"), *une avocat* or *une avocate* (*avocat*, "lawyer").[1]

This passage by Damourette and Pichon, written in the thirties, is also frequently cited:

> The ease with which French, through inflection or suffixing, produces specifically feminine forms should really discourage women in predominantly masculine professions from embellishing their courageous efforts with ridiculous and grotesque masculine denominations, which are an affront to the language as well as to the most basic human instincts. Are there not those who engrave on their calling cards: *"Maître Gisèle Martin, avocat,"* and others who have their correspondence addressed to *"Mademoiselle le Docteur Louise Renaudier"*? Common sense has up to now resisted this bizarre trend; *une avocate, une doctoresse* are routinely heard, but unfortunately the tenacity of these women may carry the day.... Do they not realize that... even from the social point of view, by clinging stubbornly to this masculine title next to their feminine name and their feminine title of *Madame* or *Mademoiselle*, they only proclaim themselves to be monstrosities? In a society in which it is normal for them to exercise the professions of lawyer, doctor, and writer, it will be natural for women in these professions to have feminine denominations like those for *brodeuses* (embroideresses) or *cigarières* ("cigar makers").[2]

The facts are not so simple as these texts may suggest. On the one hand, it is not true that the modern French norm (whether of 1930 or 1980) creates feminine forms so naturally. The situation is no doubt different in spoken French, which is much less constrained by academic restrictions and thus still faithful to the preclassical tradition which "the sanitizing work of the pedants has succeeded in separating from the written language," frustrating "literary creativity and, consequently, the normal expansion of natural and useful formations."[3] But a certain rigidity of official French hesitates to derive feminine forms based on masculine agentive nouns: we do not find *écrivaine* (*écrivain*, "writer"), *témoine, policière* (*policier*, "policeman"), *menuisière* (*menuisier*, "carpenter"), *savante* (*savant*, "scientist" or "scholar"), *ingén-*

ieuse (ingénieur, "engineer"), professeuse (professeur, "professor"),
metteuse en scène (metteur en scène, "director"), compositrice (compositeur, "composer"), or autrice (auteur, "author").[4] (Some of these
words exist as feminine adjectives, but not as nouns.)

For another thing, even if these words did not arouse the ire of
intellectuals and purists, their authorization would do little to abolish
inequality. The quest for equality has already made considerable progress, and French society has not waited for *ministresse* to replace *femmeministre*, or for acceptance of the title *Madame la Mairesse* ("Madame
Mayor"), to increase the number of professions open to women. "The
fact that the feminine is absent from the dictionary results in the
absence of feminine rights from the legal code," wrote de Gourmont in
1902.[5]

However, French society has been working toward equality between
the sexes for a long time, while derived feminine formations are still
rather rare (except, we repeat, in the living uses of the spoken language).
Such derivations have not even been encouraged by this social evolution, or by the ideologies linked to them; thus, we cannot say that "as
long as mentalities do not change, language will lag behind."[6] Language
does not evolve at the same pace as mentalities, which themselves
change less rapidly than laws. Languages are able to provide precious
evidence about social development and its representations precisely
because successive states of knowledge and culture leave their marks
upon it. But each new phase overtakes the last, so that the heaviness of
the language speaks to us of the past, not of the present. Thus, for
example, it is useless to denounce women's use of expressions whose
forms imply masculine anatomy, and to call them "machistes", as in
the case of the Italian words *fottere* (Fr. *foutre*, "fuck"), and the related
se ne fotte (Fr. *elle s'en fout*, "she doesn't give a damn").[7] For it is
characteristic of language that the literal meaning is demotivated through
frequent usage, thus preventing any association with the ideology
underlying the words when they appear.

Many expressions referring to women reveal a clearly negative connotation. In French,

> une *femme galante* is an immoral woman, while un *homme
> galant* is a well-bred man ... une *femme savante* ("educated") is ridiculous, un *homme savant* is respected. Une
> *femme légère* is a woman of easy virtue; if a man is *léger*, he
> has an easy wit. Similarly, we find *fille* or *femme facile*

("easy"), but not *homme facile;* or *une femme de petite vertu* ("a woman of small virtue"), but never *un homme de petite vertu.*"[8]

These expressions reflect a historical inequality, or the appropriation of speech, as of other instruments of power, by the masculine component of earlier societies. They are not images of contemporary relations between the sexes. It is true that such phrases can be shocking. It may even be true that they contribute to the establishment or preservation of a certain mentality. But if such is indeed the case, there is no linguistic obstacle to a program of reform through which feminists, like so many others, could leave their signature upon the language. Certain asymmetries have already been redressed through the acceptance of *historienne, avocate, actrice*—although not *factrice (facteur,* "mailman"), except jokingly—*sculptrice* (but this is not accepted by all women), and *étudiante.* The limits to this sort of endeavor are determined by the language itself. Users may not, after all, transform it at will (see chapter 8). They have the power to modify the institutions and laws of the society, or even, through revolution, to change the structure of the relations underlying the community. But they do not have the authority (or, it seems, the conscious desire) to transform the social nature of the bonds between individuals, which is the foundation of any human collectivity. Similarly, it is possible to alter the lexicon, for example, feminine nouns of agency or profession—but not to modify the phonological and morphosyntactic structures which determine the typological properties of the language.

The reason for this resistance to change is the archaic nature of idioms. Syntax is relatively static. The representations thus fossilized are from the earliest stages of the society. Populations isolated from major economic and social movements, in nonindustrialized communities, are those whose languages exhibit the greatest concentration of archaic features. In the domain of phonology, we find clicks (see chapter 1). In morphology, we see number systems based on 5, 12 or 20; dense and complex networks of adverbs of time and place; and the descriptive abundance and precision, or metaphorical richness, of classifiers, e.g., morphemes indicating the forms of objects. The variety of the latter, moreover, is limited by the common use of objects with simple forms, for in no language do we find a classifier referring to irregular zigzags or polygons with unequal sides, or any contour other than that of the most elementary geometric figures.

Additionally, in the domain of syntax, archaic features include the rich marking of spatial, temporal, and agentive relations indicating in the most precise detail who does what to whom with (or through, or for, or toward) what or whom. The features concentrated in this type of language have not usually survived in areas where industrial or assimilated societies have developed. In the latter case, they are dispersed among languages, with the syntax evolving on certain points and remaining conservative on others. Thus, in Israeli Hebrew, the masculine / feminine distinction in the second person singular and plural is maintained in the pronouns as well as in verbal morphology, in all tenses and forms, while the language has derived a "modern" possessive structure with a verb "have" (see chapter 10).

These variations in evolution reveal that the bonds between linguistic time and social time are subtle and interwoven with sharp asymmetries. In particular, the reciprocal action between languages and societies over hundreds of thousands of years has not resulted in languages which are the simple reflection of the class struggle, nor, more generally, of superstructures. This fact has not always been recognized, judging from the duration of the reign of the Soviet linguist Marr, who stated, for example:

> Simultaneous with the appearance of collective property, and as a corollary to the division of all action into the name of the person (active) and the name of the result or production of the action (passive), then, with the advancement of production to a new level (progressing, along with the formal manifestation of thought, from a synthetic structure to an analytical structure), the passive was divided into two distinct objects, direct and indirect. The appearance of collective property similarly effected the division of the active into two subjects—the collective totem or the group, and the individual totem. Also linked to this is . . . the division . . . of the totem into . . . collective subject . . . and singular subject, the appearance of the individual subject coinciding with that of private property.

Thus there would be

> a clear link between general concept and material infrastructure, between production and the social relations of production. . . . The feminine gender is not a simple formal detail: it illustrated the creation of the word at a stage at which, in the material infrastructure, the masculine social principle

219

triumphed over the feminine principle; gender expressed this *fait accompli:* matriarchy, essentially feminine, had given way to patriarchy, essentially masculine, but not yet fully so: women retained an independent position in production, where matriarchal right was still preserved.[9]

We know that Stalin long promoted Marr's sovereignty (which continued in the Soviet Union for sixteen years after the linguist's death), before finally denouncing it in the famous article published in *Pravda* on June 20, 1950. At last, official channels had recognized an obvious scientific fact: languages are not purely and simply superimposed upon a social infrastructure. Still, it is important to emphasize that the following declaration was no doubt inspired less by scientific precision than by Stalin's instinct for political opportunism:

> Language is radically different from a superstructure. Let us take, for example, the Russian society and language. In the course of the past thirty years, the former capitalist base has been liquidated in Russia, and a new socialist base has been built. Accordingly, the capitalist superstructure has been liquidated and a new superstructure corresponding to the socialist base has been created. New socialist institutions have replaced the former political and judicial ones. But despite all this, the Russian language has remained essentially what it was before the October Revolution. . . . Russian vocabulary has changed to some degree . . . in that it has been enriched with a considerable number of new words and expressions which arose in the wake of the new socialist economy, the new socialist State and its culture . . .; the meaning of many words and expressions has changed . . .; a certain number of old words have disappeared from the vocabulary. On the other hand, the basic lexicon and grammatical system of Russian, which constitute the foundation of the language, have been preserved in their integrality. . . . The language is not generated by any specific old or new base within a given society, but by the entire course of the society's history . . . over the centuries. The language was not created by any class, but by . . . all classes of the society. . . . It is no secret that, before the October Revolution, Russian served Russian capitalism and bourgeois culture every bit as well as it presently serves the socialist regime. . . . The same must be said of Ukrainian, Belorussian, Uzbek,

> Kazakh, Georgian, Armenian, Estonian, Latvian, Lithu-
> anian, Moldavian, Tatar, Azerbaijani, Bashkir, Turkmenian,
> and other languages of the Soviet nations, which have also
> served the former bourgeois regime of those nations just as
> they now serve the new socialist regime. It could not be
> otherwise. Language ... develops precisely ... in order to
> serve all members of the society regardless of their class
> identity.[10]

Thus, while language may certainly lend itself to class usage, there
is no class language.

This text emphasizes the difference between the lexicon and the
grammar, which is much more resistant to spontaneous (and especially
intentional) change. This does not however imply that the most structured parts of languages cannot also adapt to sociocultural evolutions.
In the spirit of the antiracism espoused by certain anthropologists of
the twenties, Sapir wrote: "When it comes to linguistic form, Plato
walks with the Macedonian swineherd, Confucius with the head-hunt-
ing savage of Assam."[11] Still, it is clear that grammars adapt to their
sociocultural milieu just as living organisms adapt to their environment. The biologist S. J. Gould, replying to an attack on the neo-
Darwinian theory of evolution, affirms that the very structure of organisms provides the criterion of their ability to adapt. Thus, animals with
a constant body temperature are a priori better able to survive in a
period during which the milieu undergoes major thermal modifications.[12] Similarly, a recursive linguistic structure such as the embedding of relative clauses (as in the French *l'enfant qui voulait acheter le
jouet dont le camarade qu'il admirait avait parlé a fini par l'obtenir*,
"the child who wanted to buy the toy that the playmate he admired
had talked about finally got it") is more likely to be preserved in the
language of a written culture than in an oral one, where the burden
upon memory is incompatible with communicative circumstances. And,
in fact, we observe that embedded relatives are much more frequent in
written languages than in others. The evolution of the grammar of
languages along neo-Darwinian lines is therefore not to be excluded.

It is still true, however, that the lexicon evolves more quickly.
Stalin's text again recalls that the dynamics of the lexicon cannot be
compared with that of more structured domains. This explains its
historical value as an ideological warehouse. The names of social institutions and human activities provide illuminating evidence about the
history of societies. Thus, the Daco-Romanian language has two verbs

"work:" one, *a lucra*, comes from the Latin *lŭcrāri*, "earn money" and originally took the sense of "work" in the territory occupied by the free communities of Walachians who were independent of the Byzantine emperor; the other verb, *a munci*, comes from the Old Slavic *mončiti*, which meant "torture (oneself):" the evolution toward the meaning of "work" was in this case accomplished in liaison with the feudal legislation of work imposed upon serfs,[13] just as we know that French *travailler* comes from the late Latin *tripaliare*, from *tripalium*, "yoke, instrument of torture."

But this evidence is largely *historical*. Of course, certain phenomena on the border between lexicon and grammar may shed light upon the mental representations of various societies, because morphological analysis reveals correspondences that are still more or less transparent: thus, in Nahuatl (Mexico), the verb *nemi* "move, go," has the meaning "think (about)" if it occurs with the suffix *-lia*, indicating a participant in the action, and the prefix *ta-*, marking an indefinite goal, or the reflexive prefix *mo-*, or a doubling syllable. Thus: *ta-nemi-lia*, "he thinks," *mo-nemi-lia*, word-for-word "he moves toward himself," or "he is preoccupied;" *ki-nej-nemi-lia*, where *ki* = "him," a definite personal complement, and *nej* = doubling syllable, "he thinks about him."[14] But the forms are not always interpretable. More often, as the disparity between linguistic time and social time increases, words become demotivated and lose their ideological content, and speculations about their origins become more and more futile.

For *the progress of language carries nature along, thus culturalizing it*. In Samo (Burkina-Faso), "stammer" occurs in the same constructions as "kill," and "forget" has the same structure as "bite;" in Cèmuhi (New Caledonia), "forget" governs the same type of complement as "strike," and "rejoice" the same type as "bite;" in Guarani (Paraguay), "sleep" and "rain" (both assigned to animate agents, in the latter case a natural power) have the same compatibilities as "run," while in Georgian, "sleep" compares with "be hungry."[15] These facts alone do not permit us to attribute an activist representation of stammering, amnesia, and joy to speakers of Samo and Cèmuhi; nor to the Guaranis a view of the universe which, unlike that of the Georgians, selects for animacy. The intuitive semantics that would underly such assumptions is not absurd, but no generalization may be made from such contingent data. "Sleep" is treated differently in Guarani and in Georgian; yet originally, the societies that spoke these languages were both animist. We are missing an ancient link, a forgotten historical phenomenon, by which the divergence might be "explained."

Thus, even those parts of languages which are less resistant to change, or more accessible to our initiative, remain fields of relative inertia. It is as if languages, through the stability they provide to their users, had been shaped by the collective subconscious to furnish a guarantee against the risks inherent to the vicissitudes of living. Human languages would then be provisions for, or guardians of, the species undertaking this adventure.

Yet languages do change, however slowly in comparison with social transformations. Of course, the shocks and upheavals that communities undergo do not always have an immediate effect, and certain societies may appear to be paralyzed. Language change is even slower. Still, it is a part of the very nature of languages, and a constituent of their definition. Any theory of language that ignores this fact is doomed to failure. Not only do languages change, but they are the only systems of signs for which change is certain, observed, and attested, in the domain of sound as well as in that of meaning. We do not know if the same gestures have always been used to express the same content. But we are certain that languages continually evolve over vast periods of time, usually without the knowledge of their speakers. A quite common phenomenon, which may be observed by anyone, provides a very simple illustration: variation.

Speech Variation

Even in the most homogeneous of communities, it is clear that there is no fixed and immutable linguistic form, whether in pronunciation, syntax, vocabulary, or even morphology. Careful observation reveals that groups, and even individuals, do not use identical language in all situations. While children are acquiring the essential structure of the language, they simultaneously acquire an awareness of variations in register. This is not, then, a decorative annotation to a homogeneous language entity. Variation is an inherent feature of language use.

It may seem surprising, then, that it is only in the last fifteen years that twentieth-century linguistics has started taking into account data on variation, as a reaction against the excesses of the narrowly formalist models that dominated the sixties. These models were supposed to reflect a language ideally purified of all social and historical baggage, a language defined, in classic generative grammar, by the competence of the famous "ideal speaker-hearer." [16] But even if we accept the fact that a linguistic theory must make certain choices, such pure and definitive abstractions eventually obscure the reality of languages as systems determined by the dynamics of their everyday use. Chomsky's concepts of competence (internalized knowledge of language) and performance (observed language use), like Saussure's concepts of *langue* and *parole*, correspond to the two faces of a single reality, and not to the foundations of two incompatible linguistic theories. Thus, the study of variation is in no way a contradiction of the notion of system. If a system is characterized by its global coherence, and by its organization into discrete units (which may be contrasted by differences of nature and not of degree, e.g., phonemes), it does not follow that these units are immutable. Precisely because they are primarily defined by differences, their content may be diversified, as long as these differences are maintained. Despite appearances, variation is actually linked to the notion of system.

Dialects constitute the best-known case of variation. If we consider the dialects of a given language to be systems whose differences, although observable at all levels, do not impede verbal exchange, then dialectal variation is the rule, and total homogeneity the exception. In extreme cases, on the two opposite fringes of a dialectal group, communication may become difficult. Dialectal variation concerns entire linguistic systems. But there is also a series of fluctuations specific to segments of systems. We distinguish many discriminating variables here: sex, age, social status, professional identity, place of origin, educational milieu, lifestyle (urban or rural, fixed or nomadic, more or less stable, more or less mobile), ethnic and political identity, and imaginary representation of self. The linguistic markers that integrate these variables will be called *indices*, and will be characterized here by adjectives with the suffix *-lectal*, specifying which type of variable is encoded by each index. We will thus speak of *biolectal indices* for sex and age, variables linked to biology as interpreted by language; and *sociolectal indices* for social status, professional identity, place of origin, educational milieu, and lifestyle, all variables arising from the human aptitude for building relations among individuals and groups, and between groups and their environment. *Symbolectal indices* reflect the symbolic relationship to a language as experienced by its speakers; *ethnolectal indices* mark persons of a certain ethnic entity within a language of integration; and finally, *politolectal indices* mark political status and options.[17]

Unlike other variables, those expressed by biolectal indices belong to a systematically coded zone. These indices appear in many languages which formally mark the sexual differentiation of the species. In the domain of sound, one familiar case is the diphthongization of long or accented vowels by women speakers of Russian and Arabic. It has also been observed that Mongol women tend to pronounce / u / and / a / as / ü / and / ä / respectively, without however confusing the two sets, whose specificity dominates the system of vowel harmony (/ ü / and / ä / are called "feminine vowels" in traditional Mongol terminology). Finally, we know that men and women have quite different sound inventories in languages whose users practice a clear sexual division of labor (for example, the nomadic hunting communities of the Youkaguirs of eastern Siberia).

The indices are quite numerous in morphology; Semitic languages, and most Cushitic and Chadic languages, distinguish between the masculine and feminine form of "you," and sometimes even of "I," either with an independent pronoun or with an index affixed to the verb. In Japanese, several particles which modulate the utterance for degree of assertiveness, doubt, or question vary according to the sex of the speaker or hearer. In the case of the lexicon, many Asian, Oceanian, and American Indian languages display distinct series of nouns for family relations, and for everyday objects (tools, housekeeping utensils, arms, animals)—or different series of action verbs—depending upon whether the subject of the utterance is a man or a woman. Finally, the linguistic echo of age differences is seen in the assignation of certain words and certain styles to older members of the community, with other forms belonging to the younger members.

Viewed through the prism of discourse, data that has commonly been called "natural" is seen to be culturalized by speech. The sound articulations and morphological and lexical usages mentioned above are not the results of physiological constraints rendering one sex incapable of producing them in any other fashion. These are strictly cultural constraints, which is why biolectal indices cannot be dissociated from sociolectal indices.

This link is also apparent in all cases where forms of address (pronouns or personal indices, proper names, verbal forms) explicitly mark the type of relation between individuals of different generations or status. In fact, within structures like the family (parents and children), the household (masters and domestics), school, government, the army, religious associations, etc., forms vary with the degrees of hierarchy of age or social, economic, professional, scientific, or political position. However, the binary schema, while common, is not exclusive. Other variations, some of them coded, interact with these. Romanian and Hungarian possess, in addition to the familiar "you" (equivalent to the

French *tu*), two, and in some dialects three, polite forms depending upon the degree of distance between speakers. In Romanian, the most distant form of address, *dumneavoastră*, means literally "your lordship," and, like French (cf. *vous*), uses a plural marker, the possessive *voastră* ("your").

But this type of encoding is itself variable. The use of the plural does not always imply the honorific multiplication of the hearer. In Persian and Turkish, a plural "we" is used to refer to the speaker, through a deprecating (and thus polite) fusion of individuality with the anonymity of a collectivity. Finally, while it is true that "I" and "you" are partners in dialogue, it does not follow that no others are involved, as suggested by the hypothesis of a "personality correlation" distinguishing the interlocutors from "he," presumably a "nonperson." [18] In fact, "he" is as likely as "you" to receive linguistic markers of esteem: In Tigrinya and Amharic (Ethiopia), Romanian, and Jordanian Arabic, we observe two (and, in some Romanian dialects, three) different forms reflecting the degree of respect the speaker wishes to show for the person being referred to. In Asian languages like Japanese and Korean, these markers occur as verbal forms or special affixes, indicating whether or not one honors the person about whom one is speaking.

Other types of usage reflect more free choice. Familiar forms, including French *tu*, diminutives, and pet names, do not always stress the superior status of the user: they appear quite naturally as affectionate forms in discourse between lovers, or in speech addressed to children by their parents. Moreover, polite forms are commonly used between partners of equal status to mark distance or an absence of intimacy. Inversely, speakers who should use a polite form in accordance with their own inferior social status may in fact employ a familiar *tu* because they are not accustomed to the differential use of forms of address. A more surprising phenomenon has been attested in the Arabic dialects of Lebanon, Syria, and Jordan, where it is not unusual for a father to call his son "Father," instituting a relation of equality through the honorific promotion of the inferior member in the hierarchy. [19] Finally, variables may conflict with one another. In these cases, age generally prevails over social status: polite forms are usually preferred with an older partner, even one of inferior status.

The biolectal indices, and those sociolectal indices examined so far, while coded, still reflect a choice, since the physical and social appearance of the partner is the visible criterion for their use. On the other hand, formal markers linked to variables of professional identity, place of origin, milieu, lifestyle, ethnic identity, and symbolic representation do not appear to be immediately conscious. This is true for sociolectal indices of the phonetic order, including, in France, the rolled / r / specific to certain geographical areas and rural milieus; the closing of *è* (ɛ) to *é* (e) in syllables not ending in a consonant; and the consistent opening of *o* in syllables with final consonant. This last results in the identical pronunciation of *pomme* (/ pɔm) / and *paume* (/ pom /) and of *sole*(/ sɔl) / and *saule* (/ sol /) in the south and certain parts of the north and east of France, as opposed to the center, the west, and the Paris region.

But other variables interact with these. Lifestyle may trigger the amendment of habits acquired in childhood, as when professional life induces an individual to move frequently and thus to adopt the articulatory usages of different zones. However, the phonetic model is not necessarily real. Many adopt a pronunciation that they have not heard among any precise group of speakers, and which they consider more appropriate to their function or to the social role they wish to play. Thus we observe the interference of another variable, the psychosymbolic representation, encoded by symbolectal indices.

These indices are even more unconscious than those considered above. Thus, certain phonic particularities are endorsed and substituted for usages acquired in the region of origin, which are now involuntarily censured. Such a process of unconscious assimilation to articulatory practices perceived as prestigious is currently at work among certain French speakers: determined to speak "elegantly," they go so far as to replace the / e / of past participles of regular -*er* verbs, as well as the -*ez* of the second person plural in the present, with the more "pointed" / ɛ / of the bourgeoisie of the larger cities in the north of France, particularly in Paris. Thus we find *parlé* and *parlez* pronounced like the imperfect *parlais*, that is with a final / ɛ / "like in Paris," while in fact, in many parts of the country, the tendency is on the contrary to close final / ɛ / , including in all three persons of the singular of the imperfect or conditional (*parlais, parlais, parlait; parlerais, parlerais, parlerait*), pronouncing them all / e / .

Thus discourse, as the interactive construction of meaning—but also as a confrontation between individuals seeking a means of verbal self-affirmation—includes an entirely subjective component. The speaking subject is a desiring subject. And the symbolectal indices reflecting this desire may transcend the others and, by dominating them, reveal the hidden face of speech. In the many cases where neither sex, nor age, nor any of the social variables command linguistic indices of fluctuation, it is clear that the decisive factors are symbolic ones:

speakers are motivated by the drive to purge themselves of the emblems of an "inferior" social group, or to identify themselves with an ideal community through imitation of sounds, whether through the resurrection of obsolete pronunciations, the adoption of new articulatory habits, or intellectual hypercorrection. An illustration of the latter is the making of nonstandard liaisons in French—for example, pronouncing the *t* of *avait* in *il avait un plan* ("he had a plan")—when, in fact, a clear pause separates *avait* and *un*, a fact which should preclude liaison. In a study of the principal political speeches given in France during a given period, it was observed that the higher the speaker's position in the hierarchy of political life, the more of these liaisons (which are erroneous hypercorrections) occurred—as if a politician's status required him to project the respectable image of one for whom spelling is self-evident, and who wants everyone to know it.[20] But phonetics is not the only factor. Speakers express their individuality in a style which is heard or read in their choice of vocabulary (modern or archaic), and of syntax (strict or relaxed).[21]

True symbolectal indices may be distinguished from *signals*, defined as voluntary or involuntary externalizations of sentiments. Signals are frequently reinforced by intonation which, as we have seen, does not always lend itself to uniform interpretation. When linguistic traces of fluctuation do not correspond to "objective" variables like sex, age, or status, but rather to changing emotions, the existence of traces (generally prosodic) may at best be observed; it is not always possible to assign to each trace a fixed content subsuming the diversity of affective phenomena under a given formal fact. Like symbolectal indices, signals describe spirals of subjectivity through the random flow of words. Human beings continually record their individuality in the creases of the language, despite the requirements and limitations of grammar. Speech fluctuations are another trace of this individuality.

Ethnic identity is also etched into the language. The necessity of this phenomenon provides a key to certain otherwise unexplainable progressions. Ethnolectal indices are invested with a function which has been labeled ethno-demarcative:[22] the specified group imprints upon the language its desire to be recognized as different. Such desires are stronger along national boundaries, where the immediate environment increases the need for contrastive identity. This explains, for example, the fact that the Gascons in the southern Gironde region, living near the old border between Aquitaine and the Celts and Bituriges, have preserved the stems *tir-* and *bir-* (abandoned elsewhere) for the future of the verbs *ténguer* ("hold") and *vénguer* ("come"). In Israeli

Hebrew, we find interesting minimal pairs based on contrasting stress: *xerút* ("freedom"), *tikvá* ("hope"), and *bimá* ("stage") are accented on the last syllable; when the first syllable of these same words is stressed, we obtain *xérut* (the Herut political party), *tíkva* (the name of the Israeli national anthem) and *bíma* (the Bima national theater troupe). This latter accentuation is characteristic of Yiddish, while the former is based upon classical Hebrew. And since accented words in Yiddish designate typical Israeli realities, it appears that European Jews who spoke Yiddish, when talking among themselves about phenomena arising within their own milieu, accented the words according to their native language. Many other examples, from very diverse cultures, could be given to illustrate this linguistic affirmation of social identity.[23]

These ethnic "signatures" are a sign of linguistic vitality. At the other extreme, we find populations who are not only powerless to affirm their identity and express themselves through language variation, but who in fact make minimal use of language. This is an impressive phenomenon of linguistic deprivation, corollary to a kind of social dereliction. Examples may be found in Europe: "Separated from the idioms of their ethnic and social traditions, cut off from the use of those of the dominant milieu, ... the wretched peasants of Basento (Italy) ... are literally speechless. They exhibit a profound and radical verbal deficit."[24] Human social space is by nature discursive; and if avenues of dialogue are blocked by poverty and isolation, speech gives way to stammering, as social life is all but extinguished.

Still, the study of variation as a sign of vitality must not obscure the recurrences which determine language. We have said that variation is linked to the notion of system. This is also true in another sense. We must resist the rigidity inspired by a misinterpretation of the sociolinguist Labov;[25] as a result of this attitude, one might wish to explain away, as cases of variation, so called deviant, spoken, or dialectal structures. In reality, these structures have their own grammar. Speech fluctuations, which constitute the history of the language (as we have seen, for example, in the case of pronominal forms of address), are in no sense arbitrary or haphazard phenomena. They are systematic, and governed by the dialectic of constraints and initiatives. Variation is inherent to the norm, but not in the way that free will is inherent to obligation. The two are indivisible components of language, and socio-operative linguistics treats them as such.

12

Love of Language

Language, Speech and Discourse

All linguists speak of language, speech, and discourse. But the requirement of explicit definitions for these terms is a goal, not a given. Still, such a goal is indispensable, for without it we give the impression that linguists, tacitly selecting one aspect or another, do not all address the same subject matter. Thus, as we end our journey through the territory of speech, let us summarize the fields, subjects, and disciplines under consideration; let us, in other words, describe the basic concepts as they are defined by implicit agreement among contemporary linguists of various schools. Speech (*langage*) is the first of these terms. It is an aptitude which defines the human species. The study of speech is the consideration of the relationship between humanity and this aptitude since its "origins," about which linguistics itself has little to say. It includes the examination of nonverbal forms (gestural speech, sign languages, etc.), and of pathology (various types of aphasia).

Alongside the notion of speech is that of language (*langue*). We refer here to the abstract concept, and not to any specific idiom. This is the complex domain of those features which describe us in our defining relationship with the code and our use of it.

Our interest may be further extended to *a* language, that is a given system of systems which is used in discourse and which classifies signs (i.e., pairings of sound with meaning) according to form and function. This characterization implies various features, the application of which is to be verified for real languages.

If, however, we intend to study *languages*, we must, through a process of induction, study as many as possible in terms of phonology, morphosyntax, and lexicon. We are then no longer concerned with general language properties, but with living systems which lie at the heart of communicative behaviors in specific human societies, and which help to differentiate them. Comparisons between languages will further the quest for universals; and, against the background of these universals, the components of a typology may be distinguished. For all of the linguistic itineraries outlined above, this book has tried to contribute to the identification of some guideposts.

Finally, the linguist may examine discourse. There are, however, two ways to do so. Some investigators do not separate a text from the particular linguistic system that it embodies. Instead, they relate that system to another system, converting discourse into a new configuration expressing the same meaning. This is the intoxication of the translator, a vast and fascinating tautology. It is a fundamental enterprise, unique to the dialogic species, and at the heart of all relations between nations. Translation is a consuming (but hardly gratuitous) passion for the transferral of meaning into other words. This passion has filled immense libraries, and reflects a boundless preoccupation with Babel. At its extreme, it becomes an end in itself. Translation, the quest for the most perfect equivalency between homosemic messages in two heterogeneous systems, is merely another aspect of the love for languages.

But there is another kind of passion for discourse. Translation is a desperate effort to contain variations of meaning; by contrast, written and oral texts reveal an obsession with the opaque complexity of the phenomena through which meaning is continually renewed. Such texts bring into play multiple factors of construction and deconstruction of meaning.

The fundamental faculty of speech (*faculté de langage*) stands apart from the other domains discussed here: it is not a concept which inspires passion. *A* language is an object whose contours may be epis-

231

temologically determined. (The very use of the indefinite article focuses attention on the generic, and invokes the classifying process of reason rather than the longings of the imagination.) But the concept of *language* (*la langue*), and the manifold territory of *languages* (*les langues*), do inspire different forms of real devotion.

The Passion for (Self) Expression

For users of a given language, the act of speaking and the knowledge of the system are indivisible. Situations that distinguish between the two are rare, an illustration of their essential unity. Thus, foreigners who learn a language as adults or who, since childhood, have been exposed to it along with their native language, often understand the second language better than they speak it. Such users, more comfortable with reception than with production, know the essentials of the grammar and lexicon but can spontaneously express themselves only in their own language. They, therefore, experience a dissociation which to the linguist is quite suggestive: what is received is *langue;* what is produced (more or less successfully) is *parole.*

In the vast majority of cases, however, the two are closely connected. We may set aside the basic narcissism of those who talk "to hear themselves speak," and who are quite fascinated with their own production; in general, the speaker's attachment to language has all the importance of a regulatory function. It is a condition of social and psychological stability. There are, of course, cases of voluntary detachment from a vernacular; but these may be explained. The descendants of immigrants who, in a given generation, adopt as their unique or principal language that of the host country, do so because the symbolic value of a system of communication perceived as a mirror of their new citizenship becomes more powerful for them. This attraction may, in fact, become as strong as the attraction of their original language was for the first immigrants at the intersection of two cultures. Certain groups may even adopt a prestigious neighboring language. But this is in order to escape the political and social isolation imposed by the use of a minority language in a highly centralized state. If they do not find powerful enough historical reasons to defend their own idiom, they may abandon their national language. The tendency is aggravated when the neighboring language has a writing system, which confers upon it a vague (and objectively unjustifiable) prestige. Examples could include the Bats and the Andis of the Caucasus, with respect to two "prestigious" languages, respectively Georgian and Avar. Such also appears to be the case of the Byelorussians with respect to Russian.[1] Finally, there are semipathological cases of aversion for a native language, a form of mother-hatred. The example represented by Wolfson has often been cited.[2]

But these cases remain marginal. In most situations, speakers are attached to their language as a domain of symbolic appropriation. Through it, they experience their relationship to the group that shares this linguistic domain. As the term clearly implies, they enter into *communication*. The human race is characterized by society; speakers thus become devoted to the language that constitutes the basis of that society.

The Metalinguistic Fantasy

Linguists try to speak of language in external terms. We must try to assure a cohesive discourse, and escape the circular trap of using language to discuss language. Consequently, we invent a metalanguage: a descriptive model which, while using words of the language itself, attenuates the effects of this inextricable circularity. In order to do this, the metalanguage must extract those words from the uncertainties of speech, and impose upon them a scientific rigor. But to what extent can the linguist hope to succeed in this endeavor?

For example, some researchers have proposed to identify two semantic invariables, or minimal and universal features of meaning, underlying the word *mare*, represented by the notations +EQUINE and +FEMALE. These do not of course exhaust the many referential features corresponding to the notion of "mare," but are considered sufficient for the metalanguage because they permit the opposition of *mare* to *stallion* (+EQUINE, +MALE) and *cow* (+BOVINE, +FEMALE). Partisans of this type of analysis, when reminded of its circularity, generally respond (see chapter 3) that these notations are not English words, but terms of a metalinguistic lexicon of objective properties not integrated into any language. But how can we be sure that the linguist does not interpret these semantic components through an intuitive grasp of lexical items which, in their written form, are identical to the conventional labels of the metalanguage?

It may be, then, that the only real metalanguage is that which has long been available to any schoolchild: the technical grammatical terms such as *singular, first person, preposition, adjective, subordinate*, etc.

233

These are metalinguistic words which, while specialized in their technical use, do not reflect any formalized metalanguage. They avoid the dilemma of such systems, a dilemma that arises from at least two facts: on the one hand, "we are ... obliged to recognize a multitude of metalanguages, because of the diversity of languages, or because of the diversity of linguistic theories;" on the other hand, even if this difficulty did not exist, linguistics (itself a primary formalized language) would still require "a secondary formalized language to verify its consistency." But there is no such thing; "natural discourse must try to account for formalized language."[3] This natural system escapes the verdict that is so often addressed to logical metalanguage—"there is no metalanguage."[4] We can better understand and appreciate this verdict when we read Lacan's words: "No language could tell the truth about the truth, since truth defines itself by what it speaks, and has no other means to do so." And elsewhere: "Meaning always refers to meaning, since a thing may only be shown by a sign. . . . It is only by suppressing his own mediating discourse, and by opening himself up to the flow of real words, that the analyst can effect a revealing interpretation of them."[5]

The more or less universal existence, at least in cultures with a grammatical tradition, of metalinguistic lexicons containing terms like those we have cited suggests that certain individuals have always paid conscious attention to the unconscious process of natural speech behavior, and have made it a topic of ordered discourse—in short, they adopt a scientific approach to language. In a similar manner, other spontaneous human phenomena including social behavior, the exchange of goods, and mental and affective conduct, have inspired the reflection which is the foundation of the social sciences.

But linguists do not always content themselves with traditional designations of language entities. They may retain those that they find useful, perhaps adding their own creations, in order to construct a descriptive and explanatory system of the language, a system that expresses itself in limpid form and with measured complexity, while still clearly revealing the depth of their vision. This has been accomplished by some of the greatest linguists, including Saussure, Meillet, and Benveniste, to name only those writing in French. For them, recourse to scholarly dichotomies, comparative reconstruction, or the sketching of a system of enunciation are expressed in prose that is both elegant and rigorous, fertile as well as readable. No additional key is needed to decipher it.

But the desire for a "scientific" system in a form to be borrowed from the natural sciences (without adequate information about their problems and methods) sometimes produces a kind of formalizing inflation. Linguists, the imperious authors of this expansion, are themselves victimized by it. Exhilarated by the formulae they invent, they may lose themselves in a series of games that refer only to each other. Or, intoxicated by their own discourse (which they shield from reality, and thus from any risk of contradiction), they devote themselves to a rhetoric that feeds upon the intellectual fashions of the day and delights in the circularities so dear to all pure rhetoric.

This enslavement to formalization represents a serious delusion. It is certainly important to reject the prescientific continuity between the observed world and the impressionistic discourse which, in the past, was often used to describe it; but while it is true that the quest for a metalanguage responds to this need, it is pointless to become obsessed with form. It has not been proven that the accumulation of algebraic equations can generate more illuminating explanations, nor that these equations help us to discover new facts. Moreover, the current practice of providing various glosses for formulae that should be self-explanatory suggests that this objection is implicitly recognized.[6] As for autarkic dissertations, they are an interesting illustration of the passion for linguistic discourse. This represents an ancient tendency in the history of reflection upon language: triviality of content is less obvious when disguised by sophistication of form. Inspired by this taste for majestic discourse, grammatical passion may use language as a mere pretext, and allow it to be obscured by its own jargon. Or, charmed by a metalanguage, the linguist may simply engage in play instead of mastering a useful tool.

Such work is largely inaccessible, and so remains largely unknown. Those who do not participate in scientific research find it difficult to conceive of the social (or even intellectual) utility of an enterprise whose very abstruseness seems designed to confuse the uninitiated. But even for other nonlinguistic researchers, especialy those in the social sciences, this type of work remains opaque. Linguistics must reject esoteric formalism in order to face a fundamental challenge: instead of becoming a scholastic pursuit with no apparent importance for the work of other researchers, linguistics must try to be a discipline capable of elucidating social and historical realities.

Languages as Love Objects

Are the desires of speakers oriented toward the language itself? This "instrument" which we have unconsciously shaped through the ages, and which we sometimes dream of dominating entirely (see chapter 8), is not a smooth surface of abstraction. For the speaker, and for the linguist in particular, language may become an obsession. But can we equate the basic human attachment to language, that inalienable territory at the center of the self, with the pleasure of the grammarian who chooses (and is chosen by) the study of language, not simply to make a living but through real devotion? And are there not those who are indifferent or hostile to languages? And even linguists who do not like languages?

All speakers are inspired by the desire for self-expression. The love of languages, however, is not universal. It is an odd passion in that it cultivates a series of systems designed to accomplish what a single language can do by itself. This desire for possession quite naturally includes the native or dominant language. But it is true that bilingual environments promote the love of languages. That is, at least, when these environments are not created by a political or social necessity which depreciates the value of the native language on the linguistic "market," and forces users to pay the necessary price of learning a more expensive, but more profitable, language of prestige.

"Glossophiles" are in no way troubled by the reproduction *ad infinitum* of the same content, which others may find absurd. For such devotees, languages are love objects. They enjoy the associations between certain sounds and certain meanings; they appreciate diverse types of sentence structure; they love comparing words against subtle and varying semantic grids. To express meaning, they produce foreign sounds with a pleasure akin to that of the epicure feasting on rare delicacies, or the infant nursing at the mother's breast. Mother's milk, mother tongue. The one is ingested, the other articulated, in two apparently contradictory gestures: one permits reception, the other emission. The two drives are related, however—both activities are performed with the mouth.

Some of these lovers concentrate their passion upon individual words, and compile vast inventories. One of these was Cinoc, a character created by Georges Perec.[7] For more than fifty years, Cinoc occupied the curious post of "word-killer" for Larousse: he sent several thousand words to the tomb of anonymity in order to make room for new words (sought out by other employees). Upon his retirement, Cinoc was gradually overcome by remorse for his myriad lexical crimes, and decided to edit a monumental dictionary of forgotten words, a work requiring extensive and expert research. In reality, such pilgrimages are often the work of amateurs, guided more by enthusiasm than by technical erudition. The logophile is not always a philologist.

The lover of languages is not necessarily a collector of words, however. The etymologist finds myopic pleasure in the individual histories of words, and cares little for the coherent lexicons into which they are integrated; the passionate glossophile, more of a grammarian, lovingly collects descriptions of entire languages. Some such scholars are not even content to contemplate these languages, but must learn them, and well enough to be able to converse with their native speakers. Learning a new language is as intoxicating as a new conquest. They only regret that they cannot learn them all. In this, they may appear to be worlds away from the nostalgic search for the "original" pre-Babelian language; nor do they seem to share the dreams of the apostles of Esperanto. Yet their passion for diversity is perhaps, in fact, the hidden face of a secret desire for unity.

Other enthusiasts are more disinterested. They love languages but do not aspire to use or analyze them. These Platonic lovers derive pleasure simply by listening to foreign sounds. In extreme cases, they do not even insist upon understanding what they hear. They love sound in and of itself, independent of the "parasitism" of meaning. But languages are defined precisely by this indestructible association of two aspects, neither of which is parasitic to the other. Thus "phonophilia" is a marginal case of love of languages, permitting us to better define its real components.

Does the glossophile have a "gift" for languages? Or is the acquisition of successive languages facilitated by their similarities of structure (beyond all their obvious differences), combined with powerful motivation? What is the source of this drive? Is it even practical to seek an "explanation" for a behavior whose prompting forces may rather belong in the field of psychoanalytical inquiry? The "common sense" answer has at least the merit of clarity. Even among glossophiles who seem to love languages as ends in themselves, the exhilaration of data collection is nourished by the quest for differences. Beneath the infinite diversity of languages, we are fascinated by the infinite diversity of cultures. Languages belong to the societies that speak them, and enter into the definition of these societies. For any culture, all others are a source of amazement, whether their exotic aspect arouses interest or inspires distrust. The lover of languages is captivated by "otherness"— of languages, and, by extension, of cultures. One of the goals of this book has been to provide a rational justification for this bold enterprise.

Epilogue

All speakers have some interest in language—whether they admit it or not. We are as fascinated by language as we are by ourselves. Those of us who choose language as a profession choose a technical domain and carry on ordered discourse about it. Moreover, we have good reason to make language a subject of intellectual inquiry: it is the only way we may hope to make a serious contribution to our knowledge of humanity through speech activity. Naive observation, and reversion to traditional teachings (well-intentioned as these techniques may be) cannot explain the essential properties of language. One example of this shortcoming is the illusion of a direct correspondence between sounds and letters in languages written alphabetically, and whose spelling in fact differs from their pronunciation, like French and English. Thus linguistics has more than one justification for considering itself a science.

Why is it, then, that in the past twenty-five years linguistics has lost so much of its former prestige? Why does it arouse vague feelings of disappointment? Why is it even held responsible for the esoteric aberrations of other speech-related disciplines, such as certain conceptions of literary analysis? Linguistics, concerned with the most human aspect of the human species, should be the antithesis of narrow scholasticism. Instead, it seems to have been the victim of excesses which, through undue emphasis upon refinement of form, have distorted some of its advances. An obsession with scientific precision has led linguistics to cloak itself in a false rigor which has no counterpart in even the most rigorous of sciences. This fascination with formalism has resulted in the relegation of linguistics to such a narrow corridor of technical discourse, that it seems inconceivable that the object of its inquiry is speech and humanity. For not only has linguistics been stripped of its historical and social components, but the very notion of "human" has become an abstraction; and words no longer have anything to say.

Yet the dialogic species can itself free linguistics from this predicament. For this species is not merely an object of study; human behavior subtly guides us toward an appropriate method. Of course, we cannot always take ourselves at our word(s). But, from human behavior, the linguist can rediscover dialectical thought. The way in which we construct, deconstruct, and reconstruct our languages over time by varying types against a background of naturally determined constants; our appropriation of the sign, and, through it, of the world and of its re-articulated simultaneities; the consolidation of power through language reform and writing (and, no doubt, through other techniques in the future)—these are some of the meandering itineraries of the dialogic species. Linguistics must try to appropriate the dynamic traces of these transformations—without, of course, diminishing its status as a science through a too literal emulation of its object. Humanity, the continually evolving product of a dialectic of constraints (whose future forms are unknown to us) and initiatives (whose identity will depend upon the response to imminent challenges), naturally provides the blueprint for discourse that may transcend our various disguises and address our very essence. We have only to focus our attention upon the dialogic species.

Perhaps this enterprise will regain the merit that it deserves. Perhaps linguistics, pondering speech as a reflection of humanity (its true object of study) can look forward to a great career alongside the other social sciences—with which, as we have seen, it shares essential properties. For we may one day realize that irresponsible and self-serving applications of many research results in science have placed our natural environment, and our own existence, in mortal danger. We may also appreciate the discrepancy between the almost insignificant evolution of the human brain during the past two hundred thousand years, and the fantastic advances in our knowledge of the world over that same period. This discrepancy raises many ethical and intellectual questions. In accepting this challenge, we must in no way reduce our efforts to discover the laws of the physical world and of our own biological organism (still so poorly understood); we must instead balance those efforts by taking responsibility for the applications of the knowledge obtained. This must be effected through closer attention to our psychological and social nature, as addressed by the social sciences. The necessity of such an equilibrium is perhaps much more than academic. We may even hope that the chasm between the social and natural sciences will gradually be filled. Is a harmonious resolution of the two merely a quixotic fantasy? In any case, there is no reason why we should not dare to dream.

Notes

1. Unity of Species, Plurality of Languages

1. L. Leakey, P. Tobias, J. Napier in 1964, then Y. Coppens, F. Clark Howell, J. Chavaillon, M. Taieb, and D. Johanson. Their work is cited in Y. Coppens, *Le singe, l'Afrique et l'homme* (Paris: Fayard, Le temps des sciences, 1983), to which this section is greatly indebted. See also S. R. Harnad, H. D. Steklis, and J. Lancaster, eds., *Origins and Evolution of Language and Speech* (New York: Annals of the New York Academy of Sciences, 1976), vol. 280.

2. Cf. Maurice Auroux, *L'ambiguité humaine* (Paris: Buchet-Chastel, 1983).

3. Despite this difference between capacity and realization, the term *langage* is also used in contemporary French as an equivalent for the plural *langues*. The properties ascribed to *langage* are then understood as those possessed by languages in general.

4. E. T. Hall, *The Hidden Dimension* (New York: Doubleday, 1966), p. 60.

5. On this point, and in particular on the debate over evolution from back to front or from front to back in the history of sound articulation, cf. J. Van Gineken, Les clics, les consonnes et les voyelles dans l'histoire de l'humanité, in *Proceedings of the Third International Congress of Phonetic Sciences* (Gand, 1938); C. Hagège and A. G. Haudricourt, *La phonologie panchronique* (Paris:

1. Unity of Species, Plurality of Languages

PUF, 1978), pp. 19, 57; J. Durin, Hominisation—Base articulatoire, *Revue des Etudes Slaves* (1983), 55(1):7–25. Also see, here, chapter 5.

6. G. W. Leibniz, *New Essays on Human Understanding*, 1704, Peter Remnant and Jonathan Bennett, trans. (Cambridge: Cambridge University Press, 1981), bk. 3, ch. 2.

7. Cf. N. Chomsky, *Aspects of the Theory of Syntax* (Cambridge: MIT Press, 1965), ch. 1.

8. J.-P. Changeux, *L'homme neuronal* (Paris: Fayard, Le temps des sciences), 1983, p. 355.

9. Ibid., p. 325.

10. Cf. H. Hécaen and G. Lanteri-Laura, *Evolution des connaissances et des doctrines sur les localisations cérébrales* (Paris: Desclée de Brouwer, 1977).

11. P. Broca, Perte de la parole. Ramolissement chronique et destruction partielle du lobe antérieur gauche du cerveau, *Bulletin de la Société d'Anthropologie* (1861), vol. 2, p. 219s.

12. Cf. P. D. Eimas, E. R. Siqueland, P. Jusczyk and J. Vigorito, Speech perception in infants, *Science* (1971), vol. 172, pp. 303–306; A. R. Moffitt, Consonant cue perception by twenty to twenty-four week old infants, *Child Development* (1971), vol. 42, pp. 717–731.

13. H. Hyden, Molecular basis of neuron-glia-interaction, in S. O. Schmitt, ed., *Macromolecular Specificity and Biological Memory* (Cambridge, MIT Press, 1962), pp. 55–69; J. Barbizet, Le problème du codage cérébral, son rôle dans les mécanismes de la mémoire, *Annales Médico-psychologiques* (1964), 122(1): 1–28.

14. For more details, cf. R. Husson, Mécanismes cérébraux du langage oral, de la lecture et de l'écriture, *Les Cahiers du Collège de Médecine* (1967), vol. 1–2, pp. 1–28.

15. Cf. J. Piaget, *Le structuralisme* (Paris: PUF, Que sais-je?, 1968).

16. Cf. N. Chomsky, The Formal Nature of Language, in E. H. Lenneberg, ed., *Biological Foundations of Language* (New York: Wiley, 1967); N. Chomsky and M. Halle, *The Sound Pattern of English* (New York: Harper & Row, 1968).

17. Cf. C. Hagège, *La grammaire générative. Réflexions critiques* (Paris: PUF, Coll. Le linguiste, 1976), pp. 65–68. Available in American translation, revised and updated: *Critical Reflections on Generative Grammar*, Edward Sapir Monograph Series in Language, Culture, and Cognition, trans. R.A. Hall, (Chicago: Jupiter Press, 1981).

18. Chomsky, The Formal Nature of Language.

19. C. A. Ferguson, Talking to Children: a Search for Universals, in J. H. Greenberg et al., eds., *Universals of Human Language*, vol. 1, *Method and Theory* (Stanford: Stanford University Press, 1978), pp. 203–224.

20. Ibid., p. 217.

21. A list of them can be found in W. J. M. Levelt, What Became of LAD?, in W. Abraham, ed., *Ut Videam: Contributions to a History of Linguistics, for Pieter Verburg* (Lisse: Peter de Ridder, 1975), pp. 171–190.

22. Cf. N. Chomsky, *Language and Mind* (New York: Harcourt, Brace and

World, 1968), ch. 2; also *Reflections on Language* (New York, Pantheon Books, 1975), ch. 3.

23. Cf. G. Sampson, *Making Sense* (Oxford: Oxford University Press, 1980), ch. 7–8.

2. The Creole Laboratory

1. Cf. S. J. Gould, *Ontogeny and Phylogeny* (Cambridge: Harvard University Press, 1977).

2. J.-P. Changeux, *L'homme neuronal* (Paris: Fayard, Le temps des sciences, 1983), p. 342.

3. E. Haeckel, *The History of Creation*, Lankester, trans. (New York: D. Appleton and Co., 1883).

4. Gould, *Ontogeny and Phylogeny*.

5. Cf. G. R. DeBeer, *Embryos and Ancestors*, rev. ed., (Oxford: Clarendon Press, 1951).

6. Cf. J. T. Lamendella, Relations Between the Ontogeny and Phylogeny of Language: a New Recapitulationist View, in S. R. Harnad et al, eds., *Origins and Evolution of Language and Speech* (New York: Annals of the New York Academy of Sciences, 1976), vol. 280, pp. 396–412.

7. Cf. J. von Grimm, *Über den Ursprung der Sprache* (Berlin, 1852), or L. de Rosny, *De l'origine du langage* (Paris, 1869). The ideology underlying such equations was widespread until quite recently.

8. D. Bickerton, *Roots of Language* (Ann Arbor: Karoma, 1981). Among other reviews, consult S. Begley, The Fossils of Language, *Newsweek*, Mar. 15, 1982, p. 80.

9. While not all pidgins and creoles are spoken by people of African descent, the latter do in fact constitute the majority of pidgin speakers, and thus provide an instructive example.

10. See in particular M. C. Alleyne, *Comparative Afro-American* (Ann Arbor: Karoma, 1980), and P. Baker and C. Corne, *Isle de France Creole* (Ann Arbor: Karoma, 1982).

11. M. Joos, cited by W. J. Samarin, Salient and Substantive Pidginization, in D. Hymes, ed., *Pidginization and Creolization of Languages* (Cambridge: Cambridge University Press, 1971), pp. 117–140.

12. Ibid.

13. Cf. C. Petit and E. Zuckerkandl, *Evolution moléculaire. Génétique des populations* (Paris: Hermann, Méthodes, 1976), pp. 28–30. In the area of Manchester, England, before the Industrial Revolution, most of these moths (species *Biston betularia*) had white wings which blended in with the bark of the birch trees upon which they perched; the rare black individuals were immediately visible to predator birds and thus eliminated. But when the tree trunks had been blackened with soot, the gene coded for black wing coloring (which had been preserved in the heterozygotes) allowed the black phenotype

to appear. This coloring now provided protection (since, on a black background, black wings were no longer visible). Consequently, adaptation to the new environment led to a numerical superiority of black individuals. My thanks to Monique Gasser for drawing my attention to this illustration.

3. Language Universals and Typological Differences

1. Cf. G. Steiner, *After Babel, Aspects of Language and Translation* (New York and London: Oxford University Press, 1975), ch. 2. See also C. Hagège, Voies et destins de l'action humaine sur les langues, in I. Fodor and C. Hagège, eds., *Language Reform: History and Future* (Hambourg: Buske, 1983–1984), vol. 1, pp. 11–68.

2. A. de Rivarol, *De l'universalité de la langue française, Discours qui a remporté le prix à l'Académie de Berlin* (Paris: Bailly et Dessenne, 1784). Reprinted by the Club franaçais du livre (1964), p. 99.

3. Cf. C. F. Hockett, The Problem of Universals in Languages, in J. H. Greenberg, ed., *Universals of Language* (Cambridge: MIT Press, 1963), ch. 1.

4. L. Hjelmslev, *Prolégomènes à une théorie du langage* (1942). Reprinted in Paris: Editions de Minuit, 1968), p. 138.

5. See *Colloque sur la traduction poétique*, organized by the Centre Afrique-Asie-Europe de l'Institut de Littérature générale et comparée, Sorbonne Nouvelle-Paris III (1972) (Paris: Gallimard, 1978), p. 10, especially a remark attributed to R. Etiemble.

6. J.-M. Zemb, *Vergleichende Grammatik. Franzosisch-Deutsch*, Bibliographisches Institut Mannheim, Coll. Duden-Sonderreihe Vergleichende Grammatiken (Vienna: Dudenverlag, 1978), vol. 1, p. 27.

7. Paris: Gallimard, 1982.

8. M. Joos, *Readings in Linguistics* (Washington, D.C.: American Council of Learned Societies, 1957), p. 96.

9. Cf. C. Hagège, *Le commox laamen de Colombie britannique. Présentation d'une langue amérindienne*, Amérindia, (Paris: Association d'Ethnolinguistique amérindienne, 1981), special vol. 2, pp. 87–91.

10. A. Pawley, On Meeting a Language that Defies Description in Ordinary Terms, *Kivung Congress of the Linguistic Society of Papua New Guinea*, Lae, 1980.

11. N. Chomsky, *Aspects of the Theory of Syntax* (Cambridge: MIT Press, 1965). For modern, and somewhat different, views on language, see T. Givon, *On Understanding Grammar* (New York, Academic Press, 1979), and B. Comrie, *Language Universals and Linguistic Typology* (Oxford: Blackwell, 1981).

12. L. Hjelmslev, *Le langage* (1963). Reprinted in Paris: Editions de Minuit, 1966), p. 129.

13. For more details, see C. Hagège, *La structure des langues* (Paris: PUF, Que sais-je?, 1982), pp. 39–40.

14. We are using here the semantic types defined in ch. 9, in the context of the three viewpoints theory.

15. Hence, according to innateness theories, it is assumed to be part of the genetic code. See ch. 1.

16. For more details see Hagège, *La structure des langues.*

17. G. N'Diaye, *Structure du dialecte basque de Maya* (Le Hague-Paris: Mouton, 1970), p. 219.

18. Cf. A. G. Haudricourt, Richesse en phonèmes et richesse en locuteurs, *L'Homme* (1961), 1(1):5–10.

19. Cf. G. Sampson, *Making Sense* (Oxford: Oxford University Press, 1980), pp. 63–65.

20. Chomsky, *Aspects,* p. 29.

21. Aristotle, *De Anima,* 403b, where this idea is illustrated by the word "house" *(oikos).*

22. B. Russell, *An Inquiry into Meaning and Truth* (London: Allen and Unwin, 1940), p. 33.

23. Alaska and Hawaii are separated from the rest of the country by huge expanses of land or water (and no geography book represents the Pacific Ocean as an inland lake!). Other examples include common nouns such as *constellation,* a discontinuous set of stars in both French and English; and, in French, *rouage,* the set of gears in a mechanism (e.g., a clock).

24. Chomsky, *Aspects,* p. 201, n. 15.

25. In some languages, grammar and lexicon contribute jointly to signal meaning, while in others a single domain is decisive. In French, the adverbs *demain* ("tomorrow") and *hier* ("yesterday") are associated with verb forms indicating future or past, respectively; meanwhile, Hindi has only one adverb, *kəl,* meaning "tomorrow" or "yesterday," depending on whether the verb is in future or past tense. The situation is similar in Huron, an extinct Iroquois language. For that matter, French *tout à l'heure* behaves in the same way.

26. For more details on this research, and on the language types sketched briefly here, see Hagège, *La structure des langues,* pp. 4–9.

4. Writing and Speaking

1. A. Fabre d'Olivet, *La langue hébraique restituée* (Paris, 1816–1817), Introduction, pp. xi-xii.

2. B. de Vigenère, *Traité des chiffres et secrètes manières d'écrire* (Paris, 1586), p. 3; C. Duret, *Trésor de l'histoire des langues* (Cologne, 1613), pp. 19–20.

3. J. Février, *Histoire de l'écriture* (Paris: Payot, 1959), pp. 13–15.

4. P. J. Van Ginneken, *La reconstruction typologique des langues archaiques de l'humanité* (Amsterdam: Uitgave van de N. V. Noord-Hollandsche Uitgevers-Maatschappij, 1939).

4. *Writing and Speaking*

5. G. Vico, *Scienza nuova* (Naples: 1744), 3.1.

6. J. Derrida, *De la grammatologie* (Paris: Editions de Minuit, 1967), p. 16, n. 1.

7. M. Jousse, *Le style oral* (Paris: Fondation Marcel Jousse, 1981) (1st ed., 1925), p. 257.

8. C. L. Julliot, *L'éducation de la mémoire* (Paris: 1919), pp. 33–35.

9. R. Guénon, *Introduction générale à l'étude des doctrines indoues* (Paris, 1921), p. 43.

10. *Talmud de Jérusalem* (Paris: Maisonneuve, 1972), Traité Schabbat, XVI, 1, vol. 3, p. 162.

11. *Talmud de Babylone*, Traité Guittin, 60b.

12. E. Jabès, *Le livre des questions* (Paris: Gallimard, 1963).

13. A genre exists that combines simple drawing with language graphics recording dialogues and situations: the comic strip, whose considerable success in the second half of the twentieth century has made it an element of so-called popular culture. The comic strip may be destined for an even more remarkable development in the future. Cf. U. Eco, *Apocalittici e integrati* (Milan: Fabbri-Bompiani, 1964).

14. *Naissance de l'écriture*, Cunéiformes et hiéroglyphes, Catalogue of the Exposition of May 7–August 9, 1982 (Paris: Editions de la Réunion des musées nationaux, 1982), p. 51. Contributed by B. André-Leicknam.

15. *Naissance*, p. 351. Contributed by D. Beyer.

16. J.-J Rousseau, De l'écriture, *Essai sur l'origine des langues*, Oeuvres (1826), vol. 1, ch. 5.

17. C. Nodier, *Dictionnaire raisonné des onomatopées françaises* (Paris, 1828), préface, p. 11.

18. C. Nodier, Langue organique, *Notions élémentaires de linguistique* (Paris, 1834), ch. 2. Quoted by M. Yaguello, *Les fous du langage* (Paris: Editions du Seuil, 1984), p. 182.

19. M. Foucault, *Les mots et les choses* (Paris: Gallimard, 1966), p. 103, n. 1. The author uses supporting quotations from W. Warburton, *Essai sur les hiéroglyphes des Egyptiens* (London, 1741). French trans. 1744.

20. J. Soustelle, De la pictographie au phonétisme dans l'écriture aztèque, in J. Leclant, ed., *Colloque du XXIXe Congrès International des Orientalistes*, Le déchiffrement des écritures et des langues (Paris: L'Asiathèque, 1975), p. 173.

21. V. J. Bottéro, De l'aide-mémoire à l'écriture, in *Actes du Colloque International de l'Université Paris VII*, Ecritures, systèmes idéographiques et pratiques expressives (Paris: Le Sycomore, 1982), p. 32.

22. But see J.-M. Durand, Espace et écriture en cunéiforme, in *Actes du Colloque International de l'Université Paris VII*, Ecritures, p. 63, who suggests that, independently of Akkadian influence, the progress of Sumerian notation was "one of the clearest proofs of the disappearance of this language from vernacular use. Only those unfamiliar with Hebrew or Arab mourn the absence of vowels and demand that they be written."

23. *Chanter*, which came from Latin *cantare*, was thus no longer pro-

nounced "channtère," with the final *e* constituting a syllable, but "chantèr," (as it still is today in southeast France and in certain traditional styles of dictation), and later "chanté."

24. Février, *Histoire de l'écriture*, pp. 173–179.

25. Leclant, *Colloque du XXIXe Congrès International des Orientalistes*, p. vii.

26. Février, *Histoire de l'écriture*, p. 69.

27. Jao Tsung-I, Caractères chinois et poétique, in *Actes du Colloque International de l'Université Paris VII*, Ecritures, p. 272.

28. For details on pronunciation-based writing systems, cf. C. Hagège and A. G. Haudricourt, *La phonologie panchronique* (Paris: PUF, 1978), pp. 31–37.

29. Leibniz, Letter to Father Bouvet, 1703, in the *Philosophische Schriften*, ed. Gerhardt, vol. 7, p. 25.

30. P. S. Du Ponceau, *Dissertation on the Nature and Character of the Chinese System of Writing* (Philadelphia, 1836). In chapter 3, we saw Du Ponceau's contribution to language typology in distinguishing a polysynthetic type, inspired by his knowledge of American Indian languages.

31. A. Kircher, *Prodromus coptus sive aegyptiacus* (Rome, 1636), p. 260. Quoted by J. Derrida, *De la grammatologie*, p. 120, n. 20.

32. This is the case for Ségalen and Michaux, not to mention Pound, who, obviously in error, considered Chinese characters mere pictograms, and their structure a medium for poetic expression.

33. Cf. E. Formentelli, Rêver l'idéogramme: Mallarmé, Ségalen, Michaux, Macé, in *Actes du Colloque International de l'Université Paris VII*, Ecritures, pp. 209–233. This article also recalls Mallarmé's fascination with hieroglyphics, echoed in his correspondence with the egyptologist E. Lefébure.

34. J. Gernet, Aspects et fonctions psychologiques de l'écriture, in *L'écriture et la psychologie des peuples*, Actes du Colloque (Paris: A. Colin, 1963), p. 38.

35. Cf. M. Baratin and F. Desbordes, *L'analyse linguistique dans l'Antiquité classique*, vol. 1. Les théories (Paris: Klincksieck, Horizons du langage, 1981), pp. 18, 90–93.

36. Cf. F. Desbordes, Ecriture et ambiguité d'après les textes théoriques latins, *Modèles linguistiques* (1983), vol. 2, pp. 13–37.

37. D. Arnaud, *Naissance de l'écriture*, p. 235.

38. R. S. Rattray, *Ashanti Proverbs* (Oxford, 1916).

39. For an example, see D. Noye, *Un cas d'apprentissage linguistique: l'acquisition de la langue par les jeunes Peuls du Diamaré (Nord-Cameroun)* (Paris: Geuthner, 1971).

40. French has no word for this phenomenon, called *trabalengua* in Spanish, *Zungenbrecher* in German, etc. We propose here the term *fourchelangue* (see L.-J. Calvet, *La tradition orale* (Paris: PUF, Que sais-je?, 1984), p. 10 and n. 1.

41. Cf. C. Hagège, *Le problème linguistique des prépositions et la solution chinoise (avec un essai de typologie à travers plusieurs groupes de langues)* (Paris-Louvain: Peeters, collection linguistique publiée par la Société de Linguistique de Paris, 1975), pp. 21–22.

4. Writing and Speaking

42. Cf. W. L. Chafe, Integration and Involvement in Speaking, Writing, and Oral Literature, in D. Tannen, *Spoken and Written Language,* Advances in Discourse Processes (Norwood, N.J.: Ablex, 1982), vol. 9, pp. 35–53.

43. Cf. M. Butor, Le livre comme objet, reproduced in *Repertoire II* (Paris: Editions de Minuit, 1954).

44. Cf. R. Husson, Mécanismes cérébraux du langage oral, de la lecture, et de l'écriture, *Les Cahiers du Collège de Médecine* (1967), vol. 1–2, pp. 23–28.

45. Cf. V. Alleton, *L'écriture chinoise* (Paris: PUF, Que sais-je?, 1970), pp. 63–66.

46. Despite this stylization, many poets manage to find in the graphics of the word an image of the object signified. See Claudel's reflections on graphic symbolism in *Idéogrammes occidentaux* (Paris, 1926), and on the sign *toit* ("roof") in *Oeuvres en prose* (Paris: Editions de la Péliade), p. 10.

47. P. Vernus, Espace et idéologie dans l'écriture égyptienne, in *Actes du Colloque International de l'Université Paris VII* Ecritures, p. 102.

48. Ibid., p. 106.

49. His story is recounted in the famous chapter "Leçon d'écriture" at the end of C. Lévi-Strauss, *Tristes Tropiques* (Paris: Gallimard, 1955), pp. 337–349. See Derrida, *De la grammatologie,* p. 191ff., and Calvet, *La Tradition orale,* pp. 105–111.

50. We obviously cannot deny them in this book, itself a written object.

51. Cf. C. Hagège, La ponctuation dans certaines langues de l'oralité, in *Mélanges linguistiques offerts à E. Benveniste* (Paris-Louvain: collection linguistique publiée par la Société de Linguistique de Paris, 1975), pp. 251–266.

52. Cf. M.-C. Hazaël-Massieux, L'écriture des créoles français: problèmes et perspectives dans les petites Antilles, *Fifth Biennial Conference,* Kingston, Jamaica, 1984.

53. F. de Saussure, *Cours de linguistique générale,* critical edition prepared by Tullio de Mauro (Paris: Payot, 1972), pp. 51–52, 1st ed., Geneva, 1916.

54. Rousseau, *Essai sur l'origine des langues,* ch. 8.

55. Derrida, *De la grammatologie,* Deuxième partie, ch. 1 and 2.

5. The Territory of the Sign

1. F. de Saussure, *Cours de linguistique generale,* critical edition prepared by Tullio de Mauro (Paris: Payot, 1972), p. 144.

2. We distinguish the notion of *symbol* from that of the linguistic *sign* as communicative element. Strictly speaking, the experiments discussed below do not involve symbols, since the elements of the code learned by the apes were largely arbitrary; symbols, by contrast, have some motivation.

3. C. Du Marsais, *Des tropes,* Paris, 1730. Quoted by C. Fuchs, *La paraphrase* (Paris: PUF, 1982), p. 53.

4. Many illustrations may be found in F. Brunot's *Histoire de la langue*

française (Paris: A. Colin, 1966–1968) and in a large number of other works as well.

5. H. Wallon, *Les origines de la pensée chez l'enfant* (Paris, 1945), vol. 1, pp. 41, 44, 67, 115.

6. E. Schrödinger, *What is Life?* (Oxford: 1944), p. 28ff.

7. E. T. Bell, *The Development of Mathematics* (New York: McGraw, 1945), p. 466.

8. B. T. Gardner and R. A. Gardner, Teaching Sign-Language to a Chimpanzee, *Science* (1969), 165(3894): 664–672; D. Premack, The Education of Sarah, a Chimp, *Psychology Today* (1970), 4(4):55–58.

9. Communication is only one function of languages, and we do not wish to imply that it subsumes all others (see chapter 10).

10. Cf. T. Flournoy, *Des Indes à la planète Mars* (Geneva, 1899), reprinted in Paris (Editions du Seuil, 1983), with introduction and commentary by M. Yaguello and M. Cifali.

11. R. Jakobson, Retrospect, in *Selected Writings* (Le Hague-Paris: Mouton, 1966), vol. 4, p. 640.

12. U. Eco, *The Name of the Rose* W. Weaver, trans. (New York: Harcourt Brace Jovanovich, Inc., 1983). I am grateful to B. Niederer for calling my attention to this passage.

13. E. Benveniste, Sémiologie de la langue, *Semiotica*, 1969, vol. 1; reproduced in *Problèmes de linguistique générale* (Paris: Gallimard, 1974), vol. 2, pp. 43–66.

14. Cf. Benveniste, *Problèmes de linguistique générale*, pp. 64–65, 235. Remarks on this view of two linguistics may be found in C. Hagège, Les pièges de la parole. Pour une linguistique socio-opérative, *Bulletin de la Sociètè de Linguistique de Paris* (1984) 79(1):1–47; and by the same author in Benveniste et la linguistique de la parole, *E. Benveniste aujourd'hui*, Société pour l'Information grammaticale Louvain (Paris: Peeters, Bibliothèque de l'Information grammaticale 1984), pp. 105–118.

15. This notion has long been the object of a controversy which reveals confusion on two points: first, between signifier and sign; and second, between the arbitrariness of the signifier / signified relation and that of the signifier / referent relation. Consult R. Engler, Théorie et critique d'un principe saussurien: l'arbitraire du signe, *Cahiers Ferdinand de Saussure* (1962), vol. 19, pp. 5–66, and, by the same author, Compléments à l'arbitraire, *Cahiers Ferdinand de Saussure* (1964), vol. 21, pp. 25–32.

16. Cf. *Harmonie universelle* (Paris, 1636).

17. Court de Gébelin, *Le monde primitif analysé et comparé avec le monde moderne* (Paris, 1773–1774), p. 66.

18. According to another, less traditional, interpretation, Babel (Genesis 11:1–9) is the fulfilment of destiny rather than a punishment. Cf. C. Hagège, Babel: du temps mythique au temps du langage, *Revue philosophique* (1978), vol. 4, pp. 465–479.

19. J. de Maistre, *Les soirées de Saint-Pétersbourg* (Paris: Editions du Vieux-Colombier, 1960), p. 76. Cited by H. Meschonnic, La nature dans la voix, introduction to the reedition of C. Nodier's *Dictionnaire raisonné des onomatopées françaises* (Mauvezin: Editions Trans-Europ-Repress, 1984), p. 92. Isidore of Sevilla's "etymology" of *cadaver* is recalled on p. 81.

20. Court de Gébelin, *Histoire naturelle de la parole, ou grammaire universelle et comparative* (Paris, 1778), 2. In 1816 ed., pp. 98–104). Cited by Foucault, *Les mots et les choses* (Paris: Gallimard, 1966), p. 118.

21. J.-J. Rousseau, *Essai sur l'origine des langues,* Oeuvres (1826), vol. 13, pp. 188–192. Cited by Foucault, *Les mots et les choses,* p. 118.

22. Some useful remarks on these authors and their work can be found in M. Yaguello, *Les fous du langage* (Paris: Ed. du Seuil, 1984).

23. G. de Foigny, *Les aventures de Jacques Sadeur dans la découverte et le voyage de la terre australe* (Paris, 1676), ch. 9, p. 130.

24. C. de Brosses, *Traité de la formation mécanique des langues* (Paris, 1765), p. 9.

25. M. Merleau-Ponty, *Phénoménologie de la perception* (Paris: Gallimard, 1945), p. 218.

26. D. Bolinger, Universality, in Bolinger, *Intonation,* Selected Readings (Harmondsworth: Penguin Books, 1972), pp. 313–315.

27. Cf. P. Léon, De l'analyse psychologique à la catégorisation auditive et acoustique des émotions dans la parole, *Journal de Psychologie* (1976), vol. 4, pp. 305–324.

28. Cf. C. Hagège, *La grammaire générative. Réflexions critiques* (Paris: PUF, La Collection du linguiste, 1974), p. 146.

29. Cf. T. Bearth, Is There a Universal Correlation Between Pitch and Information Value? in *Wege zur Universalien-forschung,* pp. 124–130, Sprachwissenschaftliche Beitrë zum 60, Geburtstag von Hansjakob Seiler, hrg. von G. Brettschneider und C. Lehmann (Tubingen: Gunter Narr Verlag, 1980).

30. De Brosses, *Traité de la formation mécanique des langues,* p. 9.

31. Copineau, *Essai synthétique sur l'origine et la formation des langues* (Paris, 1774), pp. 34–35. Cited by Foucault, *Les mots et les choses,* p. 123.

32. I. Hollos, Die Phasen des Selbstbewusstseins, *Internationale Zeitschrift für psychoanalyse* (1922), vol. 8, pp. 421–439.

33. I. Fonagy, *La vive voix* (Paris: Payot, 1983), p. 97.

34. Ibid., pp. 96–97.

35. V. G. Bogoraz, Chukchee, *Handbook of American Indian Languages* (Washington, 1922), vol. 2, p. 665.

36. K. Abraham, Etape prégénitale, (chapter from *Développement de la libido,* 1916), Oeuvres complètes (Paris: Payot, 1966), vol. 2, p. 246.

37. Cf. C. Hagège, *La structure des langues* (Paris: PUF, Que sais-je?, 1982), p. 25. These figures take into account mixed cases within a single language.

38. K. O. Kim, Sound Symbolism in Korean, *Journal of Linguistics* (1977), vol. 13, pp. 67–75.

6. Language, Reality, and Logic

39. I. Baudouin de Courtenay, Hominisation de la langue, *Annales de l'Université de Dorpat* (now Tartou) (Hambourg, 1893), p.153ff. The text of the speech is presented and translated by C. Hagège in A. Jacob, *Genèse de la pensée linguistique* (Paris: A. Colin, 1973), pp. 162–164.

40. Cf. C. Hagège, *La langue palau (Micronésie), une curiosité typologique* (Munich: Fink, 1985).

41. Cf. J. Haiman, Iconic and Economic Motivation, *Language* (1983), 59(4):781–819.

42. Hagège, *La structure des langues*, pp. 50–51.

43. C. Hagège, Pour un retour d'exil des périphériques, *Modèles linguistiques* (1983), 5(1):107–116.

44. Cf. J. Haiman, The Iconicity of Grammar: Isomorphism and Motivation, *Language* (1980), 56(3):515–540.

6. Language, Reality and Logic

1. L. Carroll, *Alice's Adventures in Wonderland* (New York: Potter, 1960), p. 225.

2. Cf. M. Yaguello, *Alice au pays du langage* (Paris: Ed. du Seuil, 1981), p. 159.

3. H. Schuchardt, *Brevier* (1928), p. 231. (1st ed. 1922.)

4. G. Leibniz, *Opera philosophica* (Leipzig, 1717).

5. F. Muller, *Einleitung in die Sprachwissenschaft* (Vienna, 1876).

6. W. Wundt, *Elemente der Völkerpsychologie* (Leipzig, 1911–1914).

7. M. Bréal, *Essai de sémantique* (Paris, 1897), p. 192.

8. E. Benveniste, La phrase nominale, *Bulletin de la Société de Linguistique de Paris* (1950), 46(1); reprinted in *Problèmes de linguistique générale* (Paris: Gallimard, 1966), pp. 151–167. This now-famous article is one of several which, in the last fifty years, have done a great deal to revive this very ancient notion.

9. Cf. C. Hagège, Du concept à la fonction en linguistique, ou la polarité verbo-nominale, *La Linguistique* (1984), 20(2):15–29.

10. Ibid., p. 20.

11. Ibid. This construction has also been attested in Mordvinian (USSR).

12. *Nominants,* so called because they define the noun as such. On this term, and the others used here, cf. C. Hagège, *La structure des langues* (Paris: PUF, Que sais-je?, 1982), Chap. 3.

13. Ibid., pp. 73–74.

14. E. Sapir, *Selected Writings,* D. G. Mandelbaum, ed. (Berkeley: University of California Press, 1949), p. 162.

15. B. L. Whorf, *Language, Thought, and Reality* (Cambridge: MIT Press, 1956), pp. 213–214.

16. J. Gernet, *Chine et christianisme: action et réaction* (Paris: Gallimard, Bibliothèque des Histoires, 1982).

17. E. Benveniste, Catégories de pensée et catégories de langue, *Les Etudes philosophiques*, 1958, vol. 4. Reproduced in *Problèmes de linguistique générale* (Paris: Gallimard, 1966).

18. The reader is referred to the series of studies published (under the direction of J. M. W. Verhaar) under the title *The Verb "Be" and its Synonyms* (Dordrecht: Reidel, 1968).

19. Gernet, *Chine et christianisme*, pp. 326–327.

20. Ibid., pp. 328–329.

21. F. Nietzsche, *Beyond Good and Evil*, 1886, R. J. Hollingdale, trans. (Harmondsworth: Penguin Books, 1973).

22. For more details, see C. Hagège, *La grammaire générative. Réflexions critiques* (Paris: PUF, La Collection du linguiste, 1974), p. 125, n. 1.

23. C. Serrus, *Le parallèlisme logico-grammatical* (Paris: Alcan, 1933), pp. 385–391.

24. A. Tarski, *Logic, Semantics, and Metamathematics* (London: Oxford University Press, 1956).

25. N. Beau, L'acharnement d'une mère, *Le Monde*, July 8–9, 1984, p. 10.

26. J.-J. Rousseau, *Essai sur l'origine des langues*, Oeuvres, (1826), vol. 13, pp. 220–221.

27. J. Michaelis, *De l'influence des opinions sur le langage*, (1759), French translation (1762), pp. 24, 40.

28. M. Foucault, *Les mots et les choses* (Paris: Gallimard, 1966), p. 102, n. 3.

29. Cf. L. Hjelmslev, La catégorie des cas. Etude de grammaire générale, *Acta Jutlandica* (1935–1937), 7(1):102.

30. Cf. Hagège, *La structure des langues*, p. 43.

31. Cf. J. Schmidt-Radefeldt, Structure argumentative, référence et contextualité du proverbe, in *Actes du 17e Congrès International de Linguistique et Philologie Romanes* (Aix, 1983).

32. K. Abel, *Über den Gegensinn der Urworte*, Leipzig, 1884.

33. A. Bain, *Logic*, London, 1870.

34. S. Freud, Sur les sens opposés des mots primitifs, *Jahrbuch für psychoan. psychopath. Forschungen* (1910), 2(1):179–184.

35. E. Benveniste, Remarques sur la fonction du langage dans la découverte freudienne, *La Psychanalyse* (1956), vol. 1, pp. 3–16, reproduced in *Problèmes de linguistique générale*, pp. 75–87.

36. "Relators" express relation, independently of the different meanings that may be attached to them. I introduced this term in *La Structure des langues*.

37. Cf. D. Cohen, *Aḍḍād* et ambiguité linguistique en arabe, *Arabica* (1961), vol. 8, pp. 1–29. The following examples are from the same source.

38. Ibid., p. 29, n. 75.

39. On the relationship between these categories (which were not originally linguistic) and classical Chinese poetry, see C. Hagège, *Le problème linguistique des prépositions et la solution chinoise (avec un essai de typologie à*

travers plusieurs groupes de langues) (Paris-Louvain: Peeters, Collection linguistique publiée par la Société de Linguistique de Paris, 1975), pp. 23–24.

40. Ibid., 161–174.

41. B. Russell, *Problems of Philosophy* (London: Oxford University Press, 1912), p. 219.

42. G. Stein, Poetry and Grammar, *Writings and Lectures 1911–1945*, P. Meyerowitz, ed. (London: Peter Owen, 1967).

43. C. Lévi-Strauss, *Le regard éloigné* (Paris: Plon, 1983), pp. 163–164.

44. This is the sense in which we must interpret Braque's jest (quoted in chapter 5).

7. Word Order and World Order

1. C. F. de Vaugelas, *Remarques sur la langue française*, 1647 (Paris: Chassang, 1911), vol. 2, p. 215.

2. Cf. U. Ricken, *Grammaire et philosophie au Siècle des Lumières* (Lille: PUL, 1978), p. 20.

3. J.-B. Du Bos, *Réflexions critiques sur la poésie et sur la peinture*, Paris, 1719.

4. J. Locke, *Essay on Human Understanding* (London, 1690).

5. G. de Cordemoy, *Discours physique de la parole* (Paris, 1668).

6. B. Lamy, *La rhétorique ou l'art de parler* (Paris, 1675). Some twenty editions were made of this successful work.

7. F. Fénelon, *Réflexions sur la grammaire, la rhétorique, la poétique et l'histoire (= Lettre à l'Académie)* (Paris, 1716).

8. See the recent edition of G. Girard, *Vrais principes* (Paris-Geneva: Droz, 1983, introduction by P. Swiggers, p. 13).

9. Cf. C. Hagège, Voies et destins de l'action humaine sur les langues, in I. Fodor and C. Hagège, *Language Reform: History and Future* (Hambourg: Buske, 1983–84), vol. 1, pp. 11–68.

10. Diderot, in his *Lettre sur les sourds et muets*, is more concerned with historical accuracy. See also d'Alembert's Discours préliminaire to the *Encyclopédie*, and S. Auroux, *La sémiotique des Encyclopédistes. Essai d'épistémologie historique des sciences du langage* (Paris: Payot, 1979), pp. 299–300.

11. Cf. C. Hagège, *La structure des langues* (Paris: PUF, 1982), p. 8.

12. C. Du Marsais, *Exposition d'une méthode raisonnée pour apprendre la langue latine* (Paris, 1722), and *Véritables principes de la grammaire, ou nouvelle grammaire raisonnée pour apprendre la langue latine* (Paris, 1729).

13. E. B. de Condillac, *Oeuvres philosophiques*, Georges LeRoy, ed. (Paris, 1947), vol. 1, p. 576.

14. A. de Rivarol, *De l'universalité de la langue française, Discours qui a remporté le prix à l'Académie de Berlin* (Paris: Bailly et Dessenne, 1784). Reprinted by the Club français du livre, 1964, pp. 89–90.

7. Word Order and World Order

15. T. Suzuki, *La langue close: l'univers du japonais* (Tokyo: Shinch-sha), ch. 2. Quoted by I. Tamba-Mecz, Aperçu sur les notions d'ambiguité et de paraphrase en japonais et sur leurs relations avec la lecture des idéogrammes sino-japonais, *Modèles linguistiques* (1983), 5(2):78.

16. Court de Gébelin, *Histoire naturelle de la parole, ou grammaire universelle et comparative* (Paris, 1778), p. 2. Also see J.-C. Laveaux, *Cours théorique et pratique de langue et de littérature françaises* (Berlin: A. Wever), 4 vols.

17. J.-R. Armogathe, Néologie et idéologie dans la langue française au XVIIIe siècle, *XVIIIe Siècle* (1973), p. 22, n. 5.

18. Ibid., p. 22, n. 3.

19. L. de Bonald, *Oeuvres complètes* (Paris: 1864), vol. 3, p. 452. 1st ed., 1819.

20. Cf. H. Aarsleff, *The Study of Language in England, 1780–1860* (Princeton: Princeton University Press, 1967), p. 228. Quoted by U. Ricken, La critique sensualiste à l'encontre du "Discours sur l'universalité de la langue française" d'Antoine de Rivarol, *Historiographia Linguistica* (1973), 1(1):77.

21. L. de Bonald, *Mélanges littéraires, politiques et philosophiques* (Paris: Le Clere, 1819), vol. 1, p. 295.

22. A. Goguillot, *Comment on fait parler les sourds-muets* (Paris, 1889), pp. 297–300. The bracketed additions are by M. Jousse, *Le style oral* (Paris: Fondation M. Jousse, 1981) pp. 97–99. 1st ed. 1925.

23. D. Diderot, *Lettre sur les sourds et muets*, (1751) (Geneva: Meyer, 1965).

24. Condillac, *Oeuvres philosophiques*, vol. 1, p. 577.

25. U. Domergue, *Journal de la langue française*, 1791, p. 886.

26. On this point, see chapter 9.

27. P. W. Schmidt, *Die Sprachfamilien und Sprachenkreise der Erde* (Heidelberg: Carl Winter's Universitätsbuchhandlung, 1926); C. Bally, *Linguistique générale et linguistique française* (Berne: Editions Francke, 1932), 4th ed. 1965; L. Tesnière, *Eléments de syntaxe structurale* (Paris: Klincksieck, 1959) 2nd ed. 1969.

28. Schmidt, p. 464.

29. Diderot, *Lettre sur les sourds et muets*, p. 421.

30. W. Wundt, *Elemente der Völkerpsychologie* (Leipzig, 1911–1914).

31. J. Van Ginneken, *Principes de linguistique psychologique* (Paris: Marcel Rivière, 1907; Amsterdam: E. Van der Vecht, 1907; Leipzig: Otto Harrassowitz, 1907).

32. H. Weil, *De l'ordre des mots dans les langues anciennes comparées aux langues modernes. Question de grammaire générale*, 2nd ed. (Paris: Librairie A. Franck, 1869), p. 53. 1st ed., 1844.

33. Ibid., pp. 56–57.

34. G. de Stael, *De l'Allemagne* (1813), vol. 1, ch. 12.

35. Bally, *Linguistique générale et linguistique française*, p. 201.

36. Ibid.

37. Tesnière, *Eléments de syntaxe structurale*, p. 19.

38. Ibid., p. 32.

39. On this point, see Hagège, *La structure des langues*, pp. 33–36.

40. J. Greenberg, Some Universals of Grammar with Particular Reference to the Order of Meaningful Elements, in J. H. Greenberg, ed., *Universals of Language* (Cambridge: MIT Press, 1963), pp. 58–90.

41. One known exception is Israeli Hebrew, in which we see *pahot o yoter* ("less or more"), the first element being the heavier one.

42. Cf. Hagège, *La structure des langues*, p. 26.

43. M. Grammont, *Traité de phonétique* (Paris: Delagrave, 1971), p. 379. Also see W. E. Cooper and J. R. Ross, World Order, in *Papers from the Parasession on Functionalism* (Chicago: Chicago Linguistic Society, 1975), pp. 63–111.

44. V. T. Rosenthal, *The Muqaddam* (Princeton: Princeton University Press, 1967), vol. 3, p. 391 (chapter 7, n. 55). My thanks to H. Meschonnic for this reference.

45. One might discuss this in terms of logic or physics, and argue that dimension is as objective a feature as color. But clearly the data here provides a case of linguistic, rather than logical, interpretation.

8. Wordmasters

1. D. Vairasse, *Histoire des Sévarambes qui habitent une partie du troisième continent, communément appelé Terre australe* (Paris: 1677).

2. For more details, see C. Hagège, Voies et destins de l'action humaine sur les langues, in I. Fodor and C. Hagège, eds., *Language Reform: History and Future* (Hambourg: Buske, 1983–1984), vol. 1, pp. 11–68.

3. Ibid.

4. For more details, see *ibid.*

5. A theoretical account of this may be found in the first part of M. Godelier's work, *L'idéel et le matériel* (Paris: Fayard, 1984). This opening chapter is fittingly entitled "The material and social appropriation of nature," pp. 41–163.

6. Cited by M. Yourcenar (in a rather free translation from the Latin) in the dedication of *L'oeuvre au noir* (Paris: Gallimard, 1968).

7. Cited by V. Tauli, The Future Paradigm of Linguistics, in *Proceedings of the Thirteenth International Congress of Linguists* (Tokyo: Gakushuin University, 1983), p. 889.

8. E. A. Moravcsik and J. R. Wirth, eds., *Current Approaches to Syntax* (New York: 1980), introduction, p. 17.

9. Cf. A. Sauvageot, Le langage et la pensée, *Vie et langage* (1960), vol. 103, pp. 536–539.

10. C. Nodier, *Notions élémentaires de linguistique* (Paris, 1834), vol. 12, pp. 256, 261. (*Oeuvres complètes*, Paris, 1832–1837). As for Grégoire, see n. 16 below.

11. Cf. Hagège, Voies et destins, pp. 40–41.

12. Cf. B. Quemada, Les réformes du français, in I. Fodor and C. Hagège,

eds., *Language Reform: History and Future* (Hambourg: Buske, 1983-1984), vol. 3, pp. 79–117.

13. A. Besançon, *Présent soviétique et passé russe* (Paris: Livre de poche, Coll. Pluriel, 1980).

14. This has been established through a careful analysis of the Reports made by Khrushchev and Brejnev before the 22nd and 23rd Congresses of the Communist Party of the Soviet Union, in 1961 and 1966, work carried out by P. Sériot, *Analyse du discours politique soviétique* (Paris: Institut d'Etudes Slaves, Cultures et Sociétés de l'Est, 1985), vol. 2. It is fair to add that things are currently changing, in this respect, in the Soviet Union.

15. J. Soustelle, *La vie quotidienne des Aztèques à la veille de la conquête espagnole* (Paris: Hachette, 1955), p. 114.

16. The *Rapport* of the abbé Grégoire, eighteenth-century French politician, states that "Throughout the nation, these jargons constitute so many barriers to the movement of commerce."

9. The Three Viewpoints Theory

1. On the difference between this three viewpoints theory and certain other more or less tripartite models, see C. Hagège, Les pièges de la parole. Pour une linguistique socio-opérative, *Bulletin de la Société de Linguistique de Paris* (1984), 79(1):1–47.

2. This type of structure is even more common in languages like Italian which ordinarily prepose the verb when it bears secondary information. The contrast thus obtained is illustrated in a sequence of Fellini's "La Strada:" a traveling performer tells his little assistant to announce his arrival in each town by beating on a tambourine to the chant of "è arrivato Zampano!" Confused, she inverts the announcement to "Zampano è arrivato!" This earns her a firm reprimand from her master: if the utterance begins with "Zampano," he is posited as the theme, or less informative—and therefore less interesting—element; here, however, the arriving is to be taken for granted, and the name of the person who has arrived constitutes the surprise, hence it is the element which, since unexpected, must come at the end of the utterance.

Spoken French does not generally prepose verbs in affirmative structures; instead, we find the formula *celui qui . . . , c'est* ("the one who . . . it's"). Thus, *celui qui est arrivé, c'est Zampano.* On the other hand, certain forms of written French, including journalistic style, some types of literary rhetoric, and a "humanities style," practice this preposing of the verb when it carries the less important information: *L'inspirent plus particulièrement l'amour, le sexe, les moeurs, les fantasmes, les angoisses de l'époque, le snobisme intellectuel, la psychanalyse, la drogue, l'âge, et, accessoirement, la mort* (*Le Monde*, May 15, 1979, p. 19). ("Inspire (it) particularly love, sex, custom, fantasy, the anxieties of the times, intellectual snobbery, psychoanalysis, drugs, age, and, incidentally, death.") Preposing is common in certain scientific texts: *Se pose le problème de*

... ("Poses itself the problem of ..."), *Se présente alors une difficulté* ("Presents itself then a difficulty"), etc.

3. Cf. C. Hagège, *Critical Reflections on Generative Grammar*, Edward Sapir Monograph Series in Language, Culture and Cognition (Lake Bluff, Ill.: Jupiter Press, 1981), vol. 10, p. 135.

4. Cf. S. J. Galambos and S. Goldin-Meadow, Learning a Second Language and Metalinguistic Awareness, in *Papers from the Nineteenth Regional Meeting of the Chicago Linguistic Society* (Chicago, 1983), pp. 117–133.

5. The example is cited by B. L. Whorf, *Language, Thought, and Reality* (New York: The Technology Press, 1956), p. 233.

6. Cf. J. Hinds, Shared Information in Japanese Conversation, Working Group 17: Shared Knowledge in Language Use, in *Proceedings of the Thirteenth International Congress of Linguists* (Tokyo: Gakushuin University, 1983), p. 1315.

7. The concept was originated by P. Bourdieu; among his recent works, see *Ce que parler veut dire* (Paris: Fayard, 1982), p. 83ff.

8. E. Goffman, *Interaction Ritual. Essays on Face-to-Face Behavior* (New York: Doubleday, 1967), p. 1.

9. P. Encrevé et M. de Fornel, Le sens en pratique, *Actes de la recherche en sciences sociales* (1983), vol. 46, pp. 7–8.

10. C. W. Morris, Foundations of the Theory of Signs, in O. Neurath et al, eds., *International Encyclopedia of Unified Sciences* (Chicago: University of Chicago Press, 1938), 1(1):1–59.

11. Cf. Hagège, Les pièges de la parole, *BSL*, (1984), 79(2):1–47.

12. R. Jolivet, *Descriptions quantifiées en syntaxe du français—approche fonctionnelle* (Geneva and Paris: Slatkine, 1982), pp. 184, 282.

13. However, in these languages (contrary to what is often taught), the indefinite article may very well accompany a theme, as long as the theme is supporting material (not necessarily known), and not old information. Thus, in French, we find the following example from French radio: *Une solution politique, d'accord pour la discuter* ("A political solution, agreed to discuss it.") Quoted in A. Sauvageot, *Analyse du français parlé* (Paris: Hachette, Recherches / Applications, 1972), p. 16.

14. Cf. Iyoko Hirata, *Ga* or *wa* for New Referents in a Discourse, Working Group 28: Characteristics of Japanese Expressions in News Reporting, in *Proceedings of the Thirteenth International Congress of Linguists* (Tokyo: Gakushuin University, 1983), p. 1387.

15. Excerpt from *Voyage au bout de la nuit*, 1932. Cited by J. Kristeva, Le sens et l'hétérogène, à propos du "statut du sujet," DRLAV (University of Paris VIII) (1984), vol. 30, p. 19.

16. On this distinction, and more generally on all problems related to the organization of information, see J. Perrot, in particular, Fonctions syntaxiques, énonciation, information, *Bulletin de la Société de Linguistique de Paris* (1978), 73(1):95–101.

17. Cf. M.-C. Hazaël-Massieux, Support, apport et analyse du discours, *Le français moderne* (1977), 45(2):156–164.

9. The Three Viewpoints Theory

18. Cited by H. Weil, *De l'ordre des mots dans les langues anciennes comparées aux langues modernes. Question de grammaire générale*, 2d ed. (Paris: Librairie A. Franck, 1869), p. 34. 1st ed., 1844.

19. *Iliad*, I, 84.

20. F. de Saussure, *Cours de linguistique générale*, critical edition prepared by Tullio de Mauro (Paris: Payot, 1972), p. 38.

21. N. Chomsky, *Syntactic Structures* (The Hague-Paris: Mouton, 1957); *Aspects of the Theory of Syntax* (Cambridge: MIT Press, 1965).

22. On studies which, before 1957, had given syntax an important role (Bally, Frei, Jakobson, Tesnière), see Hagège, *Critical Reflections on Generative Grammar*, pp. 168–169.

23. There is a difference between Saussure's opposition of linguistics of language and linguistics of speech, and Benveniste's distinction between semantics and semiotics. However, the two approaches are closer than has been claimed,: see chapter 5.

24. Chomsky, *Aspects*, p. 4.

25. J. L. Austin, *How to Do Things with Words* (Oxford: Oxford University Press, 1962).

26. J. R. Searle, *Speech Acts. An Essay in the Philosophy of Language* (Cambridge: Cambridge University Press, 1962).

27. Intonational curves contrasting theme and rheme are more or less coded. The utterance *il mourrait sans elle* ("he would die without her"), when pronounced with an initial middle tone and then, on *sans elle*, a high-to-low descending melody (contour 1), has the same meaning as *sans elle, il mourrait*, pronounced with an initial high-to-low melody then, on *il mourrait*, low tone (contour 2). In both cases, the meaning is "he would die separated from her presence." Symetrically, the utterance *sans elle, il mourrait* pronounced with contour 1 would have the same meaning as *il mourrait, sans elle* pronounced with contour 2. In both cases, the meaning is now "he would die if she weren't there (to help or care for him)." Beyond the theme / rheme contrast, other combinations of sequence and intonation are less clear. The utterances *moi, le ski . . .* ("me, skiing . . .") and *le ski, moi . . .* may be understood either positively or negatively, depending on intonation, which can suggest either "I like it" or "I don't like it."

28. To cite only one of the many French studies on rhetoric, see P. Fontanier, *Les figures du discours* (Paris: Flammarion, 1968), reprint of 1821 edition. In a completely different cultural context, see M.-C. Porcher, Théories sanskrites du langage indirect, *Poétique* (1975), vol. 23, pp. 358–370.

29. L. Bloomfield, *Language* (London: Allen and Unwin, 1933), p. 74; U. Eco, *La struttura assente* (Milan: Bompiani, 1968).

10. Toward a Theory of Communication

1. Cf. C. Hagège, *La structure des langues* (Paris: PUF, 1982), p. 86.

2. H. P. Grice, Logic and Conversation, mimeograph, Harvard University, 1968; reprinted in P. Cole and J. L. Morgan, eds., *Syntax and Semantics* (New York, Academic Press, 1975), vol. 3. (Speech Acts), pp. 41-58.

3. A similar view is developed by F. Jacques, particularly in *Différence et subjectivité* (Paris: Aubier-Montaigne, Coll. Analyse et raisons, 1982).

4. A precise and detailed study of the enunciative "particles" of these northern European languages, and some interesting theoretical considerations on their link to the multilingual environment of this region, were presented by M. J. Fernandez, *Discours contrastif, oralité, plurilinguisme: l'espace communicatif same, finnois, suédois (en Finlande)* doctoral thesis, University of Paris V, 1984.

5. Logical distinctions of this type may be found in various work inspired by the Anglo-American philosophy of speech, for example, O. Ducrot et al., eds., *Les mots du discours* (Paris: Ed. de Minuit, 1980). Inasmuch as these distinctions are linked to the speech acts theory of Austin and Searle, they may weaken the autonomy of linguistics within a juridico-psychological conception of the subject as "responsible for a speech act" (ibid., p. 44).

6. M. Bakhtine, *Esthétique et théorie du roman,* French translation (Paris: Gallimard, 1978), p. 39–40. Original ed., 1965.

7. See also chapter 2, an evaluation of simplicity in terms of dominant features.

8. Cf. B. Pottier, L'emploi de la préposition *a* devant l'objet en espagnol, *Bulletin de la Société de Linguistique de Paris* (1968) 63(1): 83–95.

9. Cf. Hagège, *La structure des langues,* p. 77. The data following are from the same source.

10. Cf. M. Lawrence, Structure and Function of Oksapmin Verbs, *Oceanic Linguistics* (1972), 11(1):47–66.

11. Cf. S. de Pury-Toumi, L'espace des possibles: l'exemple du nahuatl, *Bulletin de la Société de Linguistique de Paris* (1981), 76(1):359–379.

12. Cf. M. Shibatani, Passives and Related Constructions: a prototype analysis, *Language* (1985), 61(4):821–848.

13. Among them are *logophorics,* which refer to the words or thoughts of the "I": I introduced this term in C. Hagège, Les pronoms logophoriques, *Bulletin de la Société de Linguistique de Paris* (1974), 69(1):287–310.

14. Cf. M. Silverstein, Hierarchy of Features and Ergativity, in R. M. W. Dixon, ed., *Grammatical Categories in Australian Languages* (Canberra: Australian Institute of Aboriginal Studies, 1976), pp. 112–171.

15. Cf. C. Hagège, *Les catégories de la langue palau (Micronésie), une curiosité typologique* (Munich: Fink, 1985).

16. R. Thom, *Stabilité structurelle et morphogenèse* (Reading, Mass: Benjamin, 1972).

10. Toward a Theory of Communication

17. Example taken from H. Rosén, Quelques phénomènes d'absence et de présence de l'accord dans la structure de la phrase en hébreu, *Comptes rendus du Groupe Linguistique d'Etudes Chamito-sémitiques* (1964), vol. 10, pp. 78–84.

18. H. von Kleist, Über die allmähliche Verfertigung der Gedanken beim Reden, 1805, in *Sämtliche Werke* 4, Deutsche National-Literatur, vol. 150 (Berlin-Stuttgart: Speeman, 1878), p. 282ff. Cited by I. and J. Fonagy, L'intonation et l'organisation du discours, *Bulletin de la Société de Linguistique de Paris* (1983), 78(1):161–209. Among other examples, Kleist gave that of Mirabeau's famous response to the Marquis of Dreux-Brézé on June 23, 1789.

19. Cf. C. Fuchs and P. Le Goffic, Ambiguité, paraphrase et interprétation, *Modèles linguistiques* (1983), 5(2):109–136. Recall also that in 1675, the first edition of B. Lamy's *La rhétorique ou l'art de parler* already approved the assignment of rhetoric to grammar.

20. R. Barthes, speech recorded in *Le bruissement de la langue*, Essais critiques (Paris: Ed. du Seuil, 1984), vol. 4, introduction by F. Wahl, p. 21 (under the chapter title "Ecrire, verbe intransitif").

21. P. Bourdieu, L'économie des échanges linguistiques, *Langue française* (May 1977), vol. 34, pp. 17–34.

22. A well-known example in German is *Entsorgungspark*, literally "park for the expulsion of sorrows," actually meaning "nuclear waste treatment facility."

23. Cf. D. Cohen, *Aḍḍād* et ambiguité linguistique en arabe, *Arabica* (1961), vol. 8, pp. 1–29.

24. Cf. R. Witkowski and C. H. Brown, Marking Reversals and Cultural Importance, *Language* (1983), 59(3):569–582.

25. Cf. M. Yaguello, *Les fous du langage* (Paris: Ed. du Seuil, 1984), p. 31.

26. Among recent studies of these creations, presently in vogue with certain disciples of Lacan, see A. Grésillon, Mi-fugue mi-raison. Dévaliser des mots-valises, DRLAV 29 (Paris: University of Paris VIII, 1983), pp. 83–107. Some of the following examples are taken from this article.

27. M. Rheims, *Dictionnaire des mots sauvages* (Paris: Larousse, 1969).

28. Cf. C. Hagège et A. G. Haudricourt, *La phonologie panchronique* (Paris: PUF, 1978).

29. Cf. G. Bateson, *Steps to an Ecology of Mind* (New York: Chandler Publishing Company, 1972).

30. Cf. C. Kerbrat-Orecchioni, *La connotation* (Lyon: PUL, 1977).

31. Cf., in particular, M. Joos, *Readings in Linguistics* (Washington, D.C.: American Council of Learned Societies, 1957).

32. E. Benveniste, Les niveaux de l'analyse linguistique, 1964, reproduced in *Problèmes de linguistique générale* (Paris: Gallimard, 1966), pp. 119-131.

11. Speech Fluctuation

1. R. de Gourmont, *Le problème du style* (Paris: Mercure de France, 1902), p. 34.

2. J. Damourette and E. Pichon, *Des mots à la pensée* (Paris: D'Artrey, 1911–1927), vol. 1, pp. 320–321.

3. Ibid., p. 317. Spoken French is unfettered by these constraints. Among other examples, students at the *lycée* distinguish quite easily between *le prof* and *la prof*. Here, instead of a derivation of gender, we have the simple use of the masculine or feminine article before a noun made invariable through abbreviation.

4. Cf. M. Yaguello, *Les mots et les femmes* (Paris: Petite Bibliothèque Payot, 1978), pp. 118–139.

5. De Gourmont, *Le problème du style.*

6. Yaguello, *Les mots et les femmes,* p. 136.

7. Cf. N. Galli de' Paratesi, Les mots tabous et la femme, in V. Aebischer and C. Forel, *Parlers masculins, Parlers féminins?* (Neuchâtel-Paris: Delachaux et Niestél, Coll. Textes de base en psychologie, 1983), pp. 65–77.

8. Yaguello, *Les mots et les femmes,* p. 142.

9. N. I. Marr, Le langage et la modernité, lecture delivered in Leningrad, then Moscow and Tbilisi, in *Rapports de l'Institut de la culture matérielle* (Leningrad: 1932), vol. 60, p. 116ff.

10. J. Stalin, Marxism and linguistic questions, article appearing in *Pravda,* June 20, 1950.

11. E. Sapir, *Language* (New York: Harcourt, Brace & World, 1921), p. 219.

12. S. J. Gould, *Ever Since Darwin: Reflections in Natural History* (New York: W. W. Norton, 1977), p. 45.

13. Cf. A. Niculescu, Roum. lucra (a)—munci (a) "travailler," *Bulletin de la Société de Lingustique de Paris* (1983), 78(1):325–335.

14. Cf. S. de Pury-Toumi, Y rester ou s'en sortir?, *Amérinda* (1984), vol. 9, pp. 25–47, concerning the Nahuatl dialect of Tzinacapan.

15. Cf. C. Hagège, *La structure des langues* (Paris: PUF, 1982), p. 116.

16. N. Chomsky, *Aspects of the Theory of Syntax* (Cambridge: MIT Press, 1965).

17. Cf. C. Hagège, The Concept of Function in Phonology, in *Phonologica 1980, Akten der Vierten Internationalen Phonologie-tagung* (Innsbruck: Innsbrucker Beitrage zur Sprachwissenschaft, 1981), pp. 187–194.

18. E. Benveniste, Structure des relations de personne dans le verbe, *Bulletin de la société de Linguistique de Paris* (1946), 43(1):1–12; reproduced in *Problèmes de linguistique générale* (Paris: Gallimard, 1966), pp. 225–236.

19. M. R. Ayoub, Bi-polarity in Arabic Kinship Terms, in G. H. Lunt, ed., *Proceedings of the Ninth International Congress of Linguists* (The Hague, 1964), pp. 1100–1106.

20. P. Encrevé, La liaison sans enchaînement, *Actes de la recherche en sciences sociales* (1983), vol. 46, pp. 39–66.

21. Cf. A.-M. Houdebine, Sur les traces de l'imaginaire linguistique, in *Parlers masculins, Parlers féminins?*, pp. 105–139.

22. J. Allières, La fonction ethno-démarcative en linguistique, in *Actes du IIe Colloque de Linguistique fonctionnelle* (Clermont-Ferrand: C.R.D.P., 1975), pp. 173–180.

23. Cf. C. Hagège and A. G. Haudricourt, *La linguistique panchronique* (Paris: PUF, 1978), pp. 154–158.

24. T. de Mauro, Sociolinguistique et changement linguistique: quelques considérations schématiques, in *Proceedings of the XIth International Congress of Linguists (Bologna-Florence, 1972)* (Bologna: Il Mulino, 1974), vol. 2, pp. 819–824.

25. W. Labov, *Sociolinguistic Patterns* (Philadelphia: University of Pennsylvania Press, 1972).

12. Love of Language

1. Cf. C. Hagège, Voies et destins de l'action humaine sur les langues, in I. Fodor and C. Hagège, *Language Reform: History and Future* (Hambourg: Buske, 1983–84), vol. 1, pp. 11–68.

2. Cf. Wolfson, *Le schizo et les langues* (Paris: Gallimard, Coll. connaissance de l'inconscient, 1970).

3. J. Rey-Debove, *Le métalangage* (Paris: Le Robert, Coll. L'ordre des mots, 1978), p. 8.

4. The same criticism applies to Lacan's "lalangue." See M. Arrivé, Quelques notes sur le status du métalangage chez J. Lacan, DRLAV (1985), vol. 32, pp. 1–19.

5. J. Lacan, *Ecrits* (Paris: Ed. du Seuil, 1966), pp. 868, 352–353.

6. For an example of this situation in certain contemporary linguistic works, see C. Hagège, *Critical Reflections on Generative Grammar*, Edward Sapir Monograph Series in Language, Culture, and Cognition, Lake Bluff, Ill.: Jupiter Press, 1981), vol. 10, p. 126.

7. G. Perec, *La vie mode d'emploi* (Paris: Hachette, 1978, part 3, ch. 60.

Index

Index

Ainou (Japan), 195
Akkadian, 55, 101
Algonquin, 197
Alice in Wonderland (Carroll), 95–96
Alphabets, 55–56, 59, 63; adopted by oral societies, 65
Amazon, Peruvian, 28
Ambiguities, 175, 183, 184–85, 203, 213, 214; in speaker's initiative, 200–3
American English, *see* English: American
American Indian languages, 46, 132, 197, 225
American languages, 85; *see also* American Indian languages; North American languages; South American languages
American Sign Language, 76, 130
Amharic (Ethiopia), 62, 91, 113, 151, 226
Ampère, J., 146
Anagrams, 208
Analogous languages, *see* Language(s): analogous
Analysis, 24, 209; literary, 240; writing and, 52
Analyticity: tendency toward, 22, 23–25
Anaphors, 170; and anaphoric reiteration, 178
Ancien Régime, 124–29
Andis (Caucasus), 232–33
An-Nabati, Abu Bakr Ahmad ben Ali ben Washiyya: *Book of the zealot's frantic desire to learn the enigmas of ancient writing*, 64
Annals (Tacitus), 130
Anthropology, vii, 33; case-marking, 195; contribution of linguistics to, ix, 144–45; model, 211
Anticipatory sequences, 133, 136–37
Antinominalists, 82
Antiracism, 221
Antonymy, 172
Aperture, 85
Apes: training to sign, 76–80, 109
Aphasia, 10, 230; semantic, 168
Arabic, 39, 41, 86, 88, 169, 225; classi-cal, 62, 102, 112, 113, 204; forms of address in, 226; writing, 63
Aramaic, 204
Arbitrariness, 43, 44, 80, 89, 193; of the sign, 82
Areal relation, 36
Aristotle, 43, 74, 94, 104, 107, 114
Armenian, 121, 148, 221
Artaud, A., 207
Articles, 196
Articulation, 37, 83
Artifacts, 43
Artificial languages, *see* Language(s): artificial
Ascending sequences, 133–42, 144
Ashantis, 60–61
Asian languages, 32, 41, 92, 225; forms of address in, 226; ideophones in, 90
Aspectual markers, 36
Aspiration, 8–9, 88
Assertion, 78, 79, 85
Ataturk, Kemâl, 63, 148, 149, 158
Athapaskan languages (American northwest), 32
Audiberti, 205
Augustin, Saint, 59, 72, 99
Austin, J. L., 82, 182, 260n25, 261n5
"Austral" language, 83
Australia, 21, 32, 134, 197
Australian languages, 39, 197
Australopithecus, 4
Australopithecus boisei, 5
Australopithecus robustus, 5
Austronesian, 103
Autonym, 98
Autorité de l'usage (Marmontel), 128
Avantages de la langue française sur la langue latine (Le Laboureur), 118
Avar (USSR), 233
Axiological scale of beings in language, 195
Aymara (Bolivia), 101
Azerbaijani, 221
Aztec writing, 55

Ba, H. Hampaté, 60
Babel myth, 81, 146, 231
"Baby talk," 13, 20
Bain, A., 112

Index

Intonations (*Continued*)
French, 24–25; hierarchical syntactic relations indicated through, 40; in interrogation, 175; and intonational curves, 183–84, 260n27; and intonational melody, 84, 85; in oral tradition, 59; punctuation marks indicating, 66; and theme/rheme polarity, 177–78; and unity of language and speech, 183–84
Invention, 204–8
Inversions, 117, 118, 119, 121, 123; in French, 121–22, 128, 129, 130; of markers, 204; of nouns, 133; of syllables, 207
Irish, 39
Isidore of Sevilla, 82
Islam, 63
Isolating languages, *see* Language(s): isolating
Israel, 148; *see also* Hebrew
Italian, 120, 121
Italy, 148, 151

Jabès, E., 51
Jakobson, R., 77
Japanese, 31, 34, 84, 91, 173, 177; absolute synonyms in, 126; *ateji*, 64; Chinese terms in, 75; forms of address in, 226; *katakana*, 55; sexual differentiation in speech in, 225; word order in, 132; writing, 56, 63
Jargons, 77
Jespersen, O., 146–47, 153
Jordan, 226
Journal de la langue français, 125
Journal de la montagne, 127
Journalists, 148
Jousse, 59
Joyce, James, 77; *Finnegans Wake*, 33, 167
Juxtapositions, 23, 39, 91; of radicals and affixes, 45

Kabardian (Caucasus), 91
Kalam (New Guinea), 34
Karadžić, V., 148
Karok, 84–85
Kasravi, 157

Kawabata, Y.: *Kyoto*, 32
Kawi (Java), 195
Kazakh, 221
Kemâl, Mustapha, *see* Ataturk, Kemâl
Kenya, 4
Khlebnikov, 76–77
Kiowa (Oklahoma), 204
Kirchner, A., 58
Kirghiz (USSR), 156
Kleist, H. von, 199
Koraïs, 148
Koran, 63
Korea, 57
Korean, 87, 226; ideophones in, 90
Koriak (USSR), 156
Kunimaipa (New Guinea), 84
Kwakiutl (British Columbia), 194
Kyoto (Kawabata), 32

Labials, 82
Labov, W., 229
Lacan, J., 234
Laforgue, J., 205
Lamy, B., 119, 123
Language(s), viii, ix, 5, 28, 93, 109; accusative, 38, 196–97; acquisition by children, 12–13, 106, 167, 189; agglutinating, 154; analogous, 120; analysis of, 130–31; ancient religious, 62; aptitude for, 7; arbiters, 148; artificial, 146–47, 154; autonomy of writing and, 63; body, 64, 174; and capacity for self-defense, 29; centrifugal, 137–38; centripetal, 137–38; conflict over normalization of, 147, 157; conservationists, 155–57; constraint/initiative dialectic linking speaker with, 190–98; cyclic history of, 14, 93; danger to, in introduction of writing, 66; dead, 28; defined, 230–31; destiny of, and destiny of humanity, 48; development of, 7; dichotomy of speech and, 7, 13–14, 180–85, 186, 200; disappearance of, 28–29; dream of universal, 29, 146–47; ergative, 38, 196–97; faculty, 3, 6–7, 13, 30, 47, 52; genesis of, 6–7, 15, 17; homologies between, 195–96; idea of single, original, 3, 29, 205; ideal, 82–83; in-

274

181; and writing, 48–67; *see also* Psychosocial speaker
Specialization: technical lexicons for, 148
Speech, viii, ix, 16, 47, 165, 232–33; acts theory, 261n5; age differences in, 225; aptitude for, 46–47, 190, 230; biological encoding of, 190; contemplation of, 58; defined, 230; development of, 20–21; division and stratification of world through, 143–45; duality of, 76–77, 79–80; expressing the unreal, 108–9; expressive function of, 210; faculty as distinct from language, 7, 13–14; figures of, 119, 123; fixed, in writing, 51; fluctuation, 215–29; function of, 208–11; gestural, 99, 230; ideal community of, 228; and the innate, 10–15, 16; intonation in, 84; logic in, 111; natural, 234; nonverbal forms of, 230; organs, 85–87, 209; origin of, 19, 20; parts of, 37, 100; philosophy of, 261n5; phylogeny/ontogeny of, 18–20; physiology of, 87–88; and priority of spoken forms, 143; psycho-physiological foundations of, 119; rate, 198; relation with language and discourse, 230–32; relation with world, 146; relation of writing to, 48–51, 58–59, 61, 62–63, 65–67; repetition in, 60–61; simultaneity with discourse planning and transmission of, 199–200; speaker and functions of, 208–11; stratagems, 199–204; study of, as study of mankind, 188–89; symbolic value of melodies of, 84–85; variation, 223–29; varying word order basic to, 138
Spontaneity: and reflective detachment, 134–35
Staël, G. de, 136
Stalin, J., 157, 220–21
State: and codification of usage, 149; and language, 148; and linguistic unification, 155–59; *see also* Politics
Status quo, 159; dictionaries in preservation of, 149–50
Stein, G., 114

Steinthal, H., 45, 107
Storytellers, 60–61
Stress: in French, 140; word order and, 137
String(s), 97–98, 168
Structuralism, 30, 33, 49, 75, 97, 186, 189, 200, 201, 208–9, 212, 214
Structure-function relationship, 37–38, 40, 45
Structures: encoding of, 24; subordinated, 39–40
Stylistic devices, 119
Stylization, 52, 54, 57, 62, 63
Subconscious, 198, 212; collective, 223
Subject, 181, 183; and theme, 176, 177, 197; in three viewpoints theory, 165–66
Subordination, 168
Substantialist tradition, 114
Substrata, 24, 26; and learning, 20–21
Succession: immediate, 91
Sudre, J. F., 147
Sumerian, 52–53, 55, 56, 57, 60
Superlatives, 84
Suspension, 119
Suzuki, T., 126
SVO structure, 129–30, 131, 132, 133, 138
Swahili, 151
Swedish, 84, 188
Syllabaries, 59
Syllables: inversion of, 207; types of, 23
Sylvester, J., 148
Symbol(s), 90; for deferred notation of objects in absentia, 74
Symbolectal indices, 224, 227–28
Symbolism: in oral style, 60; of sound, 81, 89
Symbolization, 73; in apes, 77; capacity for, 4, 7, 73
Synonymy, 36, 43, 74–75, 126, 202
Syntax, 14, 37, 67, 121, 181, 212; ambiguity in, 200; archaic features in, 218–19; autonomy of, 167–68; choice in, 228; differentiation among languages, 38–40, 43, 46, 223; hierarchies, 14, 40; homologous structures of, 202; human subject and, 196–97; in language evolution in, 198; in lin-

ground of, 38–47; formal, 34, 35, 36; as hypotheses, 36; lexical, 43; purpose of, 47; search for, 33–35, 45, 231; substantive, 33–34, 35, 86; and typological differences, 27–47
Universe: interpretation of, 144; linguistic representation of, 209
Univocity, 147, 200
Ur inscriptions, 52
Uralic, 103; syntax, 139
Uralic-Altaic languages, 137
Usage, 96, 182, 192; class, 219–21; codification of, 149; determination of, 151
Uto-Aztecan, 101
Utterance, ix–x, 202; modifiers, 188; organization of, 102
Uzbek, 200

Vairasse, D., 82–83, 147
Variation(s), 67, 158–59, 181, 182; in speech, 223–29
Varron, 99
Vaugelas, C. F. de, 118, 148
Verbs, 45, 114, 137, 172; clauses, 101; derived from nouns, 103, 113; features of, 99, iterative, progressive, durative, 91; tenses, 23; utterances, 174; in word order, 117; *see also* Nouns
Verbants, 103
Verlaine, P., 31
Vietnamese, 32, 57, 150
Vigenère, B. de, 49
Villers-Cotterêts, edict of, 155
Virgil: *Aeneid*, 124
Vocabulary, 154, 182, 223; borrowing of, 75; choice in, 228; chromatic, 42; creation of, 149, 150–51; doubling in, 91; technical, 44; and translation, 31, 32–33
Vocal-auditory signifier: choice of, 8, 9
Vocal organs, 87, 88; *see also* Larynx; Pharyngeal muscles
Volapuk, 146
Völkerpsychologie, 189
Volney, C. de, 125
Voltaire, 179
Vowels, 40–41, 55–56, 82, 84, 86; ex-

pressive lengthening of, 84; opposition to consonants, 87; subgroups of, 41; tone in identification of, 85
Vrais principes de la langue française, Les (Girard), 119–21
VOS order, 132
VSO order, 132

Wallon, H., 75
Wan, Prince, 148, 149
Webster, Noah: *Dictionary*, 149
Weil, H., 135–36
Wenyan, 61, 106
Whorf, B. L., 104
Wilkins, 82–83
Wiyot, 84–85
Wob (Ivory Coast), 85
Wolfson, 233
Wollo province, 4
Word order, 12, 126, 132, 152, 197; ascending/descending sequences, 133–42; criteria commanding, 142; genetic and social speculations as to, 133–38; individual choice in, 127; in interrogation, 175; and meaning, 172; and natural order controversy, 116–24; and relativity of naturalness, 129–32; rigidity in, 178–79; variations of, 138–42; and world order, 116–45
Word-order debate, 116–24, 126, 129, 131, 145, 179, 181; as reflection of hierarchical relations of dependence, 133
Word-sentence coincidence, 46
Word sequence shatterers, 199–200, 205
Wordmasters, 146–59
Wordplay, 205–7, 211
Words, viii, 12, 23, 143; contingency of, 214; demiurges, 148–52, 210; determined by means of other words, 39; differentiation into types, 37; list of recommended/rejected, 151; neutral, 111–13; and objects, 81, 96; organization of, 144–45; segmentation within, 43; and signs, 71–72; sound combinations forming, 41–43; specialization of, 38; and thought, 96

European Perspectives

A Series of Columbia University Press

Julia Kristeva, *Powers of Horror*   1984
Julia Kristeva, *Revolution in Poetic Language*   1984
Richard Lowenthal, *Social Change and Cultural Crisis*   1984
Julia Kristeva, *Kristeva Reader*   1986
Daniel Roche, editor, *Journal of My Life: The Autobiography*
    of Jean-Louis Menetra   1986
Franco Basaglia, *Psychiatry Inside Out*   1987
Arnold Gehlen, *Man*   1987
Volker Meja, Dieter Misgeld, and Nico Stehr, *Modern*
    German Sociology   1987
Gilles Deleuze and Claire Parnet, *Dialogues*   1988
Michel de Certeau, *The Writing of History*   1988
Julia Kristeva, *In the Beginning Was Love*   1988
Sarah Kofman, *The Childhood of Art*   1988
Julia Kristeva, *Language: The Unknown*   1989
Gilles Deleuze, *Logic of Sense*   1989
Julia Kristeva, *Black Sun*   1989
Julia Kristeva, *Strangers to Ourselves*   1989
Claude Hagège, *The Dialogic Species*   1990